TABLE OF CONTENTS

CW00972428

DEDICATION

To the memory of James Edwin "Jeb" Bisbort (1948–1989),
the grooviest man I've ever known. Peace, Brother. —A.B.

To the memory of Walter H. Puterbaugh (1925–1981),
who tolerated my passage through the '60s, especially the loud music,
with a good nature and healthy curiosity. Peace, Dad. —P.P.

FOREWORD

Somebody once cleverly remarked, it may have been George Carlin but my memory's a bit foggy needless to say, that if you can remember the '60s, you weren't there. Truer words were never spoken. Many a Generation X–er has told me how fortunate I was to have grown up during a time in America's history when the young adult population really seemed to make a difference, politically as well as artistically. And they're right. And I do realize how lucky I am and was to have shared in the "psychedelic experience."

Graduating from high school in 1965 and having our first Top 10 record six months later, my little band, the Turtles, was instantly slung into the fast-paced world of sex, drugs, and rock and roll. And we loved every minute of it. From the first time someone passed me a "doob" through my trip with the genius who was Frank Zappa, life seemed a perpetual strobe-lit purple haze.

This is not to say that I have forgotten a single moment of that glorious decade—anything but—it's just that things were genuinely different then, that I doubt the world will ever know the likes of it again.

Without condoning the use of any drugs, I can vividly recall talking to the trees, sitting through endless Ravi Shankar concerts, hanging with the kids on the Sunset Strip, dancing naked at the Love-In in Griffith Park, watching the Who perform *Tommy* next to an also-tripped-out David Crosby, freely fornicating with any pretty lady who would have me (at least I think they were pretty), passing the boda at Grateful Dead shows, the countless concerts we performed ourselves in a somewhat altered state, and, most of all—long before actually meeting and working with them—thinking to myself how fortunate I was to be alive during the era of the Beatles.

It was the era of Warhol and Ed Sullivan; of Day-Glo VW buses; of *The Brady Bunch*, *The Partridge Family*, and, yes, *The Monkees*. I faked my way out of my draft board physical and yet had the nerve to perform at the White House. We marched at Chicago and got shot at Kent State. Our brothers went to Viet Nam in the world's most unpopular civil action and many of them never returned. We were at the dawning of the age of Aquarius and also on the Eve of Destruction. Our parents hated our long hair; couldn't understand why Twiggy was sexy; wondered if the Rolling Stones bathed; and kept asking what that smoky smell was coming from our bedrooms.

We were a generation, perhaps for the last time, that shared a common bond through our music, our art, our literature, our heroes, our communal lifestyles, and, yes, our recreational mind-expansion. We spoke in a common voice and, to the surprise of many, the world listened. And we DID make a difference.

In the years that followed, many generations have tried to emulate the achievements and the fun that history has already proven to be so meaningful. These days, new bands carry the musical banner for their contemporaries. Groups like Smashing Pumpkins and Green Day appeal to latter-day flower children. Jakob Dylan and his Wallflowers carry the torch that his father lit more than 35 years ago. Bell-bottom pants are back in fashion yet again.

Neil Young and his bandmates have been inducted to the Rock and Roll Hall of Fame. Nick at Nite is proving that the television we enjoyed as youngsters is just as entertaining to our children's children, and our favorite vinyl records have all been reissued on CD. And take a look at the overwhelming success of *Austin Powers, International Man of Mystery*...hey, one of OUR songs, "You Showed Me," is on the soundtrack. Shagadelic, Baby! What comes around, goes around.

Sure, we were "psychedelicized"...the curtains moved and the colors all ran together, but in the words of Hunter Thompson, we trod heavily on the planet and left footprints that will last forever in the sands of time.

Anybody got a light?

Howard Kaylan
St. Louis, MO

ACKNOWLEDGMENTS

The authors would like to thank Harold Bronson of Rhino Records for his sagacious editorial input and indefatigably groovy nature in steering this project through to publication. At General Publishing Group, where the book originated, we owe debts of gratitude to Jeremy Xavier for photographic research and Steve Baeck for editorial oversight. Athena Angelos helped us with photo research at the Library of Congress. At Miller Freeman Books, we are grateful to Matt Kelsey and Dorothy Cox for their conscientious work in the later stages and to Michael Kobrin for his sharp-eyed proofreading.

Finally, special acknowledgement is due our wives, Tracey O'Shaughnessy Bisbort and Carol Hill Puterbaugh, who cheefully put up with the sound of acid-rock LPs, weird movie dialogue, out-of-context laughter and other manifestations of the psychedelic era emanating from our respective office sanitariums.

SYNTHESIZING PSYCHEDELIA

THE YELLOW BRICK ROAD FROM SANDOZ TO OWSLEY

First, a revelation: "Flower Power" is as old as human civilization. Though the concept was coined by the media to describe the San Francisco scene and then got spread far and wide by a Los Angeles

singer named Scott McKenzie (who sang, "If you're going to San Francisco/Be sure to wear some flowers in your hair"), Flower Power real-

ly just became a convenient heading under which to file the legitimately wonder-filled events and images culled for this book. A trip through the psychedelic years might more accurately be described as a historic, colorful, and consciousness-raising vista along the evolutionary highway of the human species. The psychedelic culture of the 1960s was arguably the most far-reaching and pervasive of all recorded quests for enlightenment. However, it was by no means the first time that drug-induced visions had been courted and ritualized.

Long before Timothy Leary became the "Pied Piper who seduced a generation," Indians of the American Southwest and Mexico had been using special plants as sacraments in their religious ceremonies. It was, in fact, from descendants of these same Indians that Leary, in 1960, received his first dose of "magic mushrooms," which eventually launched him into

the kaleidoscopic center of the psychedelic movement. One plant that powered the Indians' heightened awareness was a cactus that grew underground—a fantastic image, is it not? The only evidence of this cactus to the naked eye were its "buttonlike protuberances" that poked above the dirt. These diamonds in the rough were mescal buttons, which when dried and eaten caused hallucinations and an altering of reality not unlike that experienced by LSD users. The primary difference between the two drugs was one of origin: mescal buttons were natural and organic, while LSD was synthesized in the laboratory.

The full scientific name for LSD is "lysergic acid diethylamide," but the hippie shorthand for the drug was, simply, "acid." LSD was synthesized in 1938 during the course of a search for a new headache cure, but its mind-expanding properties were not identified (and then

This book boasted an introduction by Eleanor Roosevelt and chapter titles such as "The Rumble," "The New Ghettos," "The Old Slums," and "The Suburbs."

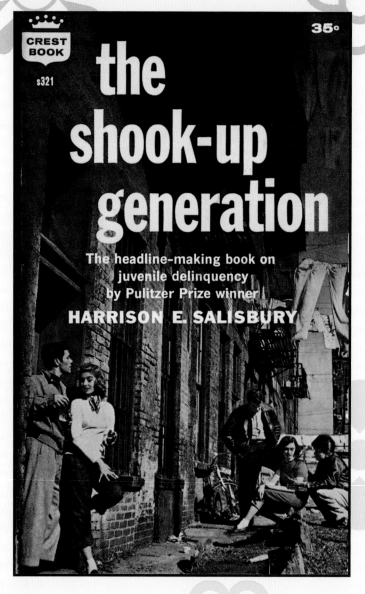

only accidentally) for another five years. How LSD thereafter fell into the hands of the counterculture of the 1960s is a long, strange trip involving curious scientists, government intelligence and military personnel, several literary figures, a group of freaks who called themselves "Merry Pranksters," some scruffy rock musicians looking to push the creative envelope, a renegade tribe of societal dropouts pulled as if by magnets to San Francisco, and, finally, the sons and daughters of middle America. Suffice to say that by the mid-'60s, the popular slogan BETTER LIVING THROUGH CHEMISTRY came to assume vastly different meanings to different generations.

In telling this tale we must bear in mind a self-evident truth: young people have always and will always be attracted to whatever new form of rebellion is available to them. As the *Encyclopedia of*

William Blake's "doors of perception" were open so wide that he could prophecy about his place (Europe) and time (1794) in a voice so loud and clear that, two centuries later, Aldous Huxley and Jim Morrison would be able to pick up the trail. Blake saw industrial progress, and "the cult of reason," as a serpent that would ultimately strangle civilization unless we sang "songs of innocence."

Psychoactive Drugs more prosaically puts it, "Almost all drug and alcohol use begins in the preteen and teenage years." Statistics further reveal that the 18-to-25-year-old age group accounts for the highest percentage of "experimenters." If we add sex and rock and roll to this anarchic equation, we find ourselves back in San Francisco circa 1966 with the Grateful Dead about to take the stage; Bill Ham cranking up his light show; Ken Kesey orchestrating conceptual insanity on the floor; and a ballroom full of dazed, day-glo creatures trying to will an elating and terrifying new counterculture into existence with drug-induced telepathy, drug-inspired music, and a drug-engendered surrender of the ego. Instead of getting caught in the soul-destroying gears of America's capitalist threshing machine, a burgeoning community of youthful dropouts chose to sing a new tune, whose lyrics beseeched, "C'mon people now, smile on your brother, everybody get together, try to love one another right now."

What made the psychedelic years unique was the naive idealism of the participants and the high-stakes game they were playing. Previously, the term "social rebel" connoted a greasy-haired, switchblade-flicking borderline criminal consumed with hatred for society and capable of random acts of violence. His drug of choice was booze, his means of escape a jacked-up car (often stolen and driven recklessly), his rock and roll conspicuously devoid of social conscience or utopian vision, and his response to trouble a flying fist or coiled chain.

Psychedelia ushered in a new kind of rebel: nonviolent, but potentially more dangerous to Western society. The participants in this revolution of the mind—even those who didn't routinely use drugs (and they were legion)—weren't undergoing the rebel rites of passage as a hormonally imbalanced prelude to resuming a straight and narrow path. No, they rejected outright the whole kit bag of American adulthood—the sleazy politics, the stultifying livelihoods, the plastic suburban pipe dream, even the "acceptable" forms of rebellion (boozing, brawling, fast cars, petty crime). They did it with total abandon, too, embracing exotic religions and psychedelic drugs while immersing themselves in music that reflected these inner odysseys. And they carried it all out on such a massive scale—at its zenith, half a million people communally frolicked in the mud at Woodstock!—that the counterculture went beyond any parent's ability to comprehend,

British-born Aldous Huxley (1894–1963) was a brilliant thinker whose lifelong interest in "visionary experience" led him fearlessly down the psychedelic path. He moved to California in 1935 and documented his pioneering trips in *Doors of Perception* (1956). He also ingested a copious amount of LSD on his deathbed to assure smooth sailing into the hereafter. Because he died the same day John Kennedy was assassinated, no one noticed.

much less control. It was a complete break with the past, a paradigm shift of unprecedented dimensions.

One countercultural pundit even branded it with a name and number: "Consciousness III" is how Yale law professor Charles Reich christened the youth-culture movement in his Bible of blissful dropout dogma, *The Greening of America*, published in 1970. Based on events that took place on college campuses and in cities like San Francisco in the late '60s, he envisioned nothing less than a wholesale retooling of society by the young. Reich prophesied: "There is a revolution coming. It will not be like revolutions of the past. It will originate with the individual and with culture, and it will change the political structure only as its final act. It will not require violence to succeed, and it cannot be successfully resisted by violence. This is the revolution of the new generation."

Wearing a gingham dress and beads around her neck, an extra had her face painted by a hippie friend as they waited with 300 other flower children to be chosen for a Greenwich Village sequence in For the Love of Ivy, starring Sidney Poitier.

Vive la révolution! Well, surely time—along with hard drugs, the shift from hippies to yuppies, the "me decade" mind-set, the Nixon and Reagan administrations, the loss of innocence and conviction, and [insert your own reason(s) here]—have conspired to abort Reich's starry-eyed notion of a new society. But despite the failure to realize utopia, it can be argued that the ideals of the era nonetheless still exert a lasting hold on the public imagination, having become embedded in the fabric of the larger culture. Just for starters, the antiwar movement, environmental awareness, strivings for gender and racial equality, military accountability, and the reclaiming of the American soul from its gray-flannel purgatory all got a hefty push from the counterculture.

It is still hard to believe that a movement of this magnitude actually occurred without more bloodshed and clampdowns in a nation where power and control historically trickled down from a humorless, conservative, WASPish, military/industrial complex. Perhaps the answer had something to do with this line from a Doors song: "They got the guns but we got the numbers." In any case, pressure from "the Establishment" was, and always is, inevitable. For a time, in the face of massive opprobrium and marshaled resources—just think back to the police riot at the 1968 Democratic Convention in Chicago—a generation held firmly to the belief that a better world was possible. This was a decade during which music, art, clothing, politics, philosophy, language, and other avenues of expression served to repudiate a world filled with assassinations, riots, war, pollution, and inequality. The message was telegraphed in all sorts of ways, essentially boiling down to Timothy Leary's oft-repeated exhortation to "Turn on, tune in, and drop out!"

THE PSCIENCE OF PSYCHEDELICS

For a word flung around as frequently as a Frisbee at a rock festival, "psychedelic" has an elusive definition. Generally credited to Dr. Humphrey Osmond (no relation to Donny and Marie), it was meant to suggest the "mind-manifesting" properties of LSD and mescaline (the drug synthesized from cactus buttons). Osmond was a British psychiatrist working in Canada on cures for mental illness and alcoholism. In 1952, he stumbled on an important link between schizophrenic mind states and those induced by mescaline. Schizophrenia, he posited, might be caused by the body producing its own hallucinogens.

Osmond's work attracted the notice of Aldous Huxley, the expatriate British writer whose classic *Brave New World* (1931) offered an unnerving premonition of a

14

world dominated by totalitarian mind control. A dignified and disciplined man, Huxley suffered all his life from a debilitating eye disease and was thus predisposed to "look within." He eagerly volunteered to take part in Osmond's drug trials. In 1953, with Osmond as his guide, Huxley took mescaline, writing about the life-altering experience in *The Doors of Perception*. Huxley borrowed his title from William Blake (1757–1827), a visionary poet who wrote, "If the doors of perception were cleansed every thing would appear to man as it is, infinite." Blake's writings also helped launch Allen Ginsberg's first mystical experience (chronicled in "Sunflower Sutra," a 1956 poem) and inspired the movement of psychedelic poster artists. *The Doors of Perception* turned many heads, none more so than a film student named Jim Morrison, whose band took its name from Huxley's tract. Before settling on the Doors, they'd called themselves the Psychedelic Rangers.

Huxley himself next went a step further by taking pure Sandoz LSD-25. He wrote of the experience: "What came through the closed door was the realization—not the knowledge, for this wasn't verbal or abstract—but the direct, total awareness, from the inside, so to say, of Love as the primary and fundamental cosmic fact." Not one to quit while he was a "head," he petitioned Osmond to devise a better word for these mind-altering drugs. In an exchange of letters from 1957, the two friends closed with competing couplets. Huxley's went: "To make this trivial world sublime/Take half a Gramme of phanerothyme." Osmond's: "To fathom hell or soar angelic/Just take a pinch of psychedelic."

And so the age of psychedelia began.

FLASH BACKWARD AND FORWARD

At the risk of further blurring the origins of psychedelia, one could make the case that the 1960s actually began on April 16, 1943. On that date, Dr. Albert Hofmann, a chemist working at Sandoz Pharmaceutical Laboratories in Basel, Switzerland, accidentally absorbed through his fingertips (another fantastic image) a derivative that he'd concocted from ergot, a fungus that grows on rye. (As a side note, Hofmann also synthesized psilocybin, the active ingredient in magic mushrooms. Never a dull moment in this gentleman's lab!)

Hofmann had spent years methodically synthesizing compounds from ergot in hopes of finding a cure for migraine headaches. With the 25th of his derivatives (dubbed LSD-25), he hit psychedelic paydirt in 1938, but he would not uncover its mind-altering properties until that fateful day five years later when he pulled an old vile full of bluish liquid off the shelf and inadvertently dosed himself.

His account of the experience, preserved in lab notes, foreshadowed the acid-induced vision quests of the '60s. "As I lay in a dazed condition with eyes closed there surged up from me a succession of fantastic, rapidly changing imagery of a striking reality and depth, alternating with a vivid, kaleidoscopic play of colors," wrote Hofmann. "Very plastic and fantastic images passed before my closed eyes....All acoustical perceptions, perchance the noise of a passing car, were translated into optical sensations, so that through each tone and noise, a corresponding colored picture, kaleidoscopically changing in form and color, was elicited."

Dr. Hofmann's mental rocket fuel fell into many hands between 1943 and 1960. Some were sinister (the Central Intelligence Agency and the Army Chemical Corps, both of which investigated the drug's potential as a brainwashing agent by dosing legions of unwitting human subjects) and others sincere (the literati: Huxley, Osmond, Ginsberg, Kesey). Still others were potentially sensational. Would anyone now believe, for example, that Henry and Claire Booth Luce, media fomenters of the "hippie threat," took LSD-25 half a dozen times in the late 1950s? Or that, in its May 1957

N1277 95¢ "...the most balanced and informative book on the subject published so far..."—Los Angeles TIMES

LSD:
The Consciousness-Expanding Drug
Edited by DAVID SOLOMON
Introduction by TIMOTHY LEARY, Ph.D.

In 1966, when this wide-selling compendium of up-to-the-minute articles and scientific studies on LSD was published, the hallucinogenic agent had not yet been declared illegal by the Federal Drug Administration. Nor had Timothy Leary, Ph.D.—who wrote the fairly straightforward introduction—issued his famous edict "Turn On, Tune In, Drop Out" to America's youth. Not that they needed any encouragement.

issue, their *Life* magazine ran a laudatory 17-page story about "magic mushrooms"? Or that Cary Grant was part of a Hollywood circle who held their own Acid Tests?

Perhaps the most surreal LSD story has to do with the administering of a megadose of acid (300,000 micrograms!) to a male Asiatic elephant in the name of science. Instead of rutting madly, which behavior the scientists had hoped to observe, the poor beast simply keeled over in a somnambulant trance. Attempts to revive the befuddled pachyderm by injecting it with other drugs wound up killing it instead. The article in the February 1963 issue of *Science* magazine that documented this misadventure did not report whether the subject saw flying elephants in the course of its trip.

Popular media-fueled myths have it that Timothy Leary was the head "head" of Haight Ashbury, so to speak. While it's true that he, along with Allen Ginsberg, passed through the Bay Area in 1960, chanting about a new "peace and love movement," the truth about who really got the costume ball rolling is considerably more complicated.

An artist who lived in Sausalito in the late 1950s—and who shall, at his request, remain nameless—remembers it like this: "When I came through during the so-called Beatnik era, everybody was already onto peyote and mescaline. And when I left to go to Mexico in 1962, LSD had come in through [Zen philosopher and writer] Alan Watts and friends in Sausalito, and Aldous Huxley in Hollywood. Huxley had just died [in 1963], using acid to pass over, taping the remaining moments. The acid was coming directly from Hofmann. I'd already had peyote in Taos in 1959, and mescaline in New York in 1960.

"I got my first acid from Watts, directly from Aldous, a nice little bottle of blue liquid, very powerful, like nothing made afterward. When I returned to SF in 1963, acid was all over the place. Leary and Alpert didn't come on the scene until much later. They had a place in Mexico and a mansion [Millbrook] they'd come by on the East Coast. When they came to San Francisco shouting, lecturing, and making a big fuss, many in the community felt they were agent provocateurs. In any case, soon after they came the government cracked down on psychedelics, and the whole scene took on a madhouse effect."

Despite his shameless self-promotion and Irish blarney, Leary indeed became the most visible proponent of psychedelics in the world. As late as 1963, he'd been a fairly straitlaced Harvard psychology professor. Already a veteran of many trips, Leary experimented in a clinical way with utilizing psychedelics in controlled situations. His most famous experiment was an attempt to rehabilitate prisoners. In a 1963 letter to the *Harvard Crimson*, he actually registered concern about the casual use of drugs. More than likely, however, he was attempting spin control, for his unorthodox methods were by then generating controversy within the academic community. Yet Leary was eventually fired, as was his colleague, Richard Alpert (later Baba Ram Dass), for the experiments.

Leary thereupon charmed his way into an idyllic base of operations, a 64-room mansion in upstate New York called Millbrook. The estate belonged to William Mellon Hitchcock, a rich disciple. From here, he started the Castalia Foundation (named after an intellectual colony in a Herman Hesse novel) with Alpert and Ralph Metzner. The trio published their own journal, *The Psychedelic Review*. Castalia became the International Foundation for Internal Freedom (IFIF), then the League of Spiritual Discovery (LSD). Another associate, Michael Hollingshead, was dispatched to set up shop in London, where he endeavored to spread the word about LSD by founding the short-lived World Psychedelic Centre (WPC).

A typical Leary pronouncement: "The second step is the realization that you have to go out of your mind to use your head." Bred in a hassle-free setting and based on blithe borrowings from *The Tibetan Book of the Dead* and ancient tenets of Taoism, Leary's philosophy spread and his credentials swelled to the point where he could fairly describe himself as High Priest of the Counterculture. In his 1968 book, *High Priest*, Leary estimates that he gave away 10 million hits of acid. One of the recipients was a stockbroker named Ron Berkowitz, later business manager for East Totem West, a psychedelic art publisher. "I was with Leary in Mexico in 1963," recalled Berkowitz, "and I took my first LSD down there. At the time about 2,000 people had taken it. Tim was saying someday millions would take it. And he was right. LSD changed what we saw. It changed what we thought. A lot of consciousness got changed at the same time."

Leary's days as an apostolic acidhead were short-lived, relative to his enduring reputation as a somewhat offbeat celebrity (including his choreographed death in 1996 and the launch of his earthly remains into space a year later). In 1967 he told a *Look* reporter, "I'm already an anachronism in the LSD movement." With that pronouncement, he may have been trying to get the media off his back while abjuring responsibility for a legion of turned-on, tuned-in dropouts he could no longer control. Perhaps he never really controlled them at all. As a March 1969

Rolling Stone review of *High Priest* put it: "Dr. Leary's well-intentioned but relentless insistence upon religion and religious ceremonies and his articulation of the LSD experience in the 'spiritual' lexicon...tend to alienate him from the head in San Francisco who drops acid and goes to the Fillmore or the freak in L.A. who takes acid and pilots his motorcycle on the freeways."

Despite "losing contact with those who already support his heterodoxies," Leary managed to remain in the public eye. Over the next three years, he was busted for pot, appealed his case to the Supreme Court (where he won), was busted again and imprisoned, and then escaped to Algeria with the help of the radical Weathermen. He lived with Eldridge Cleaver, another messianic exile from America, until they got on each other's nerves.

AS THE KALEIDOSCOPE TURNS

While it's easy to get sidetracked by Leary's glittering orbit, it's also perfectly clear that the groundwork for a psychedelic revolution was firmly in place, with or without him. Though the general public wouldn't learn much about it until 1966 or so, LSD began sending shock waves throughout the Bay Area underground as far back as 1962. This revolution of the mind circumvented the entire mechanism of mainstream Western society, enacting change on a far deeper—but, paradoxically, less quantifiable—level than that which came from the ballot box, courthouse, or classroom. It affected the way people lived to the point that it altered their perceptions of life itself, propounding what R.D. Laing dubbed "the politics of experience."

By the time the rest of the country got hip to the San Francisco scene, its idyllic underground years were ending. One of the darker days came on October 6, 1966.

The Politics of Experience
R. D. Laing

Scottish-born psychiatrist R.D. Laing (1927–1989) was already a controversial figure in his field—nontraditional treatment for schizophrenia—when his *The Politics of Experience* (1967) became both a bestseller and a buzzphrase (the groovy cover art didn't hurt). Laing believed "insanity" was often a sane adaptation to an insane time. His challenge: "Adaptation to what? To society? To a mad world?"

That's when a law passed by the state of California declaring LSD an illegal drug went into effect. The demonic implications of the date's "666" numerology were not lost on the denizens of Haight-Ashbury, who held a Love Pageant Rally in Golden Gate Park in protest. A "Prophecy of a Declaration of Independence" was read: "We hold these truths to be self-evident...The freedom of the body, the pursuit of joy, and the expansion of consciousness."

Yet illegality only served to make LSD's taking more secretive and therefore an act of rebellion with sacramental overtones. It did not stem the day-glo tide in the least, even though Sandoz Pharmaceuticals, the drug's original maker, got out of the LSD business under pressure from authorities. It fell to other sources to supply the magic potion. The medicine man who picked up where Sandoz left off was Augustus Owsley Stanley III, the black sheep of a respected Kentucky family who drifted to San Francisco after a stint in the Air Force.

With the help of a Berkeley chemistry student, Owsley began producing and selling LSD in 1965. The next year, Owsley teamed with Rock Scully (later the manager of the Grateful Dead) to set up an underground acid factory on Point Richmond, an isolated finger of land across the water from San Quentin State Prison. On October 6, Owsley officially became an outlaw. By then, he was already mass-producing huge quantities of color-coded (red, green, blue, white, purple, orange), carefully measured (exactly 250 micrograms), standard-priced (two bucks a hit), remarkably pure LSD. He produced acid tabs by the millions.

Owsley's acid batches and those of other renegade chemists acquired colorfully descriptive street names: Blue Cheer, Blue Dots, Clear Light, Green Flats, Mr. Natural, Orange Wedge, Purple Barrels, Purple Haze, Sunshine, Window Pane, White Lightning, and so on. Other mood- and mind-altering substances further fueled the head-feeding frenzy: marijuana (of which 31 different "brands" are recorded), hashish, hash oil, crystal meth, peyote, MDMA, mescaline, opium, psilocybin. The mind boggles.

"The story of that era has never been really written about adequately," claims a Bay Area poster artist. "So much was happening all over the world. I'm afraid it would take a Tolstoy to delineate the complex relations involved. There were games within games within games. For a short period of years, the eye of God opened and thousands were given a vision of the sublime."

Now let us turn our attention to the creative manifestations and spiritual pursuits of the counterculture as they tripped down what the Grateful Dead referred to as "the golden road to unlimited devotion."

You know, the place where the eye of God opened.

YOUR NAME AND EGO ARE ABOUT TO CEASE

The following is an excerpt from "Instructions for Use During a Psychedelic Session," a poetical-philosophical guide to LSD ingestion from a collection of writings by Aldous Huxley. Presumably, one's guru or flight instructor was supposed to recite this to an acid eater just prior to liftoff. Bon voyage!

O (*name of voyager*)
The time has come for you to seek new levels of reality.
Your ego and the (*name*) game are about to cease.
You are about to be set face to face with the Clear Light.
You are about to experience it in its reality.
In the ego-free state, wherein all things are like the void and cloudless sky,
And the naked spotless intellect is like a transparent vacuum;
At this moment, know yourself and abide in that state.

O (*name of voyager*),
That which is called ego-death is coming to you.
Remember:
This is now the hour of death and rebirth;
Take advantage of this temporary death to obtain the perfect state—
Enlightenment.

I CHING MEETS MR. GOODWRENCH

The following is a verbatim account by Joe McHugh, founder of East Totem West (a psychedelic graphics company), of how the *I Ching* was utilized during the peak of psychedelia:

The *I Ching* was a method of divining six lines. Various states of existence were either broken or solid, and coins and sticks were ways to divine this. We all got into *I Ching*. I really think that by using the *I Ching* I cured a leukemia case once. I ended up living with this woman and her five-year-old son in a room about the size of a table. She'd bolted from chemo six months earlier, and I was thinking of trying to get her to see a shaman in New Mexico. Then I threw a *Ching* on her, and I decided I'd interpret it as some kind of cure. Get hairs from her head, wrap them in bacon fat, boil them in a three-cornered pot, break the pot, and throw them in a stream. The *Ching* told me to do this. So I did it, and as far as I know she's been okay since. I still use *I Ching* to tell me things. It's fixed my car a number of times. My 1969 Mercury.

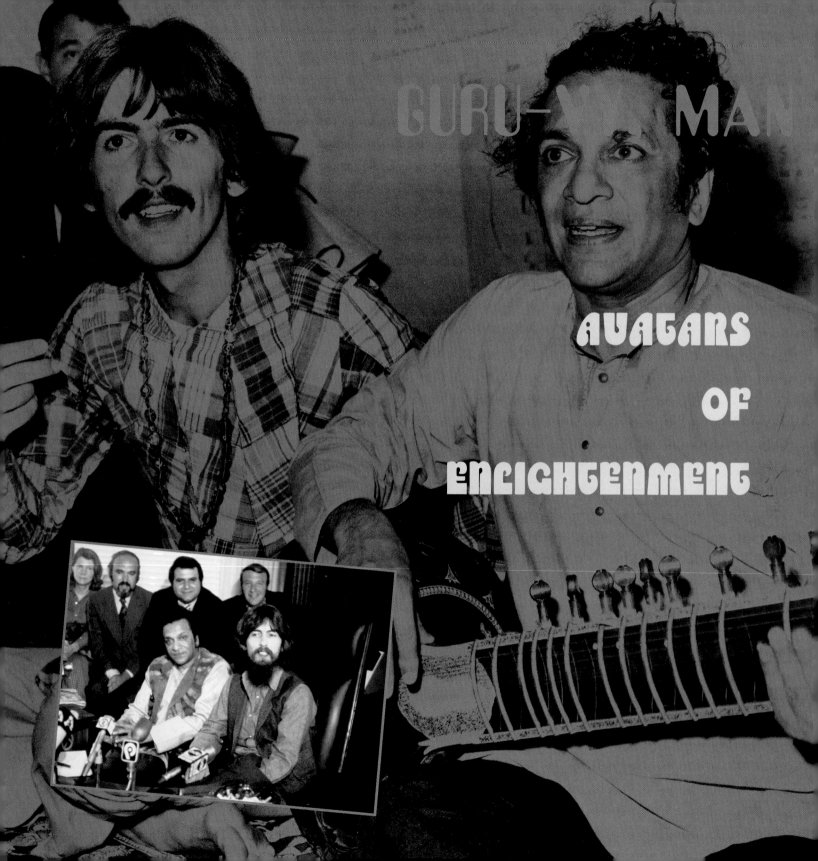

GURU-XXX MAN

AVATARS
OF
ENLIGHTENMENT

To attend to the needs of the con-sciousness-raising movement—a spiritual adjunct of psychedelia—a holy host of gurus arrived from the East (mostly India) in the 1960s. They came bearing beads, incense, sitars, philosophy, and religion. The most celebrated was Maharishi Mahesh Yogi, who became associated with the Beatles and Beach Boys.

Beatles' guitarist George Harrison met Ravi Shankar in 1965, hoping to expand his musical horizons by taking sitar lessons from a master of the instrument. He not only became infatuated with India's music, but also its spiritual, sartorial, and political life, too. Plus, he and Shankar became good friends. They're seen here at a 1967 post-*Pepper* press conference and (inset) at another press gig in July 1971, announcing a joint effort to host a benefit concert for war and famine victims in Bangladesh.

The Beatles met the Maharishi through George Harrison, whose delight in the great sitarist Ravi Shankar fed both his interest in Indian music and Indian philosophy.

As Paul McCartney related in *Days in the Life*, Jonathon Green's oral history of the English Underground, "You started to hear of the Bhagavad Gita [a portion of the *Mahabharata*, the holiest book of Hinduism] and stuff like that. And it was all a bit hazy because it wasn't like an official religion, you were chucking in bits of Kahlil Gibran, and this sort of stuff, and *Siddhartha*, which wasn't necessarily to do with it, but all seemed the same kind of thing....It was a very hectic world one was living in and this inner peace seemed to be a better thing. If nothing else, what Maharishi was suggesting was a pleasant relief from all that in order to recharge your batteries—that basically was all he said."

After recording *Sgt. Pepper's Lonely Hearts Club Band* in mid-1967, the Beatles retreated to Wales to recharge their psychic batteries with the Maharishi and his regimen of Transcendental Meditation. This brought the giggly, silver-maned guru into the spotlight, where he thrived. Soon Mike Love (of the Beach Boys) and folksinger Donovan joined the bandwagon. They and several others, including Mia Farrow and her sister, accompanied the Beatles to the Maharishi's ashram in India in early 1968. Ultimately, it turned out to be an ill-fated trip that found all the Beatles but George growing wary of the guru.

Mike Love, however, remained convinced and in fact talked his fellow Beach Boys into having the Maharishi join them on a U.S. concert tour in 1968, where he spread the TM gospel from the stage. Surrounded by a sea of flowers, pontificating in his high, nasal voice,

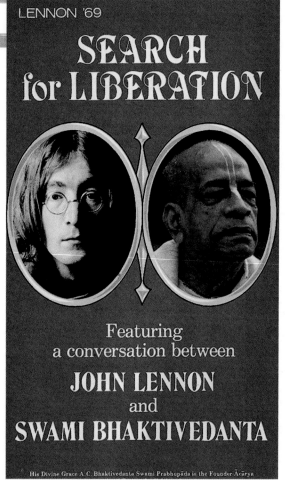

LENNON '69

SEARCH for LIBERATION

Featuring
a conversation between
JOHN LENNON
and
SWAMI BHAKTIVEDANTA

His Divine Grace A.C. Bhaktivedanta Swami Prabhupāda is the Founder-Ācārya

the Maharishi made one of rock's oddest opening acts. This outing came at a time when the Beach Boys were neither having hit singles nor making inroads with skeptical hippies. Not surprisingly, the tour was a bust, and group member Al Jardine once remarked that only the florists made any money. But one must give the Beach Boys their due: for a rock group shunned by the counterculture for a presumed lack of hipness, enlisting the Maharishi was actually a pretty hip gesture.

Before psychedelic drugs infiltrated the culture—bringing with it a hunger for spiritual guidance—many revered and respected teachers from the East had been spreading the word to small, receptive circles of eager disciples. In Southern California, British expatriate Christopher Isherwood became a follower of a Hindu monk named Swami Prabhavananda and wrote eloquently about his transcendent experiences. So did his friend and fellow writer Aldous Huxley, who lived nearby. Both men (along with thousands of others) also grew enamored of Jiddu Krishnamurti, a wise man who'd renounced the "new Messiah" title thrust upon him as a youth by the Theosophical Society. He maintained a home base north of Santa Barbara, at Ojai, but traveled the world well into his 80s, teaching and inspiring the quest for spiritual independence.

Other influential figures included Ramakrishna, who taught Swami Prabhavananda and numbered Henry Miller among his followers; Yogananda, whose best-selling

Autobiography of a Yogi (1946) was a powerful precedent for the spiritual revolution of the 1960s; and G.I. Gurdjieff, a Russian mystic, teacher, and seeker whose translated writings (most notably *Meetings With Remarkable Men*) found many admirers in the '60s.

In the Bay Area, a small colony of Zen Buddhist practitioners gravitated to the waterfront village of Sausalito, in Marin County, beginning in the early 1950s. Under the benign guidance of Alan Watts, a charismatic expatriate British theologian, they sought a "way of liberation" through Zen. More an intellectual discipline than ritualized religion, Zen struck a chord among college students, artists, and other free thinkers. Watts, a brilliant writer and thinker, told Paul Krassner of *The Realist*, "My philosophy is not concerned with what should be, but what is." Prodded by Krassner, he refused to define Zen, calling labels "degrading." Witness this exchange with Krassner:

Q: What is Zen?

A: [*Soft chuckling.*]

Q: Would you care to enlarge on that?

A: [*Loud guffawing*].

The relatively benign "yogi" (or teacher) Yogananda was the first spiritual teacher from the East to achieve widespread notice in the United States. His candid and highly readable 1946 *Autobiography* (above) was an exotic precursor to what has now been blandly marketed as New Age. The Maharishi (left) at one of his TM celebrity sessions in 1968, giving new meaning to the term "flower power."

Perhaps the best-known proponent of Zen was Gary Snyder, the naturalist/poet who served as Jack Kerouac's model for the saintly Japhy Ryder in *The Dharma Bums* (1958). As that gentle novel makes abundantly clear, Zen offers no easy path to spiritual liberation. Perhaps this explains why, outside of the provocative writings about Zen by Watts and D.T. Suzuki, it never set the hearts and minds of Middle America's kids ablaze. It was too much work.

Meher Baba's familiar face and calming presence seemed to pop up everywhere, including on a poster leaned against a tarp at the Woodstock Festival in August 1969. One of Baba's most ardent devotees (inset) was Who leader Pete Townshend. During studio sessions for *Tommy*, a pensive Townshend sports his guru's visage on a button affixed to his T-shirt. While *Tommy* can be seen as Townshend's personal spiritual odyssey, it took on universal meaning as a "rock opera." The credits on the album sleeve list composer, producer, chief engineer, cover designer, photographer, and, last but not least, avatar (Meher Baba).

Another Bay Area figure on the ramparts of mysticism was Carlos Castaneda, who found his path while an anthropology grad student at Berkeley. What began as a dissertation turned into a five-year apprenticeship with Don Juan, a Yaqui "man of knowledge" and "diablero" (black sorcerer). The result was the best-selling book *The Teachings of Don Juan: a Yaqui Way of Knowledge* (1968). If Timothy Leary had been a Pied Piper, Don Juan was an Army drill sergeant by comparison. Though he used natural psychedelic stimulants (peyote, datura, psilocybin mushrooms, *genista canariensis*), Don Juan could often be inscrutable and occasionally downright mean, and Castaneda's book ends with the student running in fear from the guru. Castaneda went back, of course, and wrote several more books about his psychedelic experiences. Stewart Brand, of the *Whole Earth Catalog*, called Castaneda and Don Juan the "frontier Boswell and Johnson" and said, "I don't have words for the importance I consider these books to carry."

In a more subtle and silent way, a guru named Meher Baba indirectly influenced millions through the words and music of his disciple, Pete Townshend of the Who. Townshend borrowed heavily from Baba's teachings for the Who's rock opera *Tommy* and his later solo work. In 1953, Baba declared himself an avatar (or divine incarnation) with the pronouncement, "I am the Highest of the High." In his 1969 obituary, *Rolling Stone* remembered Baba as "the familiar benign face on the little cards of anti-drug advice handed out at Be-Ins." Long before Nancy Reagan came along with her wooden antidrug campaign, Baba epitomized the "just say no" philosophy, and not only with drugs. He didn't just say no; he went further and said nothing at all. Baba kept a vow of silence for 43 years, communicating via sign language and alphabet board. (Here's one for the *Twilight Zone*: quiet Meher Baba died the same day as "Gabby" Hayes.)

While many hippies did not always follow the guru's advice on drugs, they admired his teachings. The following is an account by Joe McHugh, founder of East Totem West (a psychedelic graphics company), of a mind-blowing experience involving Meher Baba.

"I had a weird experience with Meher Baba once. It was a rainy February afternoon. I got out my dope box and decided to take this 'space pill' I'd been given. I was told to put it in a pipe and smoke it, and it would get me high for three days. I took one drag just to try it. I felt like I'd just stepped through the side door of an acid trip. I went in the bedroom to relax and figure out where I was. I picked up a copy of *Astral Projection*, which was a spiritual paper out of Albuquerque. I turned the page and saw a picture of Meher Baba. I looked at it, said 'Ouch,' turned the page real quick and put the paper down. Then I came back to it and told the picture, 'You're fucking with my head.'

"I threw it down on the floor and sat cross-legged on the bed. I'm looking around and thinking, 'This has never happened before with a picture. I've done it before with people, staring in someone's eyes.' So I found a picture of Gurdjieff and looked at that, but it wouldn't look back. No other picture worked. I said, 'All right, Meher Baba,' and I opened the paper again and looked at the picture. It was an experience of going through space, a multitude of forms, nothing to put my finger on. A month later, I found out that Meher Baba had died on the day I was looking at his picture. It was like I was in the draft of his pulling out."

A coda to '60s guru-mania: Columbia Records, ever eager to milk a trend, decided that guru futures might still be profitable as late as 1971. That's when they released a two-record set of spoken wisdom by Swami Satchidananda. By then, apparently, all available consciousness had been raised, as it turned out to be the worst-selling album in company history. Of the Swami's platter, a skeptical reviewer for *Fusion* magazine asked, "If Satchidananda and Professor Irwin Corey aren't one and the same person, how come you never see them together?"

In summary, what began as a

sincere pursuit of spiritual guidance—what Joseph Campbell would famously declare "following your bliss"—turned into a space race of a different sort. Inner space, so to speak, rather than outer space: who could get you to Nirvana the fastest, who could take you the furthest and highest, who offered the best afterlife benefits package. It was a massive case of attention deficit disorder, with millions of freaks trampling every imaginable path toward inner space, from the sublime to the ridiculous to the dangerous. The latter would culminate with the depraved reign over a cult of pliable, murderous androids by Charles Manson, who briefly was a resident of the Haight.

Tarot, *I Ching*, TM, T-groups, Synanon, yoga, astrology, Hare Krishna, primal screaming—you name it, we tried it. The residual effects of this alternative quest ultimately led to the New Age movement, multitudinous manifestations of which are now firmly entrenched across the land.

A sobering reality check arrived in the United States in 1970 in the rotund form of a teenaged "perfect being" called Guru Mahara Ji. Just as Tiny Tim had made long hair and Flower Power a laughingstock for all the wrong reasons, this guru, with his inscrutable babblings, gave alternative spirituality an easily satirized bad name. When Rennie Davis, a Berkeley-bred New Leftist and member of the Chicago Seven, announced that he'd become a devotee of Guru Mahara Ji, it was obvious that something—the will to address the political future? the sanity of the liberal left?—was coming to an end. Perhaps it officially came to an end when fellow Chicago Seven co-conspirator-turned-yuppie-entrepreneur Jerry Rubin began holding networking parties at Studio 54 in New York at mid-decade.

Looked at in its best light, all this dashing about in inner space brought into sharper focus the spiritual hunger of the Love Generation, who seemed willing to try anything but the mainstream religions of their elders. The Christian church, both Protestant and Catholic, got hip to this in a hurry, especially after *Time* magazine ran a cover story that asked the $64,000 Question: "Is God Dead?" Seemingly desperate measures were employed to attract the wayward sheep back into the fold of Christianity. Catholic churches, fueled by the loosening dictates of the Pope's Vatican II encyclicals, resorted to coffeehouses and folk masses. Almost every church, including the Protestant church, began hiring youthful assistant pastors who sported turtlenecks, facial hair, and peace pendants. Their mission impossible was to make church at least as interesting as smoking pot and listening to Doors albums. Some churches, like the ultraliberal Unitarians, tried hard to pursue that mixture of brotherly hipness and spiritual zeal that could be found at the intersection of Haight and Ashbury once upon a time.

Mommy, What's a Psychedelic?

The nine-minute opening track from the first album by Funkadelic is entitled "Mommy, What's a Funkadelic?" Despite lots of spacey rambling from the group's funk-psych frontman, George Clinton, the question never really gets answered, although rock critic Robert Christgau ventured a pithy response in his capsule review for the *Village Voice*: "Someone from Carolina who encountered eternity on LSD and vowed to contain it in a groove."

If you swapped "California" for "Carolina," you'd have a pretty fair definition of psychedelic, at least in its musical manifestation. *Webster's Third College Edition* defines the adjective psychedelic a bit more broadly: **1** of or causing extreme changes in the conscious mind, as hallucinations, delusions, intensification of awareness and sensory perception, etc. **2** of or associated with psychedelic drugs; specif. simulating the auditory or visual effects of the psychedelic state. (In the latter '60s, the "psychedelic state" might as well have been the 51st one in the union, with its capital being San Francisco.) Psychedelic music, logically enough, aspired to evoke the altered awareness that came with a psychedelic drug experience.

In the '60s, it was music made and received at the frontiers of consciousness by people who were looking to (in Jim Morrison's words) "break on through to the other side." Needless to say, it was not enjoyed or understood by cheerleaders, younger sisters, the malt-shop crowd, bullies, athletes (lacrosse and ping-pong players excepted), frat boys, police-men, clergymen, people who worked under car hoods, Republicans, schoolteachers (except for the hip biology teacher who later got busted for selling pot), elected officials, the Joint Chiefs of Staff, Nixon-Agnew, your parents, and your friends' parents. Everyone over the age of 30, it was safe to assume, was ignorant or disapproving of all that psychedelia represented. How could it be otherwise?

At one extreme it was confrontational music, often brutal in sound and texture. Groups like the Jimi Hendrix Experience, Big Brother and the Holding Company, Steppenwolf, the Doors, and Vanilla Fudge made what often got called "acid rock," which can best be described as psychedelia at its rawest and most intense. Bad trips as well as good, riots as well as peace, pain as well as pleasure—the whole spectrum of reality, not just the idyllic bits, were captured by acid rock. Think of the thundering momentum of Steppenwolf's "Born to Be Wild," the slo-mo Sturm und Drang of Vanilla Fudge's first album, the existential isolation of the Doors' *Strange Days*, and the pyrotechnic roar of Jimi Hendrix's guitar throughout *Are You Experienced?* The garagey side of psychedelia—represented by such combustible singles as the Electric Prunes' "I Had Too Much to Dream Last Night," the Blues Magoos' "We Ain't Got Nothin' Yet," the Music Machine's "Talk Talk," and Love's "7 & 7 Is"—also qualify as acid rock by virtue of their energy and intimation of psychic overload. That, in a nutshell, is acid rock, scourge of PTA groups and *Look* magazine.

By contrast, psychedelia could be as gentle as a spring rain, massaging the psyche with good vibes and sweetly inscrutable sounds. Stellar examples of psychedelia's blithe spirits include Pink Floyd's *Piper at the Gates of Dawn*, Spirit's languid and eponymous first album, Donovan's whimsical and exotic *Sunshine Superman* and *Mellow Yellow* LPs, and the Beach Boys circa *Smiley Smile*. The neo-psychedelic movement of the '70s and '80s yielded a new coinage, "paisley pop," and in hindsight that works nicely to describe certain poppier strains of '60s psychedelia, epitomized by some of the sunnier-sounding singles that came out of Southern California in the late '60s. Any song that mentions ice cream, candy, cinnamon, bells, flowers, rainbows, or the word *groovy* probably qualifies as paisley pop. The presence of a harpsichord, Jimmy Webb–style horn arrangements, or melismatic bah-bah-bahs is another tipoff. Personal favorites in this subgenre include "Tomorrow" by Strawberry Alarm Clock, "You Showed Me" by the Turtles, Love's "Orange Skies," the Left Banke's "Desiree," and "Yellow Balloon" by Yellow Balloon.

Often, you might find both extremes—aggression and reverie, or Luv 'n' Haight (as Sly Stone put it)—coexisting on the same piece of vinyl. Take Jefferson Airplane's *After Bathing at Baxter's*, which had songs both unnerving (Grace Slick's "Two Heads") and serene (Paul Kantner's "Saturday Afternoon"). At its best, psychedelia was a kind of musical bas-relief, encompassing varied psychic terrain. It can be argued that its ambition and imagination gave rise to "progressive rock," a genre that appeared at the tail end of the '60s and thrived during the first half of the '70s in the work of Yes, Genesis, King Crimson, Van der Graaf Generator, and others. With its emphasis on inventive, expert musicianship and its fanciful and often drawn-out musical landscapes, progressive rock was one of the fruits born of the psychedelic years.

To return to the original question—what specifically qualifies something as "psychedelic"?—here are some of the more recognizable cues:

- **Sound effects:** The sound of the guitar was the easiest indicator. Distortion, fuzztone, wah-wah, feedback, and other effects were typical of the auditory hallucinations simulated by guitarists playing in a psychedelic style. To witness the difference a decade makes, compare Eddie Cochran's '50s rockabilly version of his classic "Summertime Blues." Then listen to the psychedelic shredder into which the San Francisco bikers-on-acid trio Blue Cheer processed it. *Vive la différence!*

- **Guitar solos:** The role of the guitar was different from what had come before, too. Considerably more soloing and improvisation were done in the psychedelic era. The term "lead guitar" did not mean much before then; afterward, lead guitarists often outshone lead singers as focal points. Many groups, like the Dead and Quicksilver, didn't even have a lead singer, as in someone who stood at the mike with nothing save for maybe a tambourine to shake. The guitarists did most of the explaining, wordlessly.

•**Exotic instruments:** Psychedelic music was baroque music. Sitars, harpsichords, glockenspiels, and other exotic instruments were all part of psychedelia's boldly ecumenical reach. The Beatles tested the waters with the Indian twang of George Harrison's sitar, first heard on "Norwegian Wood." The Incredible String Band specialized in eclecticism, playing virtually anything that could be plucked or pounded. On *A Beacon From Mars*, Kaleidoscope mixed mandolin, harpguitar, harmonium, caz, and oud into their psychedelic elixir. And on *Anthem of the Sun*, the Grateful Dead were credited with playing the following, in addition to conventional rock-band instruments: vibraslap, celesta claves, harpsichord, trumpet, guiro, kazoo, timpani, orchestra bells, gong, chimes, crotales, prepared piano, finger cymbals, and electronic tape. Quite a montage of sounds they got, too!

•**Song length:** A bona fide psychedelic album generally has at least one long track (minimum length six minutes) on it. Stellar example: The Doors' first album, which ends with "The End," clocking in at a harrowing, Oedipal 11 minutes and 35 seconds. Extra points are awarded for side-long epics and double albums (like Cream's *Wheels of Fire*, which scored on both counts). Be wary of albums that outwardly look psychedelic but consist of 11 or 12 short songs under three minutes. Chances are the band sounds like Sergio Mendes and Brazil '66 or the cast of *Hair*.

•**Hair length:** If a majority of band members' hair crept past their shoulders, they were in all likelihood bona fide hippies. Make sure to steer clear of psychedelic-seeming albums whose makers are clean-shaven and smiley or potbellied swingers with beatnik facial hair; they're probably holdovers from another genre—folksingers or greaser-rockers or somesuch. A female singer in bell-bottoms with a Breck Girl hairstyle is another dead giveaway that the album within will sound more like "Guantanamera" than *Cheap Thrills*, no matter how wavy and elongated the lettering without.

•**Thematic content:** Most truly psychedelic music is not about boy–girl relationships or the pain of breaking up. If the subject of love was addressed, it was in a more universal sense, as in the Youngbloods' "Get Together." Psychedelic music is impressionistic and open to interpretation. It's about moods. It's about consciousness. It's about space. It is generally not about noun-type things or conventional "feelings." What was Country Joe's "Section 43" about? What was George Harrison saying in "Within You Without You"? What did Jim Morrison mean when he chanted "learn to forget" in "Soul Kitchen"? You don't need hard, precise answers in order to understand on some level. Suffice to say that if an album appeared to look beyond the drear of the everyday, you probably hit psychedelic paydirt.

The following chapters are about the cities and scenes where psychedelic music flowered in the '60s. Keeping in mind the loose guidelines above, let us now open the lid to the psychedelic sarcophagus and poke around a bit.

"GOT A REVOLUTION, GOT TO [REV]OLUTION"

A GATHERING OF THE TRIBES IN SAN FRANCISCO

ven though San Francisco gave rise to a lifestyle revolution on all fronts in the 1960s, people primarily know of and remember the city for its eight key musical entities: the Grateful Dead, Jefferson Airplane, Quicksilver Messenger Service, Big Brother and the Holding Company, Moby Grape, Steve Miller Band, Santana, and Country Joe and the Fish. That is the short list of musical entities whose reputa-

Janis Joplin joined Big Brother and the Holding Company in June 1965. Of her frenetic acid-blues vocals, she commented: "I don't know how to perform any other way. I've tried cooling myself and not screaming, and I've walked off feeling like nothing."

tions traveled beyond the Bay Area. But to look at this scene solely in terms of half a dozen or so bands that landed major label record contracts is like focusing on a few bits of colored glass rather than the whole rainbow of activity churning away inside the kaleidoscope of San Francisco in the mid-to-late '60s (but especially in 1966 and 1967).

What became of Fruminous Bandersnatch? Whither the Mystery Trend? Wherefore art thou, Loading Zone? Why do bands like the Other Half and Oxford Circle go unmentioned in accounts of the era? How come so few are aware that it all began with the Charlatans? Memories can be short and accounts incomplete, especially when they're reduced to a few digestible hooks by the media. All of the lesser-known groups mentioned above routinely shared bills at Bay Area ballrooms with the likes of the Dead, the Airplane, et al. However, because record contracts were not indiscriminately handed out like cheap souvenirs the way they are today, relatively few bands on this prolific scene had their music preserved.

Major-label vinyl artifacts and media accounts have only told part of the story. What about all of the lost and forgotten music? Consider that Ralph J. Gleason, a respected San Francisco news-paper journalist and elder statesman who turned his attention from jazz to rock, compiled a list of nearly 400 performing San Francisco bands in an appendix to *The Jefferson Airplane and the San Francisco Sound*, published in 1969. His methodology: "I went back and combed through all the columns I had written for the *Chronicle*, all the little notices and posters of dances and events featuring bands since the first Family Dog dance at the Longshoreman's Hall in October 1965."

Here are some personal favorite obscure band names plucked from that list: Black Shit Puppy Farm, Colossal Pomegranate, the Golden Toad, Jose's Appliances, Magnesium Water Lily, the Only Alternative and His Other Possibilities, the Recurring Love Habit, Thorstein Veblun Blues Band, the Uncut Balloon, the Universal Parking Lot, and You. (Yeah, You.)

If the San Francisco 400 had been around in the high-tech '90s, there would no doubt be a glut of

The Jefferson Airplane—Marty Balin, Jorma Kaukonen, Paul Kantner, Spencer Dryden, Grace Slick, and Jack Casady (from left)—in an outtake from the photo session for *Surrealistic Pillow*.

major- and indie-label releases or at least well-circulated DATs and a home page for every blessed one of them. Maybe we're fortunate that the limitations of technology, the constraints of the '60s music biz, and the dustbin of history have left us speculating what they sounded like. It's tempting to imagine awesome and wonderful music, but some of those lost sentinels on the psychedelic frontier surely were execrable, judging from certain obscure album releases of the time. That is to say, instead of psyche-delic wonderment, more than a few who looked and appeared to act the part of would-be psyche-delic Pied Pipers were actually pur-veyors of second-rate blues, pop, folk, and unintentionally hilarious acid-rock self-caricature. (See pages 180–183 for more on this.)

All the same, there's lots more to the story than *Surrealistic Pillow*, *Cheap Thrills*, and *Abraxis*, the three most commercially successful albums by San Francisco–based bands released in the '60s. In fact, without breaking a sweat, we came up with a list of a hundred albums from the psychedelic era that would enrich any album or CD collection (see pages 106–107 for our list of the best). Truth to tell, quite a few awesome psychedelic artifacts from San Francisco's heyday have slipped through the cracks. You haven't lived until your ears have been shredded by Blue Cheer's "Magnolia Caboose Babyfinger" (from the album *Outsideinside*) or been drawn into a vortex of fast drugs via Mad River's "Amphetamine Gazelle" (from their eponymous debut, a truly over-the-top release). If you want messages of love drizzled all over your ears like rainbows, check out It's a Beautiful Day (whose first two albums, especially the untitled debut featuring the anthemic "White Bird," are essential) and the Sons of Champlin (whose *Loosen Up Naturally* was one of the first and few double albums of the age).

Now those are psychedelic, and regardless of what drugs they're taking these days in Seattle or wherever, they just don't make 'em like that anymore.

DAWN OF THE DEAD

The roots of San Francisco's turn to psychedelia begin somewhere in the hazy changing of the guard between beatniks and hippies. The former

The Grateful Dead—Bill Kreutzmann, Bob Weir, Pigpen, Jerry Garcia, and Phil Lesh (from left)—play king of the hill in Haight-Ashbury.

were fingerpopping, jive-talking leftists who hung out at jazz dens and coffeehouses, favoring folk music, poetry, bebop jazz, facial hair, and bulky sweaters. The latter were virtual anarchists, acid-dosed revelers and dropouts who eschewed politics (why dignify a corrupt system, their logic went, by participating on any level?) and gravitated to rock music, communal dances, and other rituals of the tribe. Leaving the driving to Owsley, the rogue chemist who manufactured acid hits by the millions, the denizens of Haight-Ashbury embraced activity that had no inherent meaning, surrendering to chaos as a means of reestablishing lost connections to the true, pure soul and spirit of the human animal. The object was spiritual enlightenment or at least a good, cleansing cosmic giggle.

Jerry Garcia, on going with the flow at Kesey's Acid Tests, from a 1969 *Rolling Stone* article by writer Michael Lydon: "So you take LSD and suddenly you are aware of another plane, or several other planes, and the quest is to extend that limit, to go as far as you can go. In the Acid Tests that meant to do away with old forms, with

old ideas, try something new....When it was moving right, you could dig that there was something that it was getting toward, something like ordered chaos or some region of chaos."

Beatniks essentially belonged to the '50s, hippies to the '60s. Yet there were ties between the two subcultures, and the former loosened up San Francisco to allow for the occupation of the latter. Allen Ginsberg moved easily between decades and factions, recognizing the commonalities rather than the barriers. Poet Michael McClure, novelist Ken Kesey, deejay Tom Donahue, and Beat Generation figurehead Neal

Cassady were several others who made the transition and lingered to influence the course of events within the hippie community.

The occupation began around 1963 when students, musicians, drifters, and exiled North Beach beatniks discovered that they could rent fabulous Victorian mansions for next to nothing in an old, neglected neighborhood of blacks, Orientals, and Russian retirees known as Haight-Ashbury.

All around the Bay Area

Jefferson Airplane rock out in a TV appearance from 1968.

the elements of a scene were germinating independently. Jerry Garcia and members of what would eventually become the Grateful Dead gigged around the Palo Alto area in folk/blues/jugband ensembles with names like Mother McCree's Uptown Jug Champions. Janis Joplin was playing folk blues at area clubs and coffeehouses as far back as 1963, accompanied on and off during a two-year period by future Jefferson Airplane guitarist Jorma Kaukonen (who was then studying sociology at Santa Clara State University). Paul Kantner of the Airplane was originally a card-carrying folksinger who has cited San Francisco's Kingston Trio—three guitar- and banjo-strumming entertainers who brought folk music from campus coffeehouses into the American mainstream—as a major influence. Prior to forming Quicksilver Messenger Service, David Freiberg was part of a folk-comedy duo (David and Linda) that performed around San Francisco and even opened for Woody Allen in New York one night when the latter was doing standup comedy.

Frieberg has attributed the move from acoustic to electric music in San Francisco around mid-decade to the Beatles and the lack of work for folksingers. The shattering psychokinetic effects of LSD upon a community of laid-back potheads also served as a wake-up call to turn on and plug in. But in many ways the folk-blues influence lingered, becoming integrated into the psychedelic rock framework.

Before psychedelic music, there was a pop-folk movement around San Francisco involving groups like the Kingston Trio and the Limelighters. Bay Area

Quicksilver Messenger Service, from the cover of their 1975 reunion LP, *Solid Silver:* (left to right) Dino Valenti, David Freiberg, Gary Duncan, Greg Elmore, and John Cipollina.

musicians got into folk music through such groups but then did even more homework in trying to get at the roots of the folk canon by figuring out where the songs originated and discovering new ones. They researched sheet music and listened to field recordings done for the Library of Congress by Alan Lomax. A perfect example: "Down on Me" and "Blind Man," both of which appeared on Big Brother and the Holding Company's first album, were learned from the Lomax recordings. This kind of folk-purist approach definitely stayed with a lot of musicians who evolved into psychedelic rock and rollers.

Indeed, the first Jefferson Airplane album, *Jefferson Airplane Takes Off,* was a fairly conventional folk-rock affair. Quicksilver's debut recordings—a pair of songs that appeared on the soundtrack to a movie about the counterculture called *Revolution*—included their electrified version of "Codine," a folk song by Buffy Sainte-Marie. Early Grateful Dead sets largely consisted of retooled folk, blues, and bluegrass standards such as "I Know You Rider" and "Beat It on Down the Line." While the scene subsequently became heavily psychedelicized and fiercely original, those roots were never entirely forsaken. In fact, in the case of the Grateful Dead, they would reassert themselves after the dust had cleared on such back-to-the-basics LPs as *Workingman's Dead* and *American Beauty*, early-1970s releases that stand as the band's finest studio work.

THE FABULOUS CHARLATANS

Already, the story has gotten ahead of itself. To return to the origins of psychedelia, the band that first blazed trails into realms of altered consciousness and alternative ways of presenting music was the Charlatans. It can be argued that the musical side of the San Francisco scene began not in San Francisco but in Virginia City, Nevada, with the Charlatans' movable feast. The story of the sadly neglected Charlatans is enough to reinforce the notion that the real history of the San Francisco scene lies buried in semi-obscurity. No one who knows the scene well disputes the fact that the Charlatans got the ball rolling. But save for one unrepresentative, misbegotten, and hopelessly obscure 1966 single on the Kapp label—"The Shadow Knows" b/w "32-20 Blues"—nothing was released by the original Charlatans. A revamped version of the band recorded a generally disparaged album on the Philips label in 1969 for which departed founder George Hunter contributed only cover artwork. It wasn't until 1996 that their historic early recordings from 1966 were exhumed and issued on a British-only CD entitled *The Amazing Charlatans* (Big Beat Records).

Though the Charlatans—especially their leader, autoharp strummer, and tambourine banger George Hunter—couldn't play particularly well, they were truly where it all began. When you're a pioneer, technique takes a backseat to the quality of the ideas and their ability to shake up the status quo and launch a new movement.

According to irascible old Bill Graham, the concert promoter and Fillmore manager who saw to it that the trains ran on time in tripped-out San Francisco, the Charlatans were "the greatest." In a 1969 interview with journalist Ralph J. Gleason, he said, "To me, the Charlatans have always been the epitome of what San Francisco really was, the way they dressed, their whole style. I love them."

In the beginning, there were five Charlatans: George Hunter, Mike Wilhelm, Richie Olsen, Mike Ferguson, and Dan Hicks. Hunter was the prime mover, an L.A.-trained architect who moved up to the Bay Area and decided to "design" a band. In both their attire and music, they harked back to earlier eras in American history. They wore antique clothing that made them look like dandified outlaws and riverboat gamblers. Their repertoire of songs could have come from a player piano in an Old West saloon.

So what did their mixed bag of antique costuming and songs like "Sweet Sue" have to do with the space-age world of LSD? In Hunter's mind, the drug served as a conduit out of the polluted late 20th-century mind-set back to a world that made more sense and had more genuine style. "The nostalgia thing seemed to be on its way in," Hunter recalled in a 1976 article in *Rolling Stone*. "You could sense it was part of the whole acid thing—where people started to get concerned with what's real, the awareness of all the plastic aspects of the late Sixties and wanting to move away from that. It meant people started appreciating handmade leather goods and all that kind of stuff."

The Charlatans' wayback machine was also a means of proffering an all-American response to the British Invasion. Because everyone was mimicking the Beatles and the Stones at that point, the Charlatans took a contrarian approach and began scavanging for a strong American identity. They achieved their peculiar recontextualization of a frontier past in the psychedelic present during a mythical two-month residency at the Red Dog Saloon in Virginia City, Nevada, in the summer of 1965. You read correctly: the San Francisco scene, defined as a mix of light shows, loud electric music, and people tripping about ballrooms in costumes and on LSD, actually began at a refurbished Western saloon in an old frontier town in an adjacent state. But most of the participants (Charlatans included) trekked up from San Francisco, and the scene in the city proper escalated rapidly in the fall of 1965.

MAYBE THIS IS THE ROCK REVOLUTION

The pivotal events in the transformation of San Francisco from an underground community to an overground phenomenon were a series of dances and benefits. The first was "A Tribute to Dr. Strange" (a comic-book hero who possessed extraordinary powers) and was held at Longshoreman's Hall on October 16, 1965. Its organizers were a group of friends that included Chet Helms, who later ran the Avalon

Grace Slick, featured on this Fillmore poster, was originally in the Great Society, a folk-rock staple of the early San Francisco scene. Two of their songs, "White Rabbit" and "Somebody to Love," became hits for Jefferson Airplane, which she joined in October 1966.

Ballroom, and Alton Kelley, one of the key poster artists on the San Francisco scene. They called themselves the Family Dog, and there were direct ties between their group and the architects of the Red Dog madness from the previous summer.

"A Tribute to Dr. Strange" featured three bands: the ubiquitous Charlatans; the Great Society, a group that included Grace Slick prior to her joining the Jefferson Airplane; and the Marbles (whoever they were). A second Family Dog dance concert, "A Tribute to Sparkle Plenty," was held on October 24. Again it featured the Charlatans, as well as New York folk-rock-jugband favorites the Lovin' Spoonful. "A Tribute to Ming the Merciless" followed on November 6, with music and theater provided by a skeptical, hippie-baiting band from Los Angeles, the Mothers of Invention, led by Frank Zappa.

Also on November 6, 1965, another titan of the SF music scene made his first foray into concert promotion. Bill Graham organized a benefit to raise legal funds for the San Francisco Mime Troupe, an improvisational theater troupe whose political comedy skits resulted in trouble with the law on grounds of obscenity. Big-name poets (Ginsberg, Ferlinghetti) and jazzman John Handy appeared at "Appeal I," as it was dubbed, but the real attractions were the space-age sounds of the Jefferson Airplane and the attendees' awestruck sense of community. Films were projected on bedsheets nailed to the walls of the loft where the event was held. People came dressed in fanciful glad rags and danced free-form to the freaky new music. What was going on here?

According to Graham, reminiscing in 1990, the verdict he heard from the revelers typically went like this: "My eyes were opened. There's a new world and a new society and a new spirit."

The scene exploded—maybe "mushroomed" or "acidified" would be more descriptive verbs—from this point forward. Graham threw another Mime Troupe benefit, "Appeal II," on December 10. This time, the location was the Fillmore Auditorium. It was the first rock concert in a venue whose name would forever be associated with Graham's own.

Meanwhile, Ken Kesey—who had already been throwing wild, saturnalian LSD parties at the La Honda hangout of his Merry Pranksters—held the first of many Acid Tests on November 27 at a bookstore in Santa Cruz. The first truly public Acid Test was staged on December 4 at a residence in San Jose after a Rolling Stones concert. Departing concertgoers were handed leaflets that cryptically read "Can YOU Pass the Acid Test?" The Grateful Dead, who had just changed their name from the Warlocks, provided the music—free-form jamming around their blues-based repertoire—and as Kesey recalled in a 1997 interview with *Mojo* magazine, they were always the last to leave: "I remember we used to have to kick them out after everyone else had left. They wanted to keep partying and playing long after the parties were over!"

On January 8, 1966, Kesey zeroed in on San Francisco, holding an Acid Test that drew 2,400 crazies to the Fillmore Auditorium. Again, the Grateful Dead—house band of the Acid Tests—played, while film, light, and sound equipment abetted the hallucinogenic drugs to create a mass environment of disequilibrium that promoted a collective sense of creative anarchy.

Jerry Garcia, lead guitarist for the Grateful Dead and sky pilot of the San Francisco scene, at a free concert in Golden Gate Park.

But all this was a mere prelude to the biggest ball of all: the Trips Festival, a three-day orgy of sight, sound, and LSD held at Longshoreman's Hall from January 21 to 23, 1966. Posters promised "revelations," "the unexpected," an "electronic experience," and "a new medium of communication and entertainment." They also included the following commentary: "The general tone of things has moved on from the self-conscious happening to a more jubilant occasion where the audience participates because it's more fun to do so than not. Maybe this is the rock revolution. Audience dancing is an assumed part of all the shows and the audience is invited to wear ecstatic dress and bring their own gadgets."

On February 4, Bill Graham promoted his first nonbenefit concert at the Fillmore Auditorium. By April 1966, after a spell of alternating weekend bookings with Graham at the Fillmore, Chet Helms took his own laid-back, less-harried style of concert promotion with him to the Avalon Ballroom. Though Graham was more a thoroughgoing, type A professional and Helms an on-the-bus kindred spirit, both men's venues offered countless nights of intensely psychedelic wonderment at the outer limits of sight and sound. The bills are enough to make one pray for the invention of a Wayback Machine or, alternatively, an accelerated delving by record companies into tape vaults (such as the Grateful Dead have done with their ongoing "Dick's Picks" series of archival concert releases, sold by mail order through the band's merchandising division).

IF YOU'RE GOING TO SAN FRANCISCO...

In 1966, the turning of summer into fall witnessed a subtle changing of the guard in the rapidly evolving world of rock, with the baton passing from London to San Francisco. For all intents and purposes, the British Invasion was cooling down. England continued to swing like a manic pendulum as the cheerful pop sounds of Merseybeat gave way to the drumming of the London Underground, with all its multimedia clubs, psychedelic bands, and political-social activism (see pages 54–75). Yet San Francisco seized the momentum as the center of rock and roll's wildly expanding universe.

As a matter of fact that almost seems too coincidentally convenient for this argument, the Beatles performed their last live show in San Francisco on August 29, 1966. Jefferson Airplane's first album, *Jefferson Airplane Takes Off*, was released days later. In 1967, the dam broke and the music of San Francisco gushed out to the world in torrents of singles and, especially, albums (see pages 49–52).

As these acid trips for the ears found their way into the suburban bedrooms of middle America, the consciousness of those with receptive ears was forever altered—and you didn't even need to ingest LSD for that to be true. The music itself was so powerful a messenger that a contact high was ensured as listeners found themselves transported to heady new realms by bands who had blotted up and recast the psychedelic experience in musical form. As Donovan sang in "Fat Angel," a jazzy, stoned salute: "Fly Jefferson

Airplane/Gets you there on time." Exactly what Donovan meant by "there" was a tantalizing, coded mystery that most over-30s and absolutely no members of straight society were ever likely to figure out.

BE-INS, LOVE-INS, AND GIMME AN F...

As the year 1967 commenced, San Francisco was still Shangri-la. For a while, through the spring and into the summer, it remained a golden time and place, but the spirit began heading south like the sun not long after the Summer of Love ended. The irony is that for many if not most, that's where their awareness of San Francisco began. The year opened with an event that ranks as possibly the highwater mark in the life of Haight-Ashbury. Organized by an informal committee that included such Beat elders as Allen Ginsberg and Michael McClure, the January 14 "Human Be-In" endeavored to bring together the various clans—old beats and young hippies, Berkeley activists and apolitical San Franciscans, blacks and whites, Hell's Angels and love children—for a peaceful afternoon of rapture, meditation, and bonding on a grassy field in Golden Gate Park.

The event was announced with these words in the *San Francisco Oracle*: "A new concept of human relations being developed within the youthful underground must emerge, become conscious, and be shared so that a Revolution of form can be filled with a Renaissance of compassion, awareness, and love in the Revelation of the unity of all mankind." Poetry was read, speeches made, and music played by the Airplane, Big Brother, Quicksilver, and others. Free turkey sandwiches were handed out by the Diggers, Haight-Ashbury's righteously radical Robin Hoods of redistribution. The secret condiment that made them extra flavorful—LSD, in case you hadn't already guessed—was supplied by high chef Owsley, who also donated the turkeys. Owsley called his latest batch of acid "White Lightnin'." It was not the same kind George Jones had sung and hiccuped about in 1957, but Owsley's potion was potent as a mule kick all the same.

Mellowing out in the Panhandle, an eight-block extension of Golden Gate Park where free food and music could usually be had.

Meanwhile, across the bay in Berkeley, Country Joe and the Fish began striking blows against the empire with some stridently political yet inescapably acid-etched EPs. A boxload of home-recorded, privately pressed EPs sold one afternoon in

1967 at a Berkeley antiwar rally helped further politicize the dissident young on the other side of the bridge from apolitical Haight-Ashbury. Retailed for a mere 50 cents, it contained a crude, embryonic jugband version of their "I-Feel-Like-I'm-Fixin'-to-Die Rag."

Certainly in hindsight such an audacious release—a defiantly antiestablishment song issued on a makeshift label—stands as a precursor of the rise of independent, fuck-you labels by punk, new wave, and alternative bands in the '80s and '90s. It also points up the fact that there's less distance between hippies and punks than either might think. Both are social rebels and malcontents who invented their own subculture.

San Francisco functioned as an epicenter and magnet, drawing musicians to it. Half of Jefferson Airplane's classic lineup (group members Grace Slick, Jorma Kaukonen, and Jack Casady) had grown up on the East Coast, while drummer Spencer Dryden hailed from Los Angeles. Most of Moby Grape were from the Seattle area. Steve Miller and Boz Scaggs had called Texas and Wisconsin home before roosting in San Francisco. The Grateful Dead came up from Palo Alto, Quicksilver over from Marin County. Not only were truly native groups a relative rarity, but the bands who made Haight-Ashbury their adopted home tended to record in other places, owing to the lack

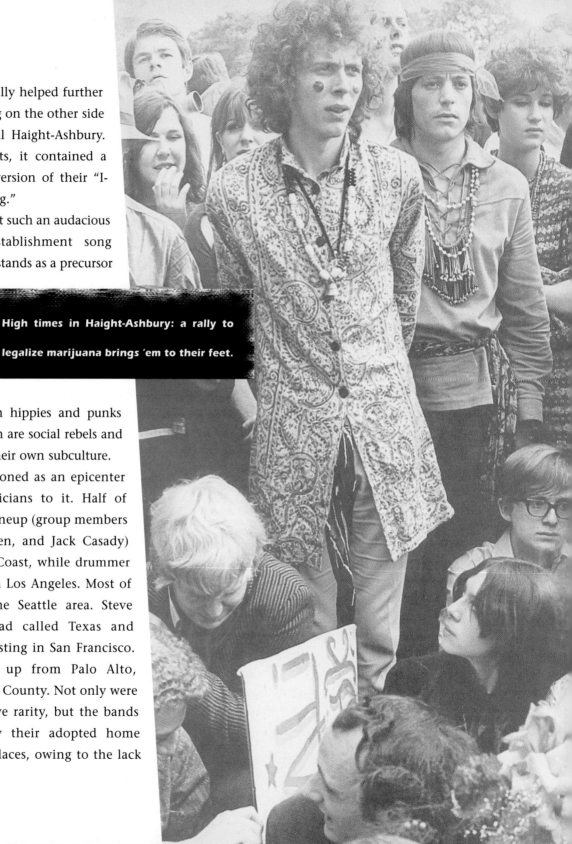

High times in Haight-Ashbury: a rally to legalize marijuana brings 'em to their feet.

of decent studios in the Bay Area. The Dead, Airplane, and Moby Grape all recorded in Los Angeles, while the Steve Miller Band jetted off to London, where they cut their first two albums at the same studios where the Jimi Hendrix Experience and the Rolling Stones were recording some of the most vital, earthshaking music of the '60s.

For all of that, the San Francisco community definitely did shape the sounds of those musicians who gravitated to it. There was a definite San Francisco sound or vibe that linked up a lot of the bands on the scene. At the height of it all, the ballrooms were staging concerts six and seven nights a week, and people were literally dancing in the streets of Haight-Ashbury. It was an embryonic journey made at the speed of sound, a century flower that bloomed and faded in the space of a few years and yet forever changed the lives of those who witnessed its brilliant unfolding.

What was responsible for this musical contagion? For starters, it was a product of acid's rapid spread; the collective raising of consciousness that this engendered; the arrival of powerful new amps and effects that made sound more descriptive; the shift in the main instruments of improvisation from jazz horns to rock guitars; the organizational efforts of personalities as diverse as Ken Kesey and Bill Graham; the literary legacy of beat poets and writers; interaction with visual artists who designed posters and light shows; the freewheeling atmosphere of the ballrooms, streets, communes, and public parks; the city's cultural heritage and adventuresome frontier ethos; and the aura of tolerance that's made San Francisco a bohemian's Shangri-la since gold rush days.

Finally, it also had a lot to do with serendipity and magic. And those kinds of things just can't be explained, only enjoyed and marveled at.

GREAT MAN THEORY REVISITED

Maybe, in actuality, the cream (including Cream, who recorded the live portions of *Wheels of Fire* during an extended run of gigs at Fillmore West) did rise to the top in San Francisco. Among scholars, the Great Man Theory of History holds that a small number of individuals—possessed of exceptional qualities and placed in extraordinary situations by dint of some charmed combination of capability, inspiration, desire, and destiny—have shaped the course of civilization.

The rock and roll corollary would be the Great Band Theory of History, which brings us back to the psychedelic sounds of the Grateful Dead, Jefferson Airplane, Quicksilver Messenger Service, Big Brother and the Holding Company, Moby Grape, Steve Miller Band, Santana, and Country Joe and the Fish. Basically, their recorded work (much of which remains in print, at least on CD), memories of gigs played during San Francisco's salad days, and the sifting mechanism of time confirm that these bands were the biggest and the best for good reason: they had the surest grasp of the '60s gestalt.

Still, we wouldn't mind flashing back via Trans-Love Airways to hear what some of the other bands on the scene were all about. What we wouldn't give to have been flies on the wall of the Red Dog Saloon in the summer of '65!

(Below) Promotional poster for the Second Annual Tribal Stomp in 1967.

(Right) *Alice's Adventures in Wonderland* and *Through the Looking Glass* by Lewis Carroll were psychedelic touchstones in the 1960s. This 1908 illustration by Arthur Rackham shows the queen, the white rabbit, and the dormouse, who was quoted by the Jefferson Airplane as having exhorted, "Feed your head." Actually, the dormouse never said any such thing.

Flower children lead a mock funeral procession through Haight-Ashbury to rid themselves of the negative hippie image and label foisted on them by the media and exploitative outside interests. The ceremony, known as "the Death of Hippie," was held on October 6, 1967, as memories of the Summer of Love were eclipsed by the reality of a rapidly degenerating Haight. At that point, the best advice might have been, "If you are going to San Francisco ... don't."

HIGH IN THE MID-'60S: SAN FRANCISCO'S TRACK RECORD

Following are lists of the most popular records by San Francisco bands from 1965 to 1970, arrayed according to highest chart position (and chart duration, in case of a tie). Year of release is provided, too. All chart information comes from *Billboard*.

Every album by a San Francisco band that made *Billboard*'s chart of Top 200 LPs during the period under study—all 68 of them—is listed below. Every single that made the Top 40—all 27 of them—is given as well. Interestingly, if just two bands—Creedence Clearwater Revival and Sly and the Family Stone—are factored out, the list shrinks to 11 Top 40 titles. If it is again reduced by the Beau Brummels, Sopwith Camel, and the Mojo Men, whose singles (however great) weren't exactly in the ballroom spirit of San Francisco's psychedelic groups, the list of hit singles dwindles to a mere six titles: two each by Jefferson Airplane and Santana, and one apiece by Big Brother and Blue Cheer.

At this point, it becomes perfectly clear that psychedelic music was an underground, album-oriented, FM-bandwidth phenomenon. In other words, it was too heavy for the Top 40.

SINGLES

1. "Everyday People," by Sly and the Family Stone (#1 for four weeks, 1968)

2. "Thank You (Falettinme Be Mice Elf Agin), by Sly and the Family Stone (#1 for two weeks, 1970)

3. "Hot Fun in the Summertime," by Sly and the Family Stone (#2, 1969)

4. "Proud Mary," by Creedence Clearwater Revival (#2, 1969)

5. "Bad Moon Rising," by Creedence Clearwater Revival (#2, 1969)

6. "Lookin' Out My Back Door," by Creedence Clearwater Revival (#2, 1970)

7. "Green River," by Creedence Clearwater Revival (#2, 1969)

8. "Travelin' Band," by Creedence Clearwater Revival (#2, 1970)

9. "Down on the Corner," by Creedence Clearwater Revival (#3, 1969)

10. "Black Magic Woman," by Santana (#4, 1970)

11. "Up Around the Bend," by Creedence Clearwater Revival (#4, 1970)

12. "Somebody to Love," by Jefferson Airplane (#5, 1967)

13. "Dance to the Music," by Sly and the Family Stone (#8, 1968)

14. "Just a Little," by the Beau Brummels (#8, 1965)

15. "White Rabbit," by Jefferson Airplane (#8, 1967)

16. "Evil Ways," by Santana (#9, 1970)

17. "Suzie Q. (Part One)," by Creedence Clearwater Revival (#11, 1968)

18. "Piece of My Heart," by Big Brother and the Holding Company (#12, 1968)

19. "Fortunate Son," by Creedence Clearwater Revival (#14, 1969)

20. "Summertime Blues," by Blue Cheer (#14, 1968)

21. "Laugh Laugh," by the Beau Brummels (#15, 1965)

22. "Stand!," by Sly and the Family Stone (#22, 1969)

23. "Hello Hello," by Sopwith Camel (#26, 1966)

24. "Commotion," by Creedence Clearwater Revival (#30, 1969)

25. "Sit Down, I Think I Love You," by the Mojo Men (#36, 1967)

26. "I Want to Take You Higher," by Sly and the Family Stone (#38, 1970)

27. "You Tell Me Why," by the Beau Brummels (#38, 1965)

ALBUMS

1. *Cosmo's Factory*, by Creedence Clearwater Revival (#1 for nine weeks, 1970)

2. *Cheap Thrills*, by Big Brother and the Holding Company (#1 for eight weeks, 1968)

3. *Abraxis*, by
   Santana (#1 for six weeks, 1970)

4. *Green River*, by
   Creedence Clearwater Revival
   (#1 for four weeks, 1969)

5. *Greatest Hits*, by
   Sly and the Family Stone (#2, 1970)

6. *Willie and the Poorboys*, by
   Creedence Clearwater Revival (#3, 1969)

7. *Surrealistic Pillow*, by
   Jefferson Airplane (#3, 1967)

8. *Santana*, by
   Santana (#4, 1969)

9. *Pendulum*, by
   Creedence Clearwater Revival (#5, 1970)

10. *Crown of Creation*, by
    Jefferson Airplane (#6, 1968)

11. *Bayou Country*, by
    Creedence Clearwater Revival (#7, 1969)

12. *Vincebus Eruptum*, by
    Blue Cheer (#11, 1968)

13. *Worst of Jefferson Airplane*, by
    Jefferson Airplane (#12, 1970)

14. *Stand!*, by
    Sly and the Family Stone (#13, 1969)

15. *Volunteers*, by
    Jefferson Airplane (#13, 1969)

16. *After Bathing at Baxter's*, by
    Jefferson Airplane (#17, 1967)

17. *Bless Its Pointed Little Head*, by
    Jefferson Airplane (#17, 1969)

18. *The Live Adventures of Mike Bloomfield
    and Al Kooper*, by
    Mike Bloomfield and Al Kooper (#18, 1969)

19. *Wow*, by Moby Grape (#20, 1968)

20. *Blows Against the Empire*, by
    Paul Kantner/Jefferson Starship (#20, 1970)

21. *Brave New World*, by
    the Steve Miller Band (#22, 1969)

22. *Cold Blood*, by Cold Blood (#23, 1969)

23. *Number Five*, by
    the Steve Miller Band (#23, 1970)

24. *Together*, by
    Country Joe and the Fish (#23, 1968)

25. *Moby Grape*, by Moby Grape (#24, 1967)

26. *Introducing the Beau Brummels*, by
    the Beau Brummels (#24, 1965)

27. *Sailor*, by
    the Steve Miller Band (#24, 1968)

28. *Shady Grove*, by
    Quicksilver Messenger Service (#25, 1970)

29. *Happy Trails*, by
    Quicksilver Messenger Service (#27, 1969)

30. *Workingman's Dead*, by
    the Grateful Dead (#27, 1970)

31. *Just for Love*, by
    Quicksilver Messenger Service (#27, 1970)

32. *Marrying Maiden*, by
    It's a Beautiful Day (#28, 1970)

33. *American Beauty*, by
    the Grateful Dead (#30, 1970)

34. *Hot Tuna*, by Hot Tuna (#30, 1970)

35. *A Long Time Comin'*, by
    the Electric Flag (#31, 1968)

36. *Your Saving Grace*, by
    the Steve Miller Band (#38, 1969)

37. *Electric Music for the Mind and Body*, by
    Country Joe and the Fish (#39, 1967)

KEY EVENTS IN THE BAY AREA COUNTERCULTURE

June 29, 1965: Charlatans' first performance at the Red Dog Saloon in Virginia City, Nevada.

August 13, 1965: Clubowner Marty Balin (of Jefferson Airplane) opens the Matrix.

October 15, 1965: First Family Dog dance, "A Tribute to Dr. Strange," held at Longshoreman's Hall.

November 6, 1965: San Francisco Mime Troupe benefit, a pivotal gathering organized by Bill Graham.

November 27, 1965: The first of Ken Kesey's many Acid Tests.

January 8, 1966: Grateful Dead play for 2,400 at an Acid Test at the Fillmore Auditorium.

January 21–23, 1966: The Trips Festival, featuring bands, light shows, and Owsley acid.

February 4, 1966: Bill Graham promotes first concert at the Fillmore, featuring Jefferson Airplane.

April 22, 1966: Chet Helms promotes first concert at the Avalon Ballroom, featuring Blues Project and Great Society.

September 20, 1966: Debut issue of the *San Francisco Oracle*.

October 6, 1966: Possession and sale of LSD outlawed in California.

January 14, 1967: The Human Be-In draws thousands to Golden Gate Park.

February 12, 1967: Underground radio debuts with midnight-to-six show on KMPX-FM.

March 23, 1968: Mayor John Shelley declares an expected Summer of Love "hippie invasion" to be unwelcome.

June 16–18, 1967: Monterey International Pop Festival.

August 9, 1967: A curious George Harrison tours Haight-Ashbury.

October 2, 1967: Famous bust of Grateful Dead's communal house at 710 Ashbury.

October 6, 1967: "Death of Hippie" parade through Haight-Ashbury protests media stereotypes.

November 9, 1967: *Rolling Stone* magazine publishes first issue.

February 1968: Violent confrontation between street people and police tactical squad.

April 1968: Every store window on Haight Street is broken during race riots following Martin Luther King's assassination.

1969: Thirty-six storefronts on crime-filled Haight Street are vacant. Street cats, it is said, are hunted for food by hungry needle freaks.

September 1969: Financially faltering Avalon Ballroom closes due to noise complaints.

December 6, 1969: Rolling Stones–sponsored free concert at Altamont Speedway marred by violence and death.

ENGLAND SWINGS

THE BRITISH UNDERGROUND SCENE

Britain's counter-culture took some cues from the goings-on in California, but the distance separating London and San Francisco prevented direct, ongoing contact between the two cities. Certain psychedelic records from the West Coast did make the transatlantic passage—the Byrds and Love are frequently cited as having influenced Pink Floyd, for instance—but the London scene developed along distinctively British lines as a response by the newly psychedelicized young to

Mick Jagger gives the Rolling Stones' demonic opus, "Sympathy for the Devil," some percussive embellishment in the studio.

the stodgy conservatism of their parochial elders.

The greatest American influence on the Brits was not a musician but a literary figure: Allen Ginsberg, the Beat Generation poet who set events in motion by organizing a reading at the Royal Albert Hall on June 11, 1965. That affair presented an international lineup of poets who read for a crowd of 6,000 bohemians high on pot, acid, and the pleasantly jarring perception of a community coming together for the first time. This group reading, billed as "Poets of the World/Poets of Our Time," marked the birth of the London Underground.

LSD hit Britain like a tidal wave. The chief emissary in the hallucinogenic revolution was Michael Hollingshead—the very man who first turned Timothy Leary on to acid. A member of Leary's League for Spiritual Discovery (LSD), Hollingshead was dispatched to London from Leary's Millbrook commune in 1966. He arrived armed with missionary zeal and 5,000 hits of acid. Before LSD was made illegal, it was handed out for free at the Institute of Contemporary Art, housed in a government building facing Buckingham Palace.

Britain's psychedelic scene, which originated in the mid-'60s and carried through to the end of the decade, was initially driven by a youthful aristocracy. They gathered at "salons"—private flats that served as hangouts for musicians, artists, intellectuals, scenemakers, and dealers—and at clubs like UFO (pronounced "you-foe"), which amounted to London's version of San Francisco's Avalon Ballroom with one crucial difference. Whereas the San Francisco ballrooms were full-time, full-fledged concert halls, British clubs like UFO operated only on certain nights. UFO was actually an old Irish dance hall rented out on weekends by Joe Boyd (a music producer and band manager) and John "Hoppy" Hopkins (photographer, journalist, and prototypical "head"). On Friday and Saturday, entering UFO was like taking a wild ride in Cinderella's psychedelic carriage. During the week it went back to being a pumpkin.

The hobbits on London's Underground scene dabbled in drugs, forged liaisons with rock musicians, read deeply, and took their consciousness-raising quite seriously. It goes without saying that psychedelic drugs provided at least some of the momentum and motivation. Smoking dope and taking acid were viewed as part of the ideological break the younger generation was making with Britain's stiff-lipped past, as well as its sexual repression and class struggles.

The differences between London and San Francisco largely had to do with the direction in which creativity and leadership flowed. In a nutshell, the London scene was organized from the top down, while San Francisco evolved from the bottom up. That is to say, San Francisco was a spontaneous, street-level scene forged by social outcasts, while the London Underground had more of an intellectual, upper-crust cast to it. In London, pop stars hobnobbed with art dealers and wealthy heirs. In San Francisco, rock musicians slummed with street people in a more egalitarian setting. In the end, the goals were essentially the same: enlightenment, community, good music, mind-expanding drugs, and a world apart from the status quo.

When they weren't fraternizing at clubs or behind the closed doors of their "salons," the underground contingent frequented new-age spaces like Indica Gallery and Bookshop. Indica became a favorite haunt of Paul McCartney's and the shop where a browsing John Lennon stumbled onto the writings of Timothy Leary. This dropout intelligentsia also founded youth-oriented publications such as the *International Times*, which tracked world politics from a youthful, leftist perspective, and *Oz*, a visually oriented periodical with cutting-edge psychedelic artwork.

A free-speech fund-raiser for *International Times* (known as *IT*, for short) became a milestone in the evolution of the British counterculture. Known as the "14-Hour Technicolor Dream," the event was held at Alexandra Palace on April 29, 1967. Tickets cost but one measly British pound, and a bevy of mind-bending musical acts performed in a carnival-like atmosphere. The program included journeyman blues artists like Alexis Korner and Champion Jack Dupree, as well as acid rockers both familiar (Pink Floyd, Soft Machine) and obscure (Giant Sun Trolley, Purple Gang).

The integration of the emerging psychedelic rock groups into a larger framework of politics, education, philosophy, and hallucinogenic drug-taking led to the blossoming of a multidimensional scene. When bands like Pink Floyd were recruited to perform at fund-raising benefits for the London Free School and *International Times*, mutual purposes were served and advanced. If the Beatles and the British Invasion bands of the early-to-mid '60s represented a postwar cultural passage from drab black-and-white to vivid Technicolor, the psychedelic epoch added yet another dimension: space. Outer and inner space.

The early years of London's musical underground were dominated by two groups—Pink Floyd and Soft Machine—who essentially became the house bands at the UFO Club for three magical months in early 1967. Pink Floyd were a quartet of art and architecture students: bassist Roger Waters, keyboardist Richard Wright, drummer Nick Mason, and guitarist

Pink Floyd in the early daze: (from left) Waters, Mason, Barrett, and Wright. Barrett's behavior grew increasingly erratic under the spell of acid, and he was officially replaced by David Gilmour in January 1968.

Roger Keith "Syd" Barrett. Nothing about their early repertoire—mostly Rolling Stones and R&B covers, including songs like "Road Runner" and "Louie Louie"—set them apart from the pack. But the lengthy instrumental freakouts they inserted in the middle of songs planted them at the forefront of the avant-garde.

Floyd first attracted attention at the "Spontaneous Underground," the name given to a series of Sunday-afternoon happenings at London's Marquee Club. As the words implied, a new culture germinated spontaneously in a nurturing underground medium whose components included drugs, music, light shows, wild costuming, free-form dancing, and offbeat behavior. A typical invitation would cryptically read: "TRIP bring furniture toy prop paper rug paint balloon jumble costume mask robot candle incense ladder wheel light self all others march 13th 5 p.m." The year was 1966, and "the Pink Floyd Sound" provided the musical ambiance at that particular happening.

For the next year, Pink Floyd were London's psychedelic Pied Pipers. Their songs orbited off into spacy soundscapes of feedback and electronic noise while back-projected light shows played off their anonymous forms. From the early days of the Spontaneous Underground to a now-legendary opening night at the Roundhouse (a converted railroad yard) to their Saturday-night gigs at the UFO Club, Pink Floyd were influential before they'd recorded a note.

Then came the records: "Arnold Layne," their first 45, a strange song about a compulsive cross-dresser. *Piper at the Gates of Dawn*, a fanciful album whose fable-like songs evinced a childlike whimsy. "Interstellar Overdrive," a lengthy instrumental album-closer that probed the outer limits of sound. "See Emily Play," a highwater mark of billowy, transcendent psychedelia and a defining moment in the Summer of Love. The latter was released as a single in Britain (where it went Top 10) and tacked onto the drastically revamped version of the *Piper* LP that appeared in America. It had been specially written for "Games of May," a Pink Floyd concert held at the Queen Elizabeth Hall on May 12, 1967. The event promised "space-age relaxation for the climax of spring—electronic compositions, colour and image projections, girls, and the Pink Floyd." In short, it apotheosized the psychedelic experience as a kind of frolicsome pagan fertility ritual.

Pink Floyd's early reputation and repertoire owed greatly to Syd Barrett, their brilliant but unstable leader. This period in their career largely remains obscure to the great mass of Pink Floyd fans who discovered them circa *Dark Side of the Moon*, four years after acid-induced psychosis forced Barrett to leave the band in April 1968. His errant, unpredictable behavior reached a sort of tragicomic nadir during an abortive American tour in the fall of 1968. During the group's appearance on *The Pat Boone Show*, Barrett responded to the straitlaced host's inanely cheerful questions with a mute, zombie-like stare. On a certain level—that of one generation regarding another with incurious disinterest across an ever-widening divide—Barrett's response seems rational enough. But in reality he had ingested so much LSD over the previous year, both willingly and unknowingly, that he could well be described as an acid casualty—one of the first, in fact. With considerable help from his erstwhile bandmates, Barrett went on to record two enchantingly eccentric solo albums—*The Madcap Laughs* and *Barrett*, both released in 1970—before abandoning music to lead the life of a recluse at his mother's home in Cambridge.

Pink Floyd sans Barrett became the unlikeliest of '70s superstars. With David Gilmour as his replacement on guitar and bassist Waters doing most of the writing, Pink Floyd retained its spacey aura. Between Barrett's exodus and their '70s breakthrough with *Dark Side of the Moon*, Pink Floyd recorded a brace of albums—*A Saucerful of Secrets*, *Ummagumma*, *Atom Heart Mother*, *Meddle*—in a pastoral psychedelic style. This less-heralded period represents some of their most compelling work. It includes the side-long "Atom Heart Mother" and "Echoes" suites—and not to mention the extraordinarily titled "Several Species of Small Furry Animals Gathered Together and Grooving With a Pict." These LPs were less inspired by hallucinogenic drugs than by the trippy natural world. "We're not a drug band," Gilmour once insisted in an interview. "Trust us." In the 1970s, the group began depicting a world of alienation and anomie on such albums as *Dark Side of the Moon*, *Animals*, and *The Wall*. The more alienated they got, the more popular they became.

The other key band on London's early psychedelic scene was the unjustly forgotten Soft Machine. For a brief spell in 1967, they were peers with Pink Floyd on bills at the UFO Club and the Roundhouse. But their lineup never stabilized, and they couldn't make their minds up whether to be a psychedelic pop band or a progressive jazz ensemble (or a little of both). Ultimately, they chose the latter course, dribbling into the mid-1970s as increasingly uninteresting instrumental noodlers. Regardless, Soft Machine were bonafide psychedelic pioneers at the outset. In their short-lived lineup of Robert Wyatt, Michael Ratledge, Daevid Allen, and Kevin Ayers, they blew minds from the same stages Pink Floyd played. Moreover, Soft Machine shared management with Jimi Hendrix and twice toured the States as his opening act. Their forte was linking discreet songs with improvisational segments so that a concert flowed like one long, uninterrupted composition. Numbers like Ayers' "We Did It Again," a trance-inducing tune in which those four words were chanted repeatedly as music swelled and ebbed behind it, would go on for half an hour.

Soft Machine, their 1968 debut, was recorded by the trio of Ayers (bass, vocals), Ratledge (organ), and Wyatt (drums, vocals). Standout tracks like "Hope for Happiness" highlight an energetic and bracingly psychedelic album, from its vertigo-inducing stereo mix to its die-cut, rotating cover (an audacious design similar to that of *Led Zeppelin III*, which appeared years later). The followup album, *Volume Two*, contained more delightfully offbeat pop-psychedelic song cycles, one of which found Robert Wyatt singing all the letters in the alphabet forwards and backwards. Inspiration visited the group again on 1971's *Thirds*, a double LP consisting of four side-long compositions. One critic proclaimed it the greatest album in pop-music history. Whether or not you consider *Thirds* the be-all and end-all of listening experiences, there's no question that compositions like "Out-Bloody-Rageous" and "Moon in June" are feats of imagination and musicianship

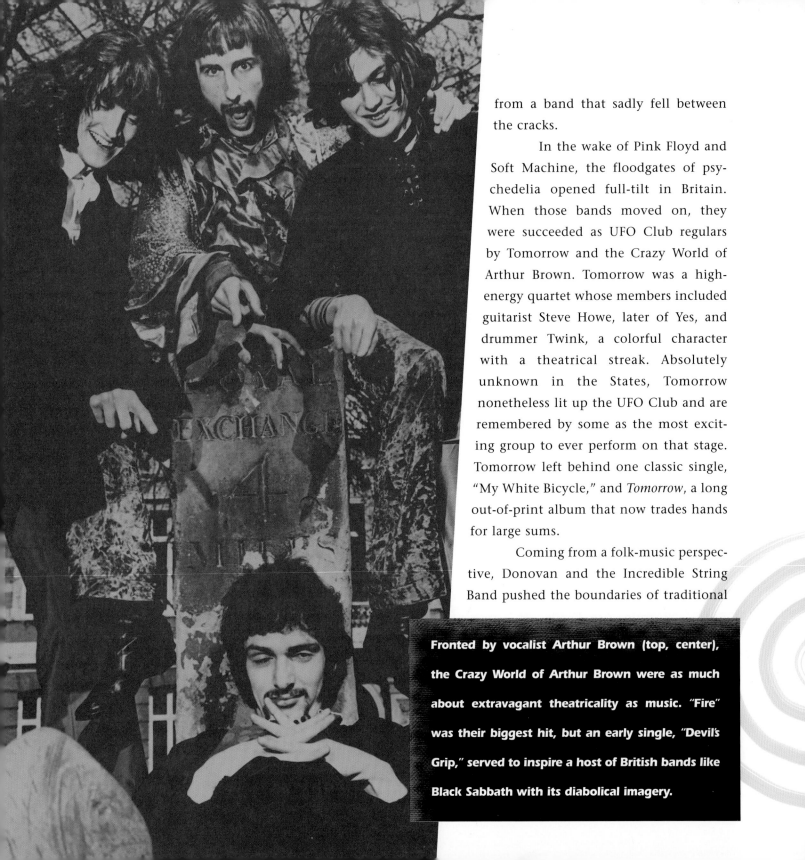

from a band that sadly fell between the cracks.

In the wake of Pink Floyd and Soft Machine, the floodgates of psychedelia opened full-tilt in Britain. When those bands moved on, they were succeeded as UFO Club regulars by Tomorrow and the Crazy World of Arthur Brown. Tomorrow was a high-energy quartet whose members included guitarist Steve Howe, later of Yes, and drummer Twink, a colorful character with a theatrical streak. Absolutely unknown in the States, Tomorrow nonetheless lit up the UFO Club and are remembered by some as the most exciting group to ever perform on that stage. Tomorrow left behind one classic single, "My White Bicycle," and *Tomorrow*, a long out-of-print album that now trades hands for large sums.

Coming from a folk-music perspective, Donovan and the Incredible String Band pushed the boundaries of traditional

Fronted by vocalist Arthur Brown (top, center), the Crazy World of Arthur Brown were as much about extravagant theatricality as music. "Fire" was their biggest hit, but an early single, "Devil's Grip," served to inspire a host of British bands like Black Sabbath with its diabolical imagery.

folk into heady new directions. Around late 1966, Donovan moved from straight folk minstrelsy to a stylishly inventive pop-jazz-Indian hybrid that yielded the hit singles "Sunshine Superman" and "Mellow Yellow," and a pair of like-named albums. Donovan captured the mood and the moment: sweet and sunny, with an enlightened, knowing wink.

The Incredible String Band also took folk music as a starting point. This chameleonic Scottish group—first a trio, then a duo, finally a quartet after they added their girlfriends—played a multitude of exotic instruments between them and did not hesitate to color their songs from a varied palette. Core members Robin Williamson and Mike Heron cooked up a woodsy world of wonder on such albums as *The 5000 Spirits or the Layers of the Onion* and *The Hangman's Beautiful Daughter*. The last of these contained their 13-minute magnum opus, "A

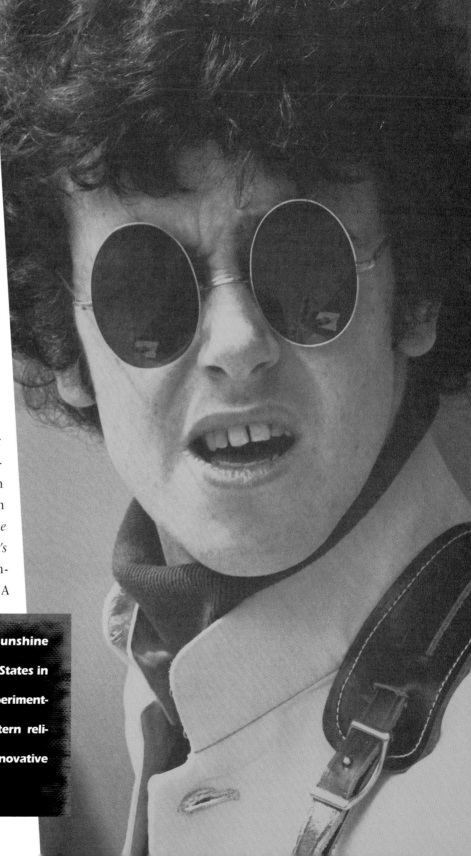

Donovan went psychedelic with "Sunshine Superman," which soared to No. 1 in the States in September 1966. The Scottish singer experimented with hallucinogens and studied Eastern religion, expanding his musical reach on innovative albums that melded disparate styles.

Very Cellular Song," written by Heron on and about an acid trip.

Other groups quite successfully overlaid a fanciful psychedelic approach upon a base of electric blues. Indeed, psychedelia found its most commercially viable expression in the work of Cream, Traffic, the Yardbirds, and the Jimi Hendrix Experience. All were schooled in blues and soul but allowed their imaginations to soar under the influence of psychedelia. Unlike the dinky rigs and setups used by the British Invasion bands, amps had grown larger and more powerful, and sound effects like wah-wah, feedback, and fuzztone had become part of the guitarist's arsenal. In the brave new world of psychedelic rock you were limited only by your imagination, and there was no lack of ways to trigger your muse: pot and acid, TM and yoga, jamming with other musicians, immersion in literature and film, getting back to nature...in short, whatever worked.

Cream appeared on the scene in June 1966. Guitarist Eric Clapton previously played with the Yardbirds and John Mayall's Bluesbreakers, while bassist Jack Bruce and drummer Ginger Baker served as rhythm section for the Graham Bond Organization. Cream were the sort of group that would have been inconceivable even two years earlier: a rock trio that approached blues-based material with the

freedom of jazz musicians. They also had something of a split personality, jamming onstage while crafting ornate psychedelic-pop miniatures in the studio. Cream peaked with *Disraeli Gears*, one of the indispensable albums from the landmark year of 1967. Songs like "Tales of Brave Ulysses" and "Sunshine of Your Love" reflected an adventuresome bent, and in this endeavor Cream were ably assisted by their collaborators—principally producer Felix Pappalardi and lyricist Pete Brown. As for their stage personas, Bruce

The Incredible String Band took their name from a Glasgow folk club. Their exotic, folk-flavored minstrelsy made them a fixture on London's underground scene. They even played at Woodstock, where this backstage photo was taken. Founders Robin Williamson and Mike Heron flank their better halves, who by this time were full-fledged, finger cymbal–clicking band members.

DISRAELI GEARS

ATCO
STEREO
SD 33-232

Side One
1. STRANGE BREW
(By Eric Clapton, Felix Pappalardi & Gail Collins;
Windfall-Pronto-Nemperor, BMI; Time: 2:45)
2. SUNSHINE OF YOUR LOVE
(By Jack Bruce, Peter Brown & Eric Clapton; Nemperor,
BMI; Time: 4:08)
3. WORLD OF PAIN
(By Felix Pappalardi & Gail Collins; Windfall-Pronto, BMI;
Time: 3:05)
4. DANCE THE NIGHT AWAY
(By Jack Bruce & Peter Brown; Nemperor, BMI; Time: 3:31)
5. BLUE CONDITION
(By Ginger Baker; Nemperor, BMI; Time: 3:25)

Side Two
1. TALES OF BRAVE ULYSSES
(By Eric Clapton & Sharp; Nemperor, BMI; Time: 2:50)
2. SWLABR
(By Jack Bruce & Peter Brown; Nemperor, BMI; Time: 2:31)
3. WE'RE GOING WRONG
(By Jack Bruce; Nemperor, BMI; Time: 3:25)
4. OUTSIDE WOMAN BLUES
(By Reynolds, Egg, BMI; Time: 2:20)
5. TAKE IT BACK
(By Jack Bruce & Peter Brown; Nemperor, BMI; Time: 3:05)
6. MOTHER'S LAMENT
(Trad. Arr. by Cream; Nemperor, BMI; Time: 1:47)

Recording engineer: Tom Dowd • Photos: Bob Whitaker • Art. Martin Sharp
Produced by Felix Pappalardi • By arrangement with Robert Stigwood
Released in the U.S.A. by special arrangement with Polydor Records Ltd.
ATCO RECORDS 1841 BROADWAY, NEW YORK, NEW YORK 10023
DIVISION OF ATLANTIC RECORDING CORPORATION © 1967 Atlantic Recording Corporation Printed in U.S.A.

The artist Martin Sharp was one of a group of upstart Australians who "invaded" the swinging London scene in the mid-'60s. With his artwork on Cream's *Disraeli Gears* album, Sharp conquered the scene, even cowriting side two's opener, "Tales of Brave Ulysses," with Eric Clapton. He was a cofounder, too, of *Oz* , a visually splashy psychedelic magazine.

and Baker were basically inveterate jazzers who nudged Clapton into long, exploratory improvisations that were also driven by Indian and world-music influences.

Among all of psychedelia's proponents, no single figure did more to advance the futuristic agenda of rock music than Jimi Hendrix. Although born in America, Hendrix eventually made his home and his reputation in England. He spent his early years as a working musician backing up soul/R&B acts like the Isley Brothers, Little Richard, and Sam Cooke. While performing in Greenwich Village with his own band, Jimmy James and the Blue Flames, Hendrix was discovered by Chas Chandler of the Animals and spirited to London, where he formed the Jimi Hendrix Experience with bassist Noel Redding and drummer Mitch Mitchell. They released their debut single, "Hey Joe," in December 1966; *Are You Experienced?* came five months later.

The question posed by that album title

could be read as a play on the band's name or a drug reference—another way of saying you're either on the bus or off the bus, as Ken Kesey and his Merry Pranksters phrased it. If there were any doubts that Hendrix was proselytizing about expanded consciousness, "Purple Haze" laid them to rest. As blatant a drug song as would be heard in the '60s, its public unveiling preceded by a month the release of *Sgt. Pepper* (which itself contained John Lennon's coded paean to psychedelic enchantment, "Lucy in the Sky with Diamonds").

For Hendrix, as for the dropout generation as a whole, drug-taking at its most idealistic was a means of opening doors to

Jimi Hendrix at Monterey, where he performed a show-stopping nine-song set on the final night. Hendrix had these words of wisdom for the Love Crowd: "It's no big story about, we couldn't make it here, so we go over to England, and America doesn't like us because, you know, our feet's too big and we got fat mattresses and we wear golden underwear, it ain't no scene like that, brother....It's so groovy to come back here and really get a chance to really play."

self-knowledge and uninhib-
ited creative expression.
Hendrix didn't just advance
rock music and the art of guitar playing on *Are You
Experienced?* With his pictorial,
otherworldly approach he
redefined it for the ages.
Rolling Stone had this to say
about *Are You Experienced?*,
which placed No. 5 on its list
of the Top 100 albums of the
period 1967–1987: "[Hendrix]
is inviting you to take a great
leap forward, to follow him into
a fourth dimension where his
Fender Stratocaster is a paint-
brush, where feedback can sing
and amplifiers shriek with pain."

Unlike the poppish,
candy-coated psychedelia one
might hear on the radio from
Status Quo ("Pictures of Match-
stick Men") or Strawberry Alarm
Clock ("Incense and Peppermints"), Hendrix delivered an
often violent and jarring world of
sound. His guitar exploded like
mortar shells on such brutally
upfront songs as "Manic Depres-
sion" and "I Don't Live Today."
Who can ever forget his version of

"The Star-Spangled Banner" at Woodstock? With its aural evocations of
"bombs bursting in air," it struck a sobering note of realism at that countercultural Elysium during the dispiriting
height of the Vietnam War. Another
highlight was his apocalyptic, electrified recasting of Bob Dylan's "All Along
the Watchtower," which caught the
darkening mood of violence that
swept across Europe and the United
States like a storm front in 1968.

On the other hand, Hendrix
could be lyrical and even tender as
he envisioned worlds beyond this
one in songs like "Spanish Castle
Magic" and "Little Wing." Ultimately Hendrix's music was about
earthly travails and heavenly tran-
scendence—the blues and beyond,
in other worlds, painted with
naked, jagged music by an artist
who held nothing back. Hendrix
was almost obsessively prolific
in the latter half of the 1960s.
According to one-time collaborator Curtis Knight, in 1965
Hendrix prophesied his own
death in five years' time. This
may explain the ferocious, sus-
tained burst of creativity that
spilled out of him over a

brief half decade. The Jimi
Hendrix Experience per-
formed 180 concerts in 1967
alone, according to the
Encyclopedia of Rock Stars. In
his lifetime, he released five
albums, including the double
LP *Electric Ladyland*. Since his
death on September 18, 1970,
an incomprehensible 300
Hendrix albums have been
released, culled from a moun-
tain of studio sessions, concert
tapes, and early (pre-Experience)
sources.

Traffic represented the
recasting of another soulful voice
in the musical context of the psychedelic age. As a teenager, Steve
Winwood had been lead singer
and organist for the Spencer Davis
Group, a hit-making white-soul
band ("I'm a Man," "Gimme Some
Lovin'") with an honest ground-
ing in blues and R&B. Caught up
in the charged spirit of the times,
Traffic came together around
Winwood as a band with a more
ambitious agenda and a hipper
name. They were the first group to
take the underground-rock ethos
forged in London and relocate it to

the country, where it could germinate in the light and sun of more natural surroundings. Traffic consisted of Winwood on vocals, keyboards, and guitar; drummer Jim Capaldi; and reedman Chris Wood. Guitarist Dave Mason was an on-and-off member. Their first single, "Paper Sun," was fragrant with the lilting sounds of sitars and flutes, over which Winwood delivered a set of lyrics that seemed to warn of the chemical excesses of the time: "Too much sun will burn," he sang with an insider's conviction.

Of their idyllic hermitage, which found them cooking up songs and living communally at a stone cottage in Berkshire, Traffic told journalist Chris Welch: "We try to get as much color into our lives as possible. We see movements and roam through the temple of our minds. We get tripped out with the countryside. It's beautiful." Traffic maintained close ties to the cottage in Berkshire all the way from *Mr. Fantasy*, their 1967 debut, through *The Low Spark of High-Heeled Boys*, their top-selling album from 1971. Traffic were a product of the times who brought an exotic, earthy soulfulness to underground rock. Psychedelia gets no more ornately entrancing than Traffic's "40,000 Headmen," from their eponymous second album.

The Yardbirds, too, got swept up in the psychedelic movement, metamorphosing from a band of blues scholars to purveyors of cutting-edge future rock. Hearing a song like "Shapes of Things" over a hometown radio station in 1966 halted many listeners (the authors of this book among them) in their tracks. The otherworldly wail of feedback from Jeff

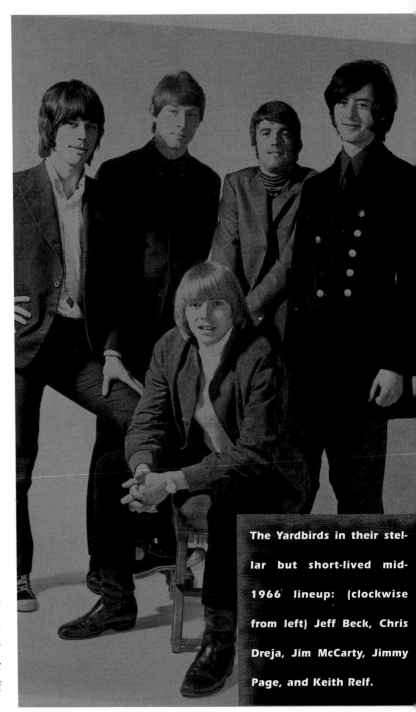

The Yardbirds in their stellar but short-lived mid-1966 lineup: (clockwise from left) Jeff Beck, Chris Dreja, Jim McCarty, Jimmy Page, and Keith Relf.

Beck's guitar and the song's stuttering fadeout were hardly standard Top 40 fare.

After Beck took over the lead guitarist's chair from Clapton, the Yardbirds rocked with a fiery, willful experimentalism. Their repertoire included psychedelic rave-ups like "Over Under Sideways Down" and forays into Middle Eastern music such as "Hot House of Omagarashid." The teenybopper mag *Hit Parader* felt moved to pose the question, "Are the Yardbirds Too Far Out?" Apparently not, as they remained a successful singles band despite their move into fastball psychedelia.

For a brief spell, Beck was joined in the Yardbirds by Jimmy Page. Here was a supergroup before that word was coined (in honor of Blind Faith, incidentally). The brief Beck–Page union yielded the blisteringly strange single, "Happenings Ten Years Time Ago" and a cameo appearance in the film *Blow-Up* (1966). Beck thereupon left to form his own group, and Page remained a Yardbird until forming Led Zeppelin (who called themselves "the New Yardbirds" for a while). Page himself unleashed some searing psychedelic solos during his Yardbirds tenure. His all-time finest blow as an axman might arguably be on the obscure Yardbirds B-side "Think About It," a feedback-driven missile lobbed into deep space (and later covered by Aerosmith).

Like the best psychedelia, the Yardbirds' music was thrilling and a little scary. Those who took hallucinogenic drugs knowingly risked a bit of sanity in hopes of breaking down the doors of perception. For someone tantalized by the promise of new horizons but unwilling to mortgage brain cells to get there, psychedelic music offered an alternative means of conveyance.

Psychedelia wasn't just a fleeting subgenre but a sweeping movement embraced by literally hundreds of bands. The brief survey of keynote psychedelic rockers offered to this point can't begin to do justice to the scope of it all. Seemingly everyone went psychedelic, with the possible exceptions of blues purist John Mayall and some of the shallower pop bands who lacked the will or imagination to make the transition. Hey, even the Dave Clark Five dabbled in it toward the tail end of their career.

The Move, a beer-drinking band from Birmingham, moved (hence, the band's name) to London and altered their sound and look in order to hook up with the underground. Though they privately eschewed drugs and never fit in with the UFO Club elite, the Move flirted with psychedelia in jaunty, twisted pop songs by prime Mover Roy Wood about getting high ("I Can Hear the Grass Grow") and flower power ("Flowers in the Rain"). The latter caused a hailstorm of controversy in Britain when it was promoted with postcards depicting then–Prime Minister Harold Wilson in a compromising position. The Move ultimately had to assign all royalties from the No.1 single to a charity designated by Wilson—an action that probably cost songwriter Wood a half-million pounds over the years.

London Underground scenemakers with still-functioning memories wax fondly about groups like AMM (who made experimental, free-jazz noise) and

The Move, 1967. (Left to right) Ace Kefford, Trevor Burton, Carl Wayne, Bev Bevan, and Roy Wood.

Eric Burdon and the Animals were typical of '60s acts that, under the influence of psychedelics, suddenly changed midstream. Under Burdon's tutelage, the "new" Animals went heavily psychedelic on albums like *Love Is* and *Every One of Us*. Burdon, in fact, became infatuated with Flower Power and the love revolution—on the West Coast of the States rather than in his native England—penning hymns of tribute like "Monterey" and "San Francisco Nights." He entitled a song "Yes I Am Experienced," an obvious rejoinder to the question posed by the first Jimi Hendrix album.

Dantalion's Chariot (which included organist Zoot Money and guitarist Andy Somers, both of whom later joined Eric Burdon's Animals). If you want to get even more obscure, psychedelic purists of the late '60s speak reverently of such psychedelic groups as Apple (no connection to the Beatles' label), the Creation (a Who-ish psychedelic foursome responsible for the period classics "Making Time" and "Painter Man"), Kaleidoscope (not to be confused with the identically named West Coast band), Koobas, the Misunderstood, Smoke ("My Friend Jack"), and the Purple Gang ("Granny Takes a Trip"). Those interested in delving deeper into the catacombs are herewith referred to Delerium's Psychedelic Archive, a comprehensive website (http://www.delerium.co.uk/archive/psychtop.html) devoted exclusively to U.K. and U.S. psychedelia. Its alphabetized listing of entries covers everything from Aardvark to Zzebra. Zounds!

Procol Harum tripped the light fandango in 1967.

68

Eric Burdon and the Animals' paean to the West Coast scene, "San Francisco Nights," entered the Top 10 the week of the Monterey Pop Festival. Burdon (front, center) guided an ever-changing lineup through a maze of hard-rocking psychedelia.

So overcome by the fumes of psychedelia was Burdon that he wrote the following lines from an essay that was printed up big on the cover of the Animals' 1967 album *Winds of Change*: "The new world [is] different from the old with new jewels to be consumed, new frontiers to be won, and much more love to be given….The games I play are mostly games of children…games of love, games of mystery, games of wonder, please excuse my games of fear and jealousy, I'm only human after all and still a student of life."

Procol Harum, though not a psychedelic band per se, offered one of the most inscrutable anthems of the age in "A Whiter Shade of Pale." The Kinks, a group given more to pastoral whimsy than trendy sounds, also made a pass at what might be called psychedelia. "Fancy," a Ray Davies–penned number from 1967's *Face to Face*, featured a hypnotic Indian-style drone. Under the direction of flute-playing leader Ian Anderson, Jethro Tull embarked on a number of eclectic tangents, particularly on their extraordinary second album, *Stand Up*, which ranged from balalaikas to a Bach Bouree. Even a group like Fairport Convention, who played electrified folk bearing a heavy traditional influence, were touched by a similarly stirring alchemy as the overtly psychedelic bands.

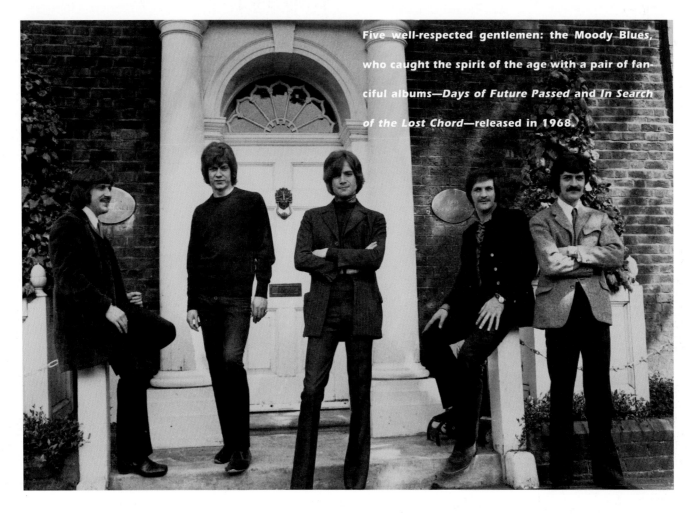

Five well-respected gentlemen: the Moody Blues, who caught the spirit of the age with a pair of fanciful albums—*Days of Future Passed* and *In Search of the Lost Chord*—released in 1968.

Following their international success with the soulful rocker "Go Now," the Moody Blues reconfigured their lineup and took a turn toward classical-rock fusion on 1967's *Days of Future Passed*. Interestingly, the original idea was to make a stereo test record: i.e., something to show off the latest advances in recorded sound. While indeed serving to demonstrate the "Deram Sound System," the album also showcased rock's broadening horizons, and the merger between the Moody Blues and the London Festival Orchestra moved contemporary music forward on yet another front in the heady year of 1967. The Moodies further delved into the classical-mystical-rock motherlode with *In Search of the Lost Chord*, which contained an ode to LSD guru Timothy Leary, "Legend of a Mind." The song was reprised nearly 30 years later on a tribute album after Leary's passing.

EXIT

The Who at the height of psychedelia: Keith Moon as court jester; Pete Townshend, foppishly turned out in frilly shirt and sequined jacket; John Entwistle, still a mod on the outside; and Roger Daltrey, who could pass for one of Robin Hood's Merry Men.

The Who weighed in with "I Can See for Miles," a Top 10 British single from 1967 that featured stuttering psychedelic guitar from Pete Townshend and lyrics about seeing through artifice and dishonesty. A song of shattering insight that implicitly drew a line between generations as bold as "My Generation" had years earlier, it remains one of the essential anthems from those turbulent times. "I Can See for Miles" appeared on *The Who Sell Out,* a brilliant album whose songs were linked by mock commercials and radio jingles. It was not just music but pop art: a snapshot of Swinging London in high gear.

More mystical than psychedelic, Tyrannosaurus Rex (later T. Rex) emerged as a product of the elfin imagination of Marc Bolan. Their first album, a fanciful, folkish affair full of dream-world imagery, appeared in the U.K. in 1968. Its title—*My People Were Fair and Had Sky in Their Hair...But Now They're Content to Wear Stars on Their Brows*—didn't exactly roll off the tongue. Already, Bolan had made his mark as a short-lived member of John's Children, writing the enticingly psychedelic "Desdemona" for them in 1967. Bolan would never lose the wide-eyed star-child persona that first surfaced in the Summer of Love, even after he became a bopping boogie-rocker with songs like "Get It On (Bang a Gong)" in the 1970s.

Late in the Summer of Love, the British pop band The Small Faces cracked the Top 40 with "Itchycoo Park," an unabashedly psychedelic ditty ("getting high with the ducks in the lake"). They followed that up with *Ogdens' Nut Gone Flake*. Mind-blowing tunes: "Happiness Stan," "Lazy Sunday," "Afterglow." *Ogdens'* broke new ground in graphics and album design.

The Small Faces took the R&B-to-psychedelia route, cutting one of the greatest of all psych-rock singles in "Itchycoo Park," which marked one of the earliest uses of phasing. (It's that "whooshing" sound.) Then came *Ogdens' Nut Gone Flake*, an album that eschewed the singles-plus-spare-tracks formula for a more ambitious, cohesive approach. Packaged in a circular cover fashioned to look like a tobacco tin, it contained such intoxicating tunes as "Tin Soldier" and "Lazy Sunday." The Small Faces' psychedelic holiday was enough to make a listener want to hang around Itchycoo Park feeding the ducks (or one's head).

Then there was this other band that can't go unmentioned. *Sgt. Pepper's Lonely Hearts Club Band*, that is. This album above all others changed the course of Western music (if not the whole of Western culture). As such, it is not only the Beatles' greatest achievement but the landmark recording of the 1960s.

"THE MAN CAN'T BUST OUR MUSIC" THE MARKETING OF PSYCHEDELIA

As the Doors, the Jefferson Airplane, and others began crash-landing near the top of the Billboard charts, record company executives began to prick up their ears to the sounds of revolution. Once Scott McKenzie made hippiedom safe for children and other living things with his Summer of Love single "San Francisco (Be Sure to Wear Flowers in Your Hair)," a communal contract signing for a bunch of San Francisco bands followed. After a certain point in 1968, when underground, album-oriented rock took off for real, a veritable feeding frenzy followed. At this point, seemingly every hair-growing, guitar-soloing, day-gloing, light-showing band in America got a record deal. The labels wanted full-length albums, not just a few test-the-waters singles, from them. This was all part of a changing of the guard as the long-playing, 12-inch, 33⅓ rpm album overtook the 7-inch, 45 rpm single in the rapidly evolving music culture.

In order to foist all these new LPs on unsuspecting daydream believers, record-company publicists had to put the hype machine into high gear. Some ads were hip, such as Warner Bros.' "God Save the Kinks" campaign and the "Win a Date With Pigpen" promo for a new Grateful Dead album. Most, however, were fulsome at best and ludicrous at worst as copywriters struggled to make bad and often bogus psychedelia sound enticing. The following are some of the most amusing attempts to make purple prose of purple haze. They're included not just for goofy fun but because these artifacts give a true flavor of the times:

On the Sons of Champlin: "The forms which we create caress our minds, and they'll take us past this place which lives by time. And the forms we are creating today are the forms which we will be some day. And the good games are the flowers of our minds forever. I love you."

On Ultimate Spinach: "You are what you dig. And if you dig grooves that go a lot deeper than yeh, yeh, yeh…if you dig sounds that trip a lot farther than most of today's 'heavy' music…if you dig original, organic music that makes most 'avant-garde' groups look like yesterday, then you're going to eat up Ultimate Spinach."

On a number of "great sound makers" from CBS Records [this from the same corporation that, in 1969, yanked the Smothers Brothers off the air for espousing antiwar sentiments]: "But the Man can't bust our music. The Establishment's against adventure. And the arousing experience that comes with listening to today's music. So what? Let them slam doors. And keep it out of concert halls…the Man can't stop you from listening. Especially if you're armed with these."

Another CBS Records dispatch: "If you won't listen to your parents, the Man, or the Establishment…Why should you listen to us?" Answer: "Because of the power of Rock, the shriek of the Blues, the doubt of Country-Folk…"

On Bobby Callender: "Sounds from the human spectrum. Where there is no clear-cut chiaroscuro…where the only charisma revolves around reality. And the only primary color is truth…daydreams littered with the changes of past and present. Echoed in concentric circles of expanding sound…"

On a band called Graffiti: "The album that'll put you on the edge of your head…and never let you off."

On a band and album called Fields: "The Fields backside is 20 minutes long and reaches two climaxes! Will you?"

On a band called Raven: "The album is as loose as it is tight. If you can dig that."

On a band and album called Blond: "From the folks who brought you Ingmar Bergman, free love, and meatballs. Sweden's new thing. They're beautiful."

On a band and album called The Baroques: "The fact is, you haven't really been turned on until you've been turned on by the Baroques."

On a band and album called Rotary Connection: "Angelica wet with wine. Tears sliding slowly up a forehead. Plastic heartbeats echoing amidst chromium rafters. Clarity of desecration. Turn yourself on with a diamond needle…travel with us in your favorite color."

On a psychedelic Japanese wunderkind named Harumi: "Two complete records in first album. Part one woven from words and wisdom of today. Part two takes you on a journey back through time—through the pomegranate forest to a fire by the river. Where the hunters of heaven sip eternal tea. And sighing strands of music flow from memories of samurai…"

On an album called *I'd Like to Get to Know You*, by Spanky and Our Gang: "(1) Open. (2) Unfold freaky 4-color poster. (3) Remove record. (4) Listen to an album that's hard to believe."

On a band and album called The United States of America: "In cuts like 'The American Metaphysical Circus,' 'I Won't Leave My Wooden Wife for You, Sugar,' and 'The American Way of Love,' the lyrics will bite your head off. And the sound…well, it's something else. Electronic…a whole new thing…places where no one's been before….The music surrounds and lifts you, and throws you around a little, too…It'll clear your head like a whiff of ammonia."

On an album called *Trilogy for the Masses*, by Ford Theatre: "Today—Scene of chaos and agony, constant change, and motion in the world of now expressed in creative rock!"

On a band and album called Songs of Innocence: "In which a vibrant confluence of mellifluous phenomenon proliferates the ignominious illations concerning the anthropocentric creed…But a totally wigged-out experience!"

On a band and album called The Fool: "Fool fathom four whose gentle lies/Make tones of oral jade/These are the pearls that see the skies/Where nothing fades/Without a key change/Into something rich and strange/Freedom ringlets all around an ear/Listen/Ding dong bell."

On a band and album called Gentle Soul: "Gentle Soul is wildflowers pressed in a bible, shadows of dawn on the wall, visions of love through a prism, views of the sea from a tower, singing from woodlands and autumn, stoned at the end of the world."

On a band and album called Moloch: "Moloch g'wan git ya…If you can't stand the heat!…electric fire and brimstone…home-cooked in Memphis…it'll likely make your ears salivate."

On a band and album called Ambergris: "Ambergris is whale puke….They play whale-rock."

No other LP in the history of popular music has been so intensely listened to, scrutinized, and revered as *Sgt. Pepper's Lonely Hearts Club Band*. Released in England on June 1, 1967, and one day later in the United States, *Sgt. Pepper* has been credited not only with altering the face of popular music but with precipitating far-reaching changes in the philosophy, lifestyle, and politics of an entire generation. It marked a radical

The Beatles, at Brian Epstein's London house, in a jubilant mood after completing *Sgt. Pepper*. Of the smoky album sessions, Sir Joseph Lockwood, esteemed head of the Beatles' British record company, looked the other way: "I knew there was some possible connection with cannabis in the studios—'smells' were noted—but I never pursued it."

break with the Top 40 format that had dominated the way pop music was marketed and received. None of its 13 songs was released as a single, per the Beatles' wishes—a move unheard of in the pop world.

Sgt. Pepper carried rock to its headiest peak. It united the counterculture at a time when young people began speaking out about everything from Vietnam to civil rights. It gave rise to the notion that rock was worthy of serious criticism and study. With its confident artistry, generous spirit, and sunny good vibes, *Sgt. Pepper* served as the unofficial soundtrack for the Summer of Love. Its reach was astounding; wherever one went in the summer of '67, a copy of *Sgt. Pepper* was bound to be playing close by. As writer Langdon Winner sagely observed, "For a brief moment, the irreparably fragmented consciousness of the West was united, at least in the minds of the young."

The term "concept album" was born with *Sgt. Pepper*. It was tied together by segues and the device of opening with the title track and then reprising it near the end of the album, which created for listeners the impression of having just heard a program by the Beatles in the guise of Sgt. Pepper's band. Though their

vaulting ambition ran the risk of alienating less adventuresome fans, *Sgt. Pepper* remained No. 1 for 15 weeks, longer than any other Beatles album.

Drawing on influences as diverse as British music hall and *musique concrète*, the Beatles liberated rock and roll from its Top 40 straitjacket. Judicious use of orchestration and exotic instruments like the sitar decorated songs that soared artfully in all directions. Although Paul McCartney takes pains to claim credit for *Sgt. Pepper* from its conception on down, the album was a solid group endeavor. In the program for his 1989–90 World Tour, McCartney rather archly stated: "I'm not trying to say [*Pepper*] was all me, but I do think John's avant-garde period later was really to give himself a go at what he's seen me having a go at." It's probably more accurate to say that McCartney instigated the Beatles' turn toward the avant-garde, but that Lennon embodied and the others embellished it.

McCartney did contribute many of the album's most openhanded, high-spirited songs: "Getting

Better," "Lovely Rita," "When I'm Sixty-Four." John Lennon's numbers tended toward surreal fantasias such as "Lucy in the Sky With Diamonds" and "Being for the Benefit of Mr. Kite," plus a caustic commentary on the workaday world, "Good Morning, Good Morning." The disparate Lennon-McCartney sensibilities merged on the album's masterful closing suite, "A Day in the Life," which concluded with a long orchestral glissando and endless piano chord carried to a silence that felt like infinity. Then there was lovable old Ringo, artlessly warbling "A Little Help from My Friends," a song about human interconnections (and

maybe drugs, depending on how you interpret the line "I get high with a little help from my friends") that struck a resonant chord with the counterculture. George contributed only one song, a tour de force of Indian music and Eastern philosophy called "Within You Without You" that showcased his growing prowess on the sitar and reverence for his teacher, Ravi Shankar.

The album was a complete package right down to its artwork: its elaborate cover collage; lyrics printed on the back cover (rock bands just didn't do that prior to *Sgt. Pepper*); a gatefold jacket that opened up to reveal a stunning portrait of the four Beatles en regalia; an inner sleeve featuring a spacy design by "The Fool," four Dutch hippie designers; and an enclosed sheet of Sgt. Pepper decals. In the wake of *Sgt. Pepper*, rock albums came stuffed with all sorts of things: lyric sheets, posters, artwork, and other objects of study for the intrepid listener.

One of us bought *Sgt. Pepper* shortly after its release at a neighborhood drugstore. The copy was monaural and cost $3.47 (roughly

The cover design for *Sgt. Pepper* was nearly as complicated as the music. Seventy-one figures were chosen by the band members from a list of their heroes. Fans spent hours scrutinizing the jacket for hidden meanings—i.e., Is that a funeral mass for the old Beatles? A pot plant? (Answers: yes, no.)

one-fifth the cost of today's CDs). It made for challenging listening to a 12-year-old who'd theretofore bought big-holed 45s and had his ear glued to the AM radio hit parade. But no one could claim to be completely unprepared for *Sgt. Pepper*, as the Beatles had been making incremental moves in that direction with the transitional albums *Rubber Soul* (1965) and *Revolver* (1966).

Before those records, the Beatles' had been lovable, globe-trotting mop-tops and growing prisoners of the clean-cut, eager-to-please image that every pop star was expected to project. Now their songs had grown more circumspect and arty, and their personalities were less "Fab Four" and more individualized. Not surprisingly, the Beatles had begun experimenting with marijuana and LSD in private. The cover of *Rubber Soul* bore wavy psychedelic lettering and a refracted, fisheye-lens photo of four unsmiling Beatles. The music within was largely acoustic and heavily Dylan-influenced, including such intimate, unplugged Beatles classics as "Norwegian Wood" and "I've Just Seen a Face."

Revolver marked a sharp turn toward ornate pop-psychedelia as the Beatles played the studio like an instrument on "Tomorrow Never Knows," "She Said She Said," and others. Their most psychedelic track from this pre-*Pepper* period was "Rain," which turned up as the B-side of "Paperback Writer" in June 1966 (between *Rubber Soul* and *Revolver*), belatedly making its LP appearance on 1970's *Hey Jude* collection. However obscure, "Rain" didn't escape the purview of Beatles historian Nicholas Schaffner, who wrote in his biography *The Beatles Forever*, "The hypnotic 'Rain' was the first articulation of a philosophy John and George were to expound repeatedly in their work over the next few years: that the outward manifestations of the material world are all nothing more than a 'wall of illusion.'"

While each of those recordings represented an artful step forward, *Sgt. Pepper* took a quantum leap. Many listeners whose minds were rapidly moving away from the constrictions of the Top 40 mentality were ready to take the trip with them. On the other hand, some Blue Meanies will passionately argue to this day that *Sgt. Pepper* was the worst thing that ever happened to rock and roll. They blame the Beatles for the pretentious excesses of progressive rock and the elevation of rock musicians to the level of "serious artists" as inimical to the spirit of the music.

However, the idea of arresting the evolution of popular music in order to hold it to some sort of mandated guidelines (short songs about dancing, teen angst, and all the other greasy kid's stuff that had become so irrelevant in these years of discord) is more intolerable than the pretentious music that issued from some quarters, inspired by the later work of the Beatles. Such an attitude is so inherently conservative that it runs counter to the basic spirit of rock and roll. Like a wild vine, it will go where it goes, and *Sgt. Pepper* endures as one of the most creative and fruitful experiments of all.

Naturally, *Sgt. Pepper* had a profound and immediate impact. Brian Wilson of the Beach Boys, who for a spell came closest to challenging the Beatles on an artistic level, scrapped his group's mythical *Smile* project, feeling that rock's greatest album had already been recorded. Frank Zappa, taking the opposite position (which is what this contrarian generally did) concocted an elaborate satire of *Sgt. Pepper* for his Mothers of Invention that mercilessly skewered the counterculture. Entitled *We're Only in It for the Money*, its savagely parodic tone was expressed in lines such as these: "Every town must have a place where phony hippies meet/Psychedelic dungeons popping up on every street." In a way, it was reassuring that the counterculture was not so doctrinaire that it couldn't absorb hits from one of its own. Zappa, a curmudgeon's curmudgeon and voice of the counter-counterculture, appended this note to *We're Only in It for the Money*: "This whole monstrosity was conceived & executed by Frank Zappa as a result of some unpleasant premonitions, August through October 1967."

Adopting the alter ego of Sgt. Pepper's Band, the Beatles reveled in the freedom it allowed. 'There was nothing they couldn't do in that last great year of unity, harmony, and collective happiness," wrote band intimate Derek Taylor.

Back on the British side, even the Rolling Stones took cues from the Beatles throughout much of the '60s, recording the psychedelic rejoinder *Their Satanic Majesties Request* hot on *Sgt. Pepper*'s heels. Often dismissed as a contrivance ill-suited to the earthy Stones, *Their Satanic Majesties Request* may be one of the more unjustly maligned albums of the decade. Granted, it does not flow as smoothly and skillfully as *Sgt. Pepper*, but certain of its songs are magnificent: the delicate, lovely "She's a Rainbow," the eerily disorienting "2000 Light Years from Home," and the brave-new-world anthem "Sing This All Together." The album's 3D jacket, which found the Stones adorned in wizard's garb and hippie finery, was as mind-blowing as the collage of famous faces surrounding the Beatles on the front of *Sgt. Pepper*. If you looked closely in the Stones' garden, you could even make out tiny, hidden Beatle faces.

In the play of light and shadows between the Beatles and the Stones, you might say that *Sgt. Pepper* took listeners on a good trip while *Their Satanic Majesties Request* flirted more with the darker side of the psychedelic experience, the scarifying maze into which lost souls having bad trips might wander. But that didn't invalidate the album; in fact, it works in a complementary way to *Sgt. Pepper*.

The Beatles' magnum opus served to challenge other ambitious musical minds. The Pretty Things, led by singer Phil May, wrote and recorded the first rock opera, *S.F. Sorrow*, a lamentably obscure milestone that is ripe for rediscovery. *S.F. Sorrow* was based on an Orwellian short story by May about one Sebastian F. Sorrow, an individual who suffers a loss of self at the hands of a soulless, technocratic society. As civilization slouches toward the millennium, *S.F. Sorrow*'s bleak futurist scenario seems more timely than ever. The Who's Pete Townshend reportedly listened to the album for the better part of a week. It is not far-fetched to surmise that some of its ambitious architecture might have influenced Townshend as he worked on the rock opera *Tommy*, the Who's double album about a deaf, dumb, and blind boy who embarks on an "amazing journey."

Sgt. Pepper

Though *Tommy*'s story line is hopelessly obscure, and becomes more so with each long-winded explanation from its composer, *Tommy* served as an archetypal metaphor for a generation that was on its own path, groping in the dark for spiritual enlightenment and redemption. As such, it was emblematic of the best instincts and motivations of the '60s, and a fitting album to close out the decade. One of the most scintillating performances at Woodstock was the Who's hypercharged set, especially the "See Me, Feel Me" medley from *Tommy* that was a highlight of the Woodstock film. With the Who as electrified seers, the crowd at

Sgt. Pepper was originally set to be a double album, but the sessions consumed so much time and money that a single LP was released in a deluxe package. As artist Peter Blake said, "Instead of the second record they got the cutouts, badges, sergeant's stripes, and so on." This was one of the extras.

Woodstock—and millions more who absorbed the experience in theaters or on record—capped the decade that had given us *Sgt. Pepper* with one more amazing journey.

LOS ANGELES

CITY OF NIGHT AT THE DAWN OF PSYCHEDELIA

San Francisco got most of the attention and was considered the more "authentic" scene, yet Los Angeles contributed its share of stars to the freak flag that unfurled over this divided nation in the late '60s. These included the Byrds, Buffalo Springfield, the Doors, Iron Butterfly, Love, Spirit, the Turtles, Steppenwolf, the Mamas and the Papas, the Mothers of Invention, and Captain Beefheart

The Mamas and the Papas (left to right: John Phillips, Michelle Phillips, Cass Elliot, and Dennis Doherty) enjoyed six Top 5 singles, including the No. 1 "Monday, Monday."

and His Magic Band. You could also throw in the Beach Boys, who were truly freakier than anyone had any inkling at the time. A highly fertile and creative scene whose resident geniuses included the likes of Frank Zappa, Brian Wilson, Van Dyke Parks (freelance producer, session

hand, and solo artist), Jim Morrison, and Arthur Lee, Los Angeles bristled with talent. There wasn't the same sense of community or countercultural dogma that bound the San Franciscans, but the brightly colored bits of glass on the L.A. scene made for a highly entertaining mosaic all the same.

In lieu of an established older neighborhood like Haight-Ashbury, the young scenemakers of L.A. hung out on the Sunset Strip while the pop-star types began inhabiting enclaves like Laurel Canyon. The miracle mile of Sunset Strip, home to clubs like the Whisky A Go Go, was where the kids gathered and paraded in increasing numbers at mid-decade, eliciting the wrath of their intolerant elders. The defining moment in L.A.'s burgeoning youthquake came when authorities attempted to clear the Strip of loiterers in November 1966. The ensuing confrontation with the authorities gave the embattled young rebels a rallying point and a profound sense of "us vs. them." The events also provided the grist for Stephen Stills' superb documentary

recounting "For What It's Worth," a song that became a hit for his group Buffalo Springfield in early '67 and was added to subsequent pressings of their already released first album.

In many respects, the L.A. musicians could not have been more different than their Haight-Ashbury counterparts. For one thing, the music coming out of L.A. generally placed more of an emphasis on vocals than guitars. From the Beach Boys to the Association, the Mamas and Papas to the Turtles, the L.A. sound was more about strong singing than lengthy guitar epiphanies. Moreover, the musicians were not as heedlessly scruffy. Think of Morrison in his leathers, the lithe and model-like Michelle Phillips, Roger McGuinn's trademark specs, Neil Young in his fringy jacket, or the groovy boutique threads worn by the trendier musicians-about-town. By and large, the L.A. contingent had shorter hair and neatly trimmed beards, and their outfits were brightly colored rock-star haberdashery (which may be one reason that fashion-conscious Londoners felt a closer bond with Los Angeles than San Francisco). The glaring exception was the Mothers, who meant to be grotesque. But they, too, could be seen as actors playing a role, to some degree—that of deliberately ugly, anti-rock stars—as opposed to the San Francisco musicians, who tended to be their own frumpy, unassuming selves everywhere they went, including the concert stage.

The differences between the two cities and their musical communities were so glaring that you could almost think of them as opposite poles within the carnivalesque world of psychedelia. This generated some actual antagonism. San Franciscans regarded L.A. as a plastic scene whose bands were slick and overproduced. Paul Kantner of Jefferson Airplane voiced that cranky sentiment in an interview from the time in which he cited the Beach Boys as Exhibit A. If you put those surfing choirboys onstage at the Fillmore, Kantner argued, "it wouldn't work."

Los Angeles, on the other hand, looked down on San Francisco as a bunch of sloppy troglodytes who couldn't get their act together in a studio or onstage. Frank Zappa once leapt to the defense of the Monkees, claiming that their albums were better produced than anything out of San Francisco. About the only thing that Zappa had in common with

Buffalo Springfield, shown at Redondo Beach in 1966, was a war of wills between Steve Stills (top left) and Neil Young (bottom left).

the similarly bilious Lou Reed was their mutual disdain for the hippie subculture of Haight-Ashbury.

An illustrative tale: When musical emissaries from the two cities began meeting to arrange billings for the Monterey International Pop Festival, attempts were made to court the Grateful Dead. In his book *Living With the Dead*, manager Rock Scully recounted the get-together between an L.A.-based contingent led by festival organizer Lou Adler and the highly skeptical Grateful Dead, who were concerned about a hidden agenda and profit motive.

Phil Lesh (the Dead's bassist): "Why do we get the impression you guys are gonna film this thing and make umpteen double albums and sell it from here to Singapore?"

Adler: "No, no, no, baby, you've got us all wrong. Where'd you ever get these crazy ideas? Look, guys, this is going to be great for everyone. The L.A./San Francisco/London axis strutting its stuff and the whole fucking world watching us. Can you dig it? It's going to be magical, baby....Hey, it doesn't get much better than this!"

Lesh: "Oh shit, now I know we're gonna get screwed!"

Simply stated, the dynamics of the scene were vastly different. Los Angeles is a faster, flatter, sunnier, and more spread-out place where the entertainment business (with the emphasis on the latter word) makes its headquarters. Commercialism wasn't quite the dirty word in Southern California that it was up in the Bay Area. Even bands as broodingly intense as the Doors carved a niche for themselves on the Top 40 without feeling like some sacred oath had been violated. They notched a No. 1 hit on their second try with an edited version of "Light My Fire" at the height of the Summer of Love. Indeed, the Doors cracked the Top 40 more times than the Jefferson Airplane, Quicksilver, Country Joe, the Dead, and Big Brother put together! It was no contest, with the final score being Doors 8, San Francisco 4 (and the Dead wouldn't launch their one-and-only chart hit, "Touch of Grey," until 1987).

The Doors' Jim Morrison was so deeply into the visionary experience, as triggered by a voluminous intake of LSD, that he went clear beyond psychedelia into another realm entirely, one in which he could see and imagine his own death and what it meant in the cosmic scheme of things. This came across in Morrison's shamanistic stage presence and in such lengthy epistles as "The End" and "When the Music's Over." Morrison described his voluble role as lyricist and vocalist with the Doors as "the feeling of a bowstring being pulled back for 22 years and suddenly let go."

In the Doors' first record-company bio—dictated by the band members in a show of self-determination that would never have happened in the early '60s—Morrison offered this philosophical insight: "I like ideas about the breaking away or overthrowing of established order. I am interested in anything about revolt, disorder, chaos, especially activity that has no meaning."

The Doors (bottom to top: Jim Morrison, Ray Manzarek, Robbie Krieger, and John Densmore): "The future's uncertain and the end is always near."

It is difficult to imagine those same words issuing from the lips of, say, Frankie Avalon or Bobby Rydell. The Doors represented a shift in sensibility of the profoundest sort. Morrison became the living embodiment of the poet William Blake's decree that "the road of excess leads to the palace of wisdom." If Blake was right, then Jim Morrison was the wisest man alive. He regularly pushed his mind and mortal frame to their limits. One night he ingested 10,000 micrograms of acid (the average dose is 250 mikes), and from the deepest depths of his psyche the Oedipal section of "The End" welled up during a performance at the Whisky.

The music on their first two albums, *The Doors* and *Strange Days*, was dark, Dionysian, and intoxicating. It was better described as acid rock than psychedelic music. Alcohol eventually replaced acid as Morrison's drug of choice, but his poetical sensibilities and the inspired musicianship of keyboardist Ray Manzarek, guitarist Robbie Krieger, and drummer John Densmore—which drew upon the freedom of jazz and the exacting temperament of classical as much as from rock and roll—carried them through six studio albums. Morrison's body finally succumbed to the abuse he'd heaped on it during his brief 27 years on the planet. He expired on July 3, 1971, in the bathtub of an apartment in Paris, to which he'd fled on a self-imposed exile with his wife Pamela after completing work on the *L.A. Woman* album.

While the Doors were the keystone band on the L.A. scene, others played significant roles. Prior to the Doors' ascent, Love was the reigning group on the scene whose success the Doors sought to emulate. They were first to sign with Elektra Records, paving the way for the Doors' discovery and signing. Love was led by the temperamental Arthur Lee, a brilliant songwriter and singer. His foil was Bryan MacLean, who'd been a Byrds roadie. Love in its original incarnation was a six-member group with three guitarists—an echo of the

early Byrds—who hit all the bases: short, combustible punk-psych songs ("7&7 Is"); a quixotic, side-long piece ("Revolution"); and a brilliantly realized concept album (*Forever Changes*). The latter was Love's finest hour, a deep and painstaking study of an unraveling life in whose downward spiral one could find beauty. The broken piece of pottery held by Lee in the rear-cover photo served as a perfect metaphor for the coming apart of this drug-soaked band and the larger crackup of the counterculture as the decade wore on (and wore out).

The Doors and Love had much in common—a passion for the edge, a penchant for getting in trouble and pushing the envelope, drug problems within the band—and at least some of their similarities may have had a psychological underpinning. Morrison bluntly attributed his flamboyant, destructive behavior to the fact that he "didn't get enough love as a kid." In 1997, Bryan MacLean explained Love's antics to *Mojo* magazine in this way: "We were creating a persona—the bad boys of rock 'n' roll! Kids who are neglected by their fathers go after negative attention, you know?" In that sense, Love were as much a gang as a band, and the fact that leader Arthur Lee is in prison as this is being written—one

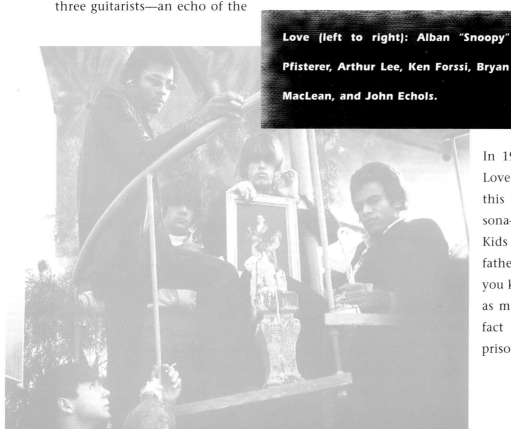

Love (left to right): Alban "Snoopy" Pfisterer, Arthur Lee, Ken Forssi, Bryan MacLean, and John Echols.

Faces that only a mother could love: the Mothers of Invention, led by the brilliant iconoclast Frank Zappa (lower right), vowed to "kill ugly radio."

through a string of late-'60s albums that left no target unscathed. Much of it was seemingly "psychedelic" (as in unconventional and unbounded by rules) without falling into formal lockstep with musical trends.

The severely intellectual Zappa eschewed drugs as mindless escapism (though he made an exception on his own behalf for cigarettes). He skewered the meaningless lives and empty mores of the older generation in such songs as "Brown Shoes Don't Make It" while lamenting the fate of their children, whom he described as "the left-behinds of the Great Society." He told older tourists who chanced to wander into a Mothers performance at the Whisky, "If your children ever find out how lame you really are, they'll murder you in your sleep." The Mothers broke every rule. Their first release, *Freak Out!*, was a double album. Their second, *Absolutely Free*, lambasted with scarifying social satire a country that absolutely was not (free, that is). The third, *We're Only in It for the Money*, parodied the Beatles and the counterculture.

Los Angeles in the 1960s teemed like a beehive with lots of different cells being worked independently. There were the Turtles, probably the brightest and funniest Top 40 band in America, several of whose members were later recruited by Zappa as Mothers in the '70s. There was Spirit, one of L.A.'s trippiest bands, whose visual symbol was guitarist Randy California's stepfather, bald-domed drummer Ed Cassidy. (California, incidentally, had been a protégé of Jimi Hendrix at the tender age of 15.)

of the early casualties of California's "three strikes and you're out" legislation—would seem to bear that out.

Using the Mothers of Invention as his vehicle, Frank Zappa sought another kind of negative attention: stirring up the animosity of a mainstream culture whose small-minded mediocrity he despised. A skilled composer, arranger, conductor, guitarist, and satirist, Zappa brilliantly navigated his Mothers

Spirit's jazz- and pop-tinged psychedelia rose from the low-key charm of their heady debut, *Spirit*, to the full-blown psychedelic roar of their classic fourth album, *Twelve Dreams of Dr. Sardonicus*. The group Kaleidoscope, which included longtime Jackson Browne sideman and guitarist extraordinaire David Lindley, made exotic records that partook of Middle Eastern and other world-music influences. Particularly worth seeking out is their album *A Beacon From Mars*.

The Byrds, after their Beatles-meets-Dylan origins, plunged into a psychedelic maelstrom with a series of recordings that included the epochal "Eight Miles High," with its John Coltrane–style solo flight by Roger McGuinn on 12-string guitar. No other group delved so deeply into the altered realities of the times without losing a grasp on their pop-band moorings, and such albums as *Fifth Dimension*, *Younger Than Yesterday*, and *Notorious Byrd Brothers* remain essential snapshots of an incense-scented, acid-drenched world in motion: a kaleidoscope whose every turn yielded some fantastic window on the age.

Then there were the Beach Boys, whose late-'60s experiments and travails were as Byzantine as any group's. Drummer Dennis Wilson, of course, found his way into Charles Manson's inner circle, while singer Mike Love discovered meditation via the Maharishi. Meanwhile, creative helmsman Brian Wilson had long since withdrawn from the rigors of touring and holed up in the studio, an obsessive genius in his element given free reign to go wild. Playing a game of can-you-top-this with the Beatles, Wilson pulled out all stops in 1966, the year that both *Pet Sounds* and "Good Vibrations" were released.

The Beatles countered with *Sgt. Pepper*. Wilson set to work on *Smile*, an album that was going to be "the culmination of all of Brian's intellectual occupations," according to business adviser and close confidant David Anderle. It would also display Wilson's love of humor, the elements, and the outdoors. All the recipes for a truly psychedelic magnum opus were in place, but the project collapsed around Wilson in tandem with his own tenuous sanity. Bits and pieces of *Smile* have been released over the years, from "Cabinessence" to "Surf's Up," but this legendary project has yet to be properly reconstructed for official release from the Beach Boys' work tapes. One can always hope.

As mentioned, the Los Angeles bands were unabashedly geared for success on a level that eclipsed their warier brethren up the coast. Steppenwolf, a hard-rock band with psychedelic designs airbrushed onto the shiny biker chrome of their music, scored with "Born to Be Wild" (first recorded reference to "heavy metal") and "Magic Carpet Ride" (a heady mental romp about getting high on and to music). The biggest album of the decade belonged to Iron Butterfly, a foursome whose signature song, "In-A-Gadda-Da-Vida," stands as the most popular long track in the storied annals of psychedelia. The L.A.-based band—several of whose members were living above the Sunset Strip club Bido

89

Lido's (a way station for the Doors and Love, among others) when keyboardist Doug Ingle composed the song—premiered "In-A-Gadda-Da-Vida" at the Whisky A Go Go one night in 1968. An open-ended piece with room for solos, it grew in length as the band members absorbed the influence of an African mass for chorus and percussion called *Missa Luba*, whose trancelike rhythms and spirituality rubbed off on them. Running for 17:05 and occupying an entire side of their second album—entitled, not surprisingly, *In-A-Gadda-Da-Vida*—this riff-driven song with its indelible drum solo in the middle became one of the touchstones of the still-evolving rock underground. It peaked at No. 4 on the album chart—not a bad showing for an "underground" record—and went on to sell four million copies. Via Iron Butterfly wings, underground rock had arrived.

On the overground, AM side of the dial, another musician with ties to L.A. cut a song that reached No. 4 on the singles chart. In one of the crowning ironies of the age, singer Scott McKenzie (born Philip Blondheim in Jacksonville, Florida) crooned "San Francisco (Be Sure to Wear Flowers in Your Hair)," a song written and produced by John Phillips of the Mamas and the Papas.

Yes, the song that sent a tide of longhairs flooding to San Francisco during the Summer of Love actually originated in Los Angeles. Maybe that's where all the trouble between the two cities began.

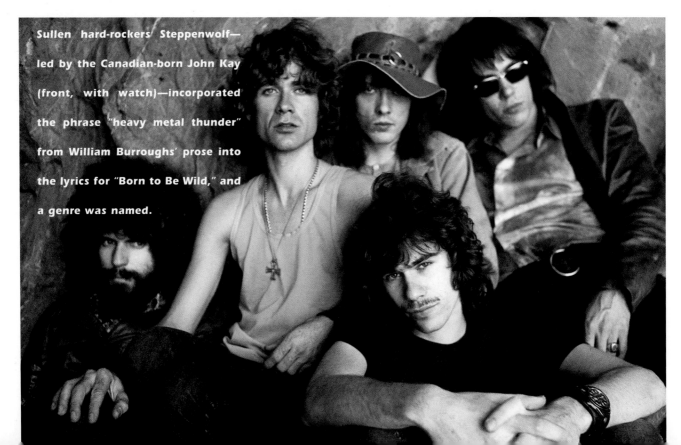

Sullen hard-rockers Steppenwolf—led by the Canadian-born John Kay (front, with watch)—incorporated the phrase "heavy metal thunder" from William Burroughs' prose into the lyrics for "Born to Be Wild," and a genre was named.

CALLING OUT AROUND THE WORLD:
OTHER CITIES AND THEIR SCENES

San Francisco, Los Angeles, and London were certainly the hubs of the music revolution in the late '60s. However, there were viable scenes in other locales across the fruited plain as developments in the hub cities trickled outward like bursts of day-glo paint on a spinning turntable. Eventually, the whole country got saturated by the music and lifestyle of the psychedelia era. Just look at the numerous volumes in the *Nuggets* and *Pebbles* series, which document local and regional scenes around the country.

Here are several cities that had active musical scenes, accompanied by some of the bands that put them on the freakadelic map.

Boston: Ultimate Spinach, Beacon Street Union, Orpheus, Earth Opera, Eden's Children, the Remains, the Standells, the Barbarians.

Detroit/Ann Arbor: MC5, the Stooges (originally the Psychedelic Stooges), the Rationals, the Amboy Dukes, the Bob Seger System, Mitch Ryder and the Detroit Wheels.

Houston/Dallas/Austin: the 13th Floor Elevators, Fever Tree, the Red Crayola, the Moving Sidewalk, Bubble Puppy, the Clique, Mouse and the Traps, Sir Douglas Quintet.

New York/Long Island: Velvet Underground, the Rascals, Lovin' Spoonful, the Cyrkle, Blues Project, Vanilla Fudge, the Vagrants (featuring Leslie West), Blues Magoos, the Hassles (featuring Billy Joel), the Strangeloves, the Illusion, the Soft White Underbelly (later Blue Öyster Cult), the Fugs, the Holy Modal Rounders, David Peel and the Lower East Side.

THE LSD-C&W CONNECTION

Look into the closets of at least a few stars from the country & western, folk, and bluegrass fields and you might be surprised at the tie-dyed skeletons hidden in the back. Which is to say that before they donned cowboy hats and the sensible, down-home personalities that are the hallmark of roots-oriented musicians, the following were once members of full-blown, honest-to-Owsley psychedelic combos. Far out!

Dan Seals: Before this well-groomed country singer started recording standard Nashville fare with titles like "Headin' West" and "Meet Me in Montana," he was a member of the duo England Dan and John Ford Coley. (Remember "I'd Really Love to See You Tonight"?) Before England Dan and John Ford Coley, both men belonged to Southwest F.O.B., a psychedelic quintet from Texas whose "Smell of Incense" just missed the Top 40 in 1968. The cover of their lone album (*Smell of Incense*, on Hip Records) depicts four naked women seated inside a plastic cube set in a cave with billowing clouds of incense. What would the country folk make of that?

Joe Stampley: One half of a honky-tonk duo with Moe Bandy, the hard-charging, cowboy-hatted Stampley might be the least likely C&W figure this side of Roy Acuff to have worn hippie threads. But on the cover of a 1967-vintage album called *Happening Now!*, by the Uniques, bandleader Stampley affects an op-art shirt loud enough to make the late Andy Warhol don shades. Stampley made a sartorial statement of another kind in the early '80s when he and Bandy recorded "Where's the Dress," a barroom-redneck putdown of the flamboyant Boy George (of Culture Club). A question for Stampley: Where's the shirt?

Jerry Jeff Walker: This venerable folk troubadour, responsible for everything from "Mr. Bojangles" to beery epiphanies with his Lost Gonzo Band, belonged to a long-forgotten psychedelic group called Circus Maximus. They cut a pair of late-'60s albums for the Vanguard label, the first of which includes the mind-blowing "Wind," eight minutes' worth of trippy poetry set to jazzy psychedelic accompaniment: "The more you learn, the less you know/The more you move, the more you go to nowhere." Chew on that, Bojangles!

Barry Tashian: Barry and Holly Tashian (his wife) are highly regarded in folk-country circles, having recorded a brace of well-received albums on Rounder. But back in 1967 Barry led one of the best (and most neglected) bands of the '60s, the Remains. They toured with the Beatles in 1966, and some who were around argue that they musically blew the Fab Four off the stage. Their forte was high-energy garage-soul, with a whiff of late-'60s headiness creeping into originals like "Don't Look Back."

Kenny Rogers: The sugar-daddy pop-country crooner with salt-and-pepper whiskers made waves in 1967 with the First Edition, who hit it big with the mind-meltingly psychedelic "Just Dropped In (To See What Condition My Condition Was In)." Just as scary as the song's evocation of mental derangement (it was written by Mickey Newbury, later a progressive country-folkie) is the fact that the persona behind "The Gambler" and a roasted-chicken franchise sang this turkey.

J.J. Cale: Would you believe that this laconic, laid-back Oklahoma picker—who has written such songs as "After Midnight" and "Cocaine"—belonged to a psychedelic cash-in group called the Leathercoated Minds? Their one-and-only album, *A Trip Down the Sunset Strip*, was produced and arranged by Cale, and it includes four Cale originals alongside versions of "Psychotic Reaction," "Eight Miles High," and "Sunshine Superman." From the liner notes: "The songs contained in this album are 'what's happening'...We sincerely hope you will be given a mental Trip Down the Sunset Strip."

Peter Rowan: A modern-bluegrass legend and Bill Monroe protégé who's recorded a string of albums for the Sugar Hill label, Rowan blew minds once upon a time as a member of Earth Opera. This trippy quintet—part of the short-lived "Bosstown Sound" hype—released two albums on Elektra that included such twisted epics as "Death by Fire" (sample lyric: "I decree that her death be by rumor, the skull gleamed.../In agreement, the room full of white teeth all clicked"). Another Earth Opera alumnus: David Grisman, the well-known "jazzgrass" mandolinist and collaborator of Jerry Garcia's on projects like *Old and In the Way*.

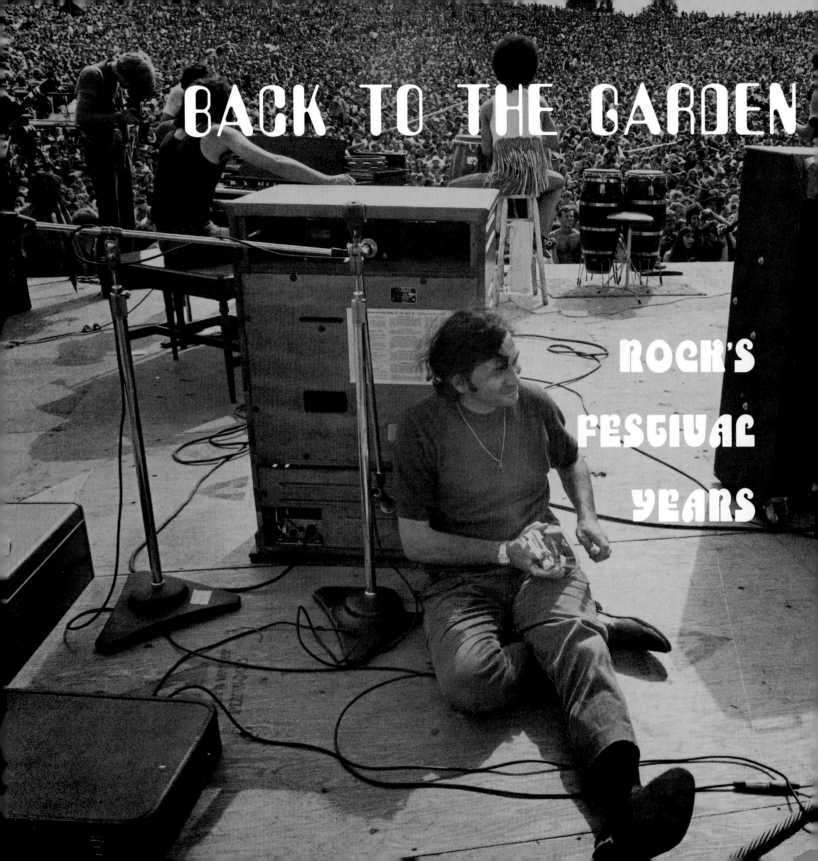

(Left) Bill Graham hangs out behind the amps during Santana's career-making set at Woodstock. (Above) Because the promoters were overwhelmed by a crowd that was "half a million strong," performers had to be helicoptered on and off Yasgur's farm.

f rock and roll concerts were a form of religion in the late 1960s, then the Holy Trinity in America were the Monterey International Pop Festival (June 16, 1967), Woodstock Music and Art Fair, An Aquarian Exposition (August 15–17, 1969), and the Concert at Altamont Speedway (December 1, 1969). The first marked the birth, the second the flowering, and the third the crucifixion of the psychedelic years.

In Great Britain, the trinity could well have been the following: First, the Festival of the Flower Children at Woburn Abbey (August 26–28, 1967), which was attended by the Duchess of Bedford, who mistook it for an actual flower show. Second, a free festival in Hyde Park, on July 5, 1969, organized by the Rolling Stones as a tribute to the recently deceased Brian Jones. Third, the Isle of Wight Festival (August 26–31, 1970). The latter was marked by great sets, poor planning, and bad sound, plus rain, mud, gate crashers, and the last public performance by Jimi Hendrix.

In between these red-letter dates came a spate of festivals, attended by freaks, nomads, predators, and prey. Among them:

Love-In, at the Palais de Sports in Paris, November 17–18, 1967. Musicians included Soft Machine and Dantalion's Chariot.

Rome Pop Festival, May 7, 1968. Italian riot police were called out to quell the crowds' excitement in the middle of a set by the Move.

Northern California Rock Festival, May 18, 1968. A mind-blowing lineup that included the Doors, the Dead, Steve Miller Band, Big Brother and the Holding Company, and Jefferson Airplane.

Swiss Rock Festival, in Zurich, June 10–11, 1968. Featuring Jimi Hendrix, Eric Burdon and the Animals, and Traffic.

Free Festival, Hyde Park, London, June 29, 1968. Psychedelia blazed with Pink Floyd (minus Syd Barrett), Tyrannosaurus Rex, Jethro Tull, and acid-folkie Roy Harper.

During his opening-day set at Woodstock, Arlo Guthrie set a Guinness record—broken the next day by John Sebastian—for use of the phrase "far out." Ravi Shankar played at both Woodstock (inset) and Monterey Pop, providing many with their first exposure to Indian music.

Newport Two-Day Festival, in Costa Mesa, California, August 4–5, 1968. What a lineup! Eric Burdon and the Animals, the Grateful Dead, Country Joe and the Fish, Canned Heat, Jefferson Airplane, Blue Cheer, Electric Flag, Iron Butterfly, Paul Butterfield Blues Band, Steppenwolf, and Quicksilver Messenger Service. One anomalous note: Sonny and Cher performed. No doubt "Laugh at Me" became a self-fulfilling prophesy.

Big Sur Folk Festival, Big Sur, California, Labor Day, 1968. This lineup of rockers and folkies (Stephen Stills, David Crosby, Van Dyke Parks, Joni Mitchell, Judy Collins, Arlo Guthrie) provided 2,000 attendees a "refreshing and relaxing weekend" on the grounds of the Esalen Institute at Big Sur. The highlight was an outdoor wedding of

Mimi Farina and Milan Melvin, a KSAN deejay. Her sister, Joan Baez, provided musical accompaniment.

Sky River Rock Festival and Lighter Than Air Fair, Sultan, Washington, September 2–4, 1968. After three days of intermittent rain, this freak-fest, held on Betty Nelson's Organic Raspberry Farm 50 miles from Seattle, turned 15,000 drenched hippies into "mud cultists." One participant dubbed it the "best freaking scene ever." The 40 scheduled acts included the Grateful Dead, It's a Beautiful Day, the Youngbloods, Country Joe and the Fish, H.P. Lovecraft, Kaleidoscope, and blues musicians James Cotton and Big Mama Thornton.

Miami Pop Festival, Hallandale, Florida, December 28–30, 1968. The eclectic lineup included the Grateful Dead, Joe Tex, Hugh Masekela, Iron Butterfly, Jose Feliciano, and Marvin Gaye.

Newport '69 Pop Festival, Newport, Rhode Island, June 20–22, 1969. Jimi Hendrix, Creedence Clearwater Revival, Joe Cocker, Jethro Tull, the Byrds, Ike and Tina Turner, Booker T. and the MG's, and Johnny Winter.

Toronto Rock Festival, June 22, 1969.

The Who blew away everyone except maybe Abbie Hoffman, who was knocked offstage by Pete Townshend when he tried to commandeer a microphone. (Opposite, bottom) Though rumors Bob Dylan might perform proved false, festivalgoers were treated to a set by the Band, his renowned backup group. (Below) Bob "the Bear" Hite of Canned Heat extends a beefy paw to the Woodstock throng, exhorting them to boogie.

Procol Harum, Steppenwolf, the Band.

Newport Jazz [sic] Festival, July 3–4, 1969. Jethro Tull, Johnny Winter, James Brown, Led Zeppelin, Ten Years After, Mothers of Invention.

Atlanta Pop Festival, Atlanta International Speedway, Atlanta, Georgia, July 4–5, 1969. The lineup for this one is roughly the same as the Newport Festival, which was running simultaneously. The best-received acts were relative unknowns Sweetwater, Pacific Gas and Electric, and Grand Funk Railroad.

Denver Pop Festival, Denver, Colorado, July 17–19, 1969. This three-day bummer was ill-advisedly held in Mile High Stadium, where seating was limited to 20,000. With Jimi Hendrix having just been named *Rolling Stone*'s Performer of the Year, there were naturally twice that many who wanted inside (and for free). Announcer Chip Monck repeatedly warned people to wet towels and washcloths and place them over their faces, because of the tear gas and pepper machines. Dubious highlight: Hendrix playing "Star-Spangled Banner," then announcing his band was breaking up.

Atlantic City Festival, Atlantic City, New Jersey, August 1–3, 1969. Roughly the same lineup as the above three festivals.

Ann Arbor Blues Festival, Ann Arbor, Michigan, August 16, 1969. This relatively small blast "brought virtually every living bluesman and 8,000 students, hippies, and blues freaks together on a small field near the University of Michigan's central campus." Artists included B.B. King, James Cotton, Mississippi Fred McDowell, Magic Sam, Howlin' Wolf, Muddy Waters, Arthur Crudup, Sleepy John Estes, and Big Mama Thornton. The trip: "65-year-old bluesmen suddenly acquiring 18-year-old groupies."

Texas International Pop Festival, Lewisville, Texas, August 30–31, 1969. Similar lineup as Newport, Atlanta, Atlantic City, and Denver.

Isle of Wight Festival, August 31, 1969. Bob Dylan and the Band took revenge on the hecklers with a riveting set.

Rock 'n' Roll Revival Concert, Toronto, September 13, 1969. A revival for veteran rockers like Chuck Berry, Gene Vincent, Bo Diddley, Little Richard, and Jerry Lee Lewis, and an unveiling of John Lennon's Plastic Ono Band, who debuted "Give Peace A Chance" and "Instant Karma." Also present: the Doors and Alice Cooper.

The Monterey Pop Festival attracted musicians and actors alike. Brian Jones rubs shoulders with Bruce Dern (above), while Harry Dean Stanton and Ren Fair share a giggle (below).

Winter's End: Three More Days of Peace and Music in Miami, Florida, December 1969. If Altamont hadn't convinced anyone the end was nigh, this debacle polished off what little shine was left upon psychedelia's bruised apple. It was a rip-off from the get-go, with the promoter promising Wavy Gravy a bunch of money for his utopian Earth People's Park if his Hog Farm would run the free kitchen, free stage, and OD tent. Gravy had proven his mettle at Woodstock. However, the promoter not only ran out of money but didn't even get the necessary permits. Plus, venal creeps like Sly Stone were demanding $35,000 to play for one hour. Only the goodwill of local bands, as well as that of Mountain and Johnny Winter (who played for free), kept the crowd from becoming unruly.

These omens notwithstanding, festivals continued to be held well into the '70s. They began to have a "been there, done that" quality, with the same musicians playing them like an inflated club circuit, the same increasingly aggressive demands for "free concerts" from unruly hordes outside the gates, and the same depressing epidemic of bad drugs and overdoses ruining what little goodwill was left in the tattered counterculture.

A personal reminiscence from Alan: Flower

Scenes from the festival years. Waiting for good food, good drugs, or Godot (top); according to the Merry Pranksters' creed, one was either on the bus or off the bus (middle); Richie Havens, the first performer to take the stage at Woodstock (bottom).

Power ended for me at the Second Atlanta Pop Festival, in July 1970. For months I'd saved my money in eager anticipation of seeing some favorite bands and enjoying a few days of pastoral hippiedom. (For its second incarnation, they'd moved the Atlanta festival to Byron, Georgia, staging it on a rural farm rather than in the oven of a raceway.) I brought a tent and supplies, fully anticipating a momentous event.

When I got there, the festival had become a test of wills between those outside and inside the gates. The tension was palpable for the first day and a half as people stormed fences, lobbed rocks and bottles, and shouted at the hired security guards—"Pigs!" "Music's for the people!" etc.— who were working-class guys just trying to make a buck. Upon investigating the teeming hordes more closely, I spotted my own brother, who was striking a pose with a group of his comrades not unlike the Marines on Iwo Jima. Instead of hoisting a flag, however, they were tearing down the fences. We briefly caught each other's eyes and glowered. It was like a scene from the Civil War, pitting brother against brother.

A personal reminiscence from Parke: There was an early-'70s rock-festival debacle I attended in a Charlotte, North Carolina, sports stadium. The lineup of talent included the likes of Wishbone Ash and Uriah Heep, who were the headliners. However, bad weather—fearsome thunderstorms, with dangerous lightning bolts sending the freaked-out crowd scurrying for cover— scuttled the outdoor event after only a few bands had played. The festival was abruptly and chaotically relocated inside a rank gymnasium on the property, into which only a fraction of the crowd could squeeze. But that was okay, because many freaks who were too stoned to boogie remained outside, where they lay face down like Civil War casualties littering a battlefield.

The absolute nadir of the festival years was the Celebration of Life Festival, held in McCrea, Louisiana, in the summer of 1971. "Celebration of Drugs, Death, and Dissolution" would have been more like it. Envision these hellish scenes, as described by journalist Chet Flippo in the pages of the July 22, 1971, issue of *Rolling Stone*:

"The festival began Thursday night—three and one-half days late—with Yogi Bahjan taking the stage, chanting and saying, 'God bless you. Let us meditate for one minute for peace and brotherhood.' 'Fuck you. Let's boogie,' responded a member of the crowd.

"A tractor pulling two flatbed trailers would come around, and six hired hands would jump off to collect endless piles of rotting watermelon rinds, empty wine bottles, discarded clothing and other assorted garbage.

"A festival worker ODed backstage and crumpled to the floor as 'Sister Morphine' was being played over the P.A. system to allay an impatient audience.

"Finally, there was dope, and it was plentiful. You had only to walk to the intersection of Cocaine Row and Smack Street (as the makeshift signs proclaimed) to find dealers hawking an estimated 30 varieties of mindbender, only two of which could be smoked. Plastic syringes, at $1 apiece, were selling briskly."

Toto, I don't think we're in Woodstock anymore.

ROCK FESTIVAL SURVIVAL GUIDE

For the undaunted and unsinkable pilgrims who continued to flock to festivals, *Big Fat* magazine ran a "Survival Guide" in their May 1970 issue that gives a flavor of the times. Excerpts include:

- "There is one cardinal rule: share. Share your food, water, dope, body, mind and whatever else you have."

- "It's hard to say what the best way to get somewhere is, but suffice it to say that driving is bad but walking is worse. Arriving early is a good idea."

- "BRING WATER. Twelve hours in the sun can make you very thirsty. Local water may or may not give you dysentery or some other loathsome disease, so why chance it?"

- "Food is nice, too, but not quite as essential as water....If it's free, far out. If it's not, be prepared for an incredible rip-off."

- "There will probably be some Johnny on the Spot–type portable toilets....Chances are about half of them will be dirty, smelly, crowded, and generally a drag. Try to find one in an out-of-the-way place."

- "If you're going to use dope...bring your own. If you don't, you risk buying poison dope from some long-haired shmuck and you also risk paying up to two dollars a joint—the going rate at the Newport Jazz Festival last year."

- "If you think someone is a narc, ask him. If he is, and he doesn't tell you, you are being illegally entrapped and an arrest won't stand up." (Yeah, right.)

- "It's real easy to get an infection in the middle of millions of sweating people."

- "Bring a sleeping bag and at least one plastic ground cloth. Rain can be groovy, but it you're really tired and want to sleep it'll drive you crazy if you don't have something to keep it off you."

- "Try to camp close enough to a staging area or speaker so you won't get screwed when 100,000 people sit in front of you before you wake up."

Good night, John-Boy.

LIVE FAST, DIE YOUNG: MONTEREY'S MORBID LEGACY

Though the psychedelic years seemed to hold much promise, the writing may have already been on the wall at the Monterey Pop Festival, at least in hindsight. Within seven years of the festival, seven who performed at Monterey would be dead to "unnatural causes": Janis Joplin, Jimi Hendrix, Otis Redding, Cass Elliott, Ron "Pigpen" McKernan, Alan Wilson, and Brian Cole (of the Association). None was over 30 years old. An eighth casualty, Brian Jones of the Rolling Stones, was an emcee and eminent presence—the only member of the Stones or Beatles in attendance at the festival. On Jones' arm was Nico, the ghostly Velvet Underground *chanteuse* who has since passed on as well.

To be fair, Redding's death was not related to excess. The greatest soul singer of them all died when his chartered plane went down in an icy lake. But regardless of cause, the sheer number of untimely passings (see table below) is eerie indeed. And the death toll has continued to mount with the passing years: Keith Moon (the Who), Bob "the Bear" Hite (Canned Heat), Mike Clarke (the Byrds), Gene Clark (the Byrds), Mike Bloomfield (Electric Flag), Paul Butterfield (Butterfield Blues Band), Laura Nyro, John Cipollina (Quicksilver Messenger Service), Jerry Garcia (Grateful Dead), Al Jackson (Booker T. and the MG's).

Name	Date of Death	Age at Death	Cause of Death
Otis Redding	December 10, 1967	26	airplane crash
Brian Jones	July 3, 1969	27	drowned in own pool; ruled "death by misadventure"
Alan Wilson	September 3, 1970	27	drug overdose
Jimi Hendrix	September 18, 1970	27	inhalation of vomit following barbiturate intoxication
Janis Joplin	October 4, 1970	27	drug overdose
Brian Cole	August 2, 1972	29	drug overdose
Ron "Pigpen" McKernan	March 8, 1973	27	liver failure
Cass Elliot	July 29, 1974	30	choking

ESSENTIAL ALBUMS OF THE LATE '60S

Here is a list of the 100 albums that best reflect the era under discussion in this book. They are bounded more by a period of time—the latter half of the '60s, and the years 1967–68 in particular—than the term *psychedelic*. That is to say, they have more to do with enlightened music-making and widened horizons than with a narrowly defined sound (typified by fuzztone and wah-wah, "raga rock," side-long epics, lyrics about "the canyons of your mind," etc.). All the same, you won't find Bob Dylan or Aretha Franklin here, because they weren't, um, *psychedelic* enough for this particular list.

In the context of their times, each of these albums rewarded multiple listenings in a variety of settings, from contemplative still life (boy at his lava lamp) to communal frenzy (strobe lights flashing and stoned bodies grooving wildly). They still hold up as music and as artifacts of an era when music mattered more than you can believe or imagine.

ALBUMS (arranged alphabetically by artist and then chronologically for artists with multiple entries):

1. Amboy Dukes: *Journey to the Center of the Mind*
2. Animals, Eric Burdon and the: *Love Is*
3. Barrett, Syd: *The Madcap Laughs* (U.K. only)
4. Beach Boys, the: *Smiley Smile*
5. Beacon Street Union: *The Eyes of the Beacon Street Union*
6. Beatles, the: *Revolver*
7. Beatles, the: *Sgt. Pepper's Lonely Hearts Club Band*
8. Beatles, the: *Magical Mystery Tour*
9. Beau Brummels: *Triangle*
10. Big Brother and the Holding Company: *Cheap Thrills*
11. Blue Cheer: *Vincebus Eruptum*
12. Blue Cheer: *Outsideinside*
13. Blues Magoos: *Psychedelic Lollipop*
14. Bonzo Dog Band: *Urban Spaceman*
15. Brown, Arthur: *The Crazy World of Arthur Brown*
16. Buckley, Tim: *Goodbye and Hello*
17. Buffalo Springfield: *Buffalo Springfield Again*
18. Byrds, the: *Fifth Dimension*
19. Byrds, the: *Yesterday and Today*
20. Canned Heat: *Boogie With Canned Heat*
21. Captain Beefheart and the Magic Band: *Safe as Milk*
22. Captain Beefheart and the Magic Band: *Trout Mask Replica*
23. Charlatans, the: *The Charlatans*
24. Count Five: *Psychotic Reaction*
25. Country Joe and the Fish: *Electric Music for the Mind and Body*
26. Cream: *Disraeli Gears*
27. Cream: *Wheels of Fire*
28. Deviants, the: *Ptoof!*
29. Donovan: *Sunshine Superman*
30. Doors: *Doors*
31. Doors: *Strange Days*
32. Electric Prunes: *The Electric Prunes*
33. Fairport Convention: *Unhalfbricking*

34. Family: *Music in a Doll's House*
35. Fever Tree: *Fever Tree*
36. Fugs, the: *The Fugs First Album*
37. Grateful Dead: *Anthem of the Sun*
38. Grateful Dead: *Aoxomoxoa*
39. Incredible String Band: *The 5,000 Spirits or the Layers of the Onion*
40. Iron Butterfly: *In-A-Gadda-Da-Vida*
41. It's a Beautiful Day: *It's a Beautiful Day*
42. Jefferson Airplane: *Surrealistic Pillow*
43. Jefferson Airplane: *After Bathing at Baxter's*
44. Jethro Tull: *Stand Up*
45. Jimi Hendrix Experience: *Are You Experienced?*
46. Jimi Hendrix Experience: *Axis: Bold as Love*
47. Jimi Hendrix Experience: *Electric Ladyland*
48. Kaleidoscope: *A Beacon from Mars*
49. King Crimson: *In the Court of the Crimson King*
50. Kinks, the: *Face to Face*
51. Love: *Forever Changes*
52. Mad River: *Paradise Bar & Grill*
53. MC5: *Kick Out the Jams*
54. Moby Grape: *Moby Grape*
55. Moody Blues: *In Search of the Lost Chord*
56. Mothers of Invention: *Freak Out!*
57. Mothers of Invention: *Absolutely Free*
58. Mothers of Invention: *We're Only in It for the Money*
59. Move, the: *The Move* (U.K. only)
60. Nice, the: *Thoughts of Emerlist Davjack*
61. Parks, Van Dyke: *Song Cycle*
62. Pearls Before Swine: *One Nation Underground*
63. Pink Floyd: *Piper at the Gates of Dawn*
64. Pink Floyd: *A Saucerful of Secrets*
65. Pretty Things: *S.F. Sorrow*
66. Procol Harum: *Procol Harum*
67. Quicksilver Messenger Service: *Quicksilver Messenger Service*
68. Quicksilver Messenger Service: *Happy Trails*
69. Rascals, the: *Time Peace/Greatest Hits*
70. Rolling Stones: *Aftermath*
71. Rolling Stones: *Flowers*
72. Rolling Stones: *Their Satanic Majesties Request*
73. Santana: *Santana*
74. Seeds, the: *Future*
75. Small Faces: *Ogdens' Nut Gone Flake*
76. Soft Machine: *Soft Machine*
77. Sons of Champlin: *Loosen Up Naturally*
78. Sopwith Camel, the: *The Sopwith Camel*
79. Spirit: *Spirit*
80. Spirit: *The Family That Plays Together*
81. Status Quo: *Messages from the Status Quo*
82. Steppenwolf: *Steppenwolf*
83. Steppenwolf: *Steppenwolf the 2nd*
84. Steve Miller Band: *Sailor*
85. Stooges, the: *The Stooges*
86. Strawberry Alarm Clock: *Incense and Peppermints*
87. Ten Years After: *Ssssh*
88. 13th Floor Elevators, the: *Psychedelic Sounds*
89. Tomorrow: *Tomorrow*
90. Traffic: *Dear Mr. Fantasy*
91. Traffic: *Traffic*
92. Vanilla Fudge: *Vanilla Fudge*
93. Velvet Underground: *Velvet Underground and Nico*
94. West Coast Pop Art Experimental Band: *Part One*
95. Who, the: *The Who Sell Out*
96. Who, the: *Tommy*
97. Woodstock: *Music from the Original Soundtrack and More* (various artists)
98. Yardbirds, the: *Over Under Sideways Down*
99. Youngbloods, the: *Earth Music*
100. Zombies, the: *Odyssey and Oracle*

TWO ROCK CRITICS WHO NEVER TOOK ACID REMINISCE ABOUT THE LATE '60S

The following is a transcript of a conversation between this book's authors on the subject of growing up absurd in the late '60s. Like most adolescent members of Woodstock Nation, we grew up in a setting other than San Francisco, Los Angeles, New York, or London. That is to say, those were the hotspots that got all the attention, but the great majority of us watched it all unfolding from the hinterlands, plugging in via records and *Rolling Stone* and whatever hometown scene managed to germinate.

Alan Bisbort (AB) spent his teen years in Atlanta, Georgia, and Parke Puterbaugh (PP) grew up in Greensboro, North Carolina. Neither was exactly a hub of the counterculture. They were like most places in America at that time in that their hippie enclaves took cues from the larger scenes while swirling in some distinctively local or regional character of their own. You didn't have to head to San Francisco with a flower in your hair to be part of the movement. Indeed we think our experiences are typical of a far greater number of people who watched it all from a distance and then interpreted it in their own ways.

The inspiration for broaching these subjects in dialogue form came from Paul Nelson and Lester Bangs, who took a similar approach in their jointly authored 1981 biography of Rod Stewart with a chapter entitled "Two Jewish Mothers Pose as Rock Critics." In it, they taped a discussion about the subject of their book and transcribed the results. For us, taking the same approach seemed a fresh, spontaneous way to dredge up adolescent memories of growing up in psychedelic times. Our stories and experiences are no doubt similar to a lot of others who have lived to tell the tale.

AB: Probably a good place to start, at least from my perspective, is the Doors, because they're more or less how I entered the side door of psychedelia. Seeing how I wasn't an acidhead, the closest approximation to the state of mind one associates with psychedelics was the music. The summer of '67, when all that stuff was happening in San Francisco, coincided with the arrival in my neighborhood of the half brother of the most wild of my friends. His mother couldn't take care of him, so he came from Los Angeles, bringing with him his clothes and one album, which was the first Doors album. I remember he called his half brother and me into the room and placed this magical disc on the turntable and proceeded to expound while it was playing on how this was the touchstone of a new way of looking at things. We, of course, agreed with him.

At some point toward the end of the summer the half brother was packed off to some reform school on the West Coast, but in the interim he had done his damage. First of all, he was the first person I ever saw smoke pot. It was like watching someone degenerate over the course of an entire summer, and then watching an entire neighborhood degenerate along with him. He got people into sniffing glue: you'd put a paper bag over your head and put this Pester's Model Glue in there and just breathe until you were overcome.

PP: Did you try it?

AB: No, I was horrified. I mean, you'd be in these packed rooms with these "good kids" from middle-class families excitedly grabbing the bag and placing it over their heads. Meanwhile, the Doors are playing through the whole summer, over and over again. It was like every parent's worst nightmare, exactly what the Joe Pynes of the world were saying was going to happen if this hippie ethic were to take over. And you could see over the course of the summer that people's sideburns were growing longer, their hair was growing over their collars, they were wearing flare bottoms and out-and-out bell-bottoms. By the time school came in, which would have been 10th grade for me, we had all completely turned our back on mainstream society. There was no turning back. It was like a neighborhood full of hippies of the mind, if not the physical realm. It was like he had done his job and was packed off. But the Doors album was what did the job, I think.

He was a scary guy. One of those things that's part of the myth of psychedelia and hippies is that it was all an "everybody's a brother"

thing. I think there was always an element there like this half brother, who was a borderline criminal and a predator who was charismatic and influential and Pied Piper-ish. There was nothing really "peace and love" about him at all. His idea of a good time was to try to kill one of the neighborhood dogs with a cherry bomb. He had us out there shooting pellet guns at passing cars. This was the Summer of Love?!

I never was an acidhead and I hated the smell of incense and patchouli and I hated all that bogus peace-and-love lip service. But what I did like was that it was a totally new and nonjudgmental way to look at life. You could look and act the way you wanted, listen to what music you wanted. It was like entering an exotic new world.

PP: It was like a whole new world of expression had opened up, and it was such a contrast to the Wally-and-Beaver world that you got from living in suburbia, going to church with your parents, watching the harmless sitcoms, digesting the whitewashed material that was presented to you in school. Behind the façade, there was this whole festering world underneath that very benign-looking middle-class world we all inhabited. Once you started probing behind the lives that went on in these seemingly innocuous suburban neighborhoods, these terrible scripts were being lived out. I think very definitely this was a generational sort of break as profound as any in human history, where this massive chasm opened up between generations. Part of the crowbar for that was the mind-altering drugs, which I think just totally shattered all the preconceptions that you'd been force-fed growing up, as well as furthering this sense of apartness from our parents' generation and all the things their lives represented.

AB: I agree, and I think the backdrop to all that, besides the fact that there were drugs, were the totally new, expansive musical forms, the artwork, the visuals that attended it, the underground newspapers and magazines, and the political situation. I mean, you lived every day with the body count in the news. Starting in 1963, when people started getting shot in high office, it was like the entire decade was littered with bloody corpses. This was pointed out as something you needed to grow up and enter. Well, the adult world was this horror show, and who wanted it, you know? In my own house, I couldn't have people over. My father was having problems, but then everybody's house was somewhat like that.

PP: Wasn't it Roxy Music who sang, "In every dream home a heartache"?

AB: I was already predisposed to think the adult world sucked and they didn't know what the hell they were talking about. I was intuitively counting the minutes, if not the seconds, when I could be free of that and go off to wherever it was that I was going to go when I was old enough.

Another stereotype, which was never true, was that hippies didn't work. I worked my ass off. I went to high school, but I worked jobs all the time. Every penny I earned went to albums and magazines. I wouldn't have this archive if I hadn't spent every penny I made buying up stuff that I found to be magical, and I wouldn't have hung onto it unless I thought it had some sort of alchemical power. I became very absorbed in these little relics and ramifications of the psychedelic culture, especially the albums. I would spend literally hours by myself in my room listening to these albums over and over again. To me, it was the only thing worth breathing for.

PP: You know that Beach Boys song "In My Room"? That would describe great chunks of my adolescence. I worked menial jobs, too, delivering newspapers and washing trucks, and every penny went into albums. I would make trips downtown every Saturday, and I had a whole route of places marked out where I'd go see what had come in or what was there.

AB: That's exactly what I used to do.

PP: I'd go look at albums I hadn't yet bought but thought about buying, and if they were still there, I thought, "This is the day I'll buy it, if nothing else is available." The choices in those days were much more reasonable in number. It's not like we were deluged with product the way we are now. That much stuff did not come out in album form, so I can remember anticipating the release of some album for months that I heard was in the works. Every time I'd go downtown I'd check to see if it was out yet, or if something else had come out in the meantime. I can even remember the prices from the stickers at the different stores: $3.47, $4.37, $3.98, $4.98. And I would take whatever I bought home, and it would be a sacred moment.

AB: Everything had to be right, though. You couldn't just run into the house and throw it down. If the TV was too loud in the other room or you were hassled by your mother: "Where have you been? Why don't you get a haircut?" Or whatever. The moment had to be right. I recall that your room was right in the middle of your house. I lucked out in that I commandeered the basement, which nobody else wanted to live in. I just said, "Look, I'll live down there." I positioned my bed so that I could see the bottom of the stairwell, and if they wanted to say anything to me, they flicked the light on and off. I had the music on so loud I couldn't hear them, so that was the only way they could communicate with me. I would turn the stereo down, get up and go, "Yeah? What do you want?" "Do you want pot roast or Brunswick stew tonight, honey?" "Oh, goddamn, I don't want either one." And then, you know, "Is that music?"

PP: In some of the worst moments, my father would pop into my room and pretend to start twisting to the music. [Both laugh hysterically.]

AB: My father would never do that! I wish he had. God knows what he thought of the caterwauling guitars rising up from the basement.

PP: But, you know, these were commandments carved on vinyl, handed down from the mount and received with much ceremony and fanfare. It was a private ritual, for me. I couldn't listen to music as a background for other activity or even really appreciate it in situations where there was somebody else around and we were trying to talk or do something.

AB: At the same time, whenever a report would come due in school and I had to give a production to the class on some subject, I would always choose something related to rock music. I found this report I did in 10th grade. It was the fall after that guy had corrupted me and the rest of the people in my neighborhood. I gave a report in composition on Don Van Vliet [Captain Beefheart]. These are the first two sentences of my report: "Don Van Vliet was born in 1941 in Glendale, California. At age five, he decided that civilized American life was a gigantic fraud." [Both laugh.] That was my report! You could just see the aghast expressions.

PP: I can remember vividly the first time I heard something that I could identify as psychedelic, as something that took a step beyond rock and roll as I'd known it and seemed part of an altered reality. Again, we keep coming back to the Doors, but it was "Light My Fire" and especially the flip side of the record, "The Crystal Ship." It was this crazy song that didn't have a chorus, it was very linear, mostly played on piano, which you didn't often hear, with this fractured poetic narrative about something that seemed far beyond the realm of anything that was ever talked about in a pop song. At that point, I bought the "Light My Fire" single, and it whetted my appetite to hear the whole album. Before that, it used to suffice to buy a single, because you knew that was the best song and the rest of the album was generally crappy filler: cover versions of the hits of the day or retreaded songs that everyone did like "Fortune Teller." But at that point, here was a B-side as good and intriguing as the A-side that sounded like nothing I'd ever heard before. I saved all my pennies, quite literally, so I could buy that first Doors album.

That whole summer of '67, I didn't have any mentoring experiences quite like the one you described with the delinquent from California, but my next-door neighbor and I were on the same wavelength, and we would sit around each other's rooms for hours on end listening to music: the Doors, the Rolling Stones, Cream, Jefferson Airplane. Beyond that, there were many late summer nights after the family had gone to bed where I would quietly have that record on. It would be dark, no one else up, and the album would just conjure a whole mood of mystical reverie and deep thought.

AB: The whole world would look different after you listened to that music. You'd go into the world of junior high school or whatever, and everything seemed different, exciting, like you had some secret knowledge or the beginnings of it. I loved it because it fed into my utter disdain of the normal school experience.

On the weekends, I'd take the bus downtown, because I was too young to drive. I went to all the head shops and bought the magazines, bought more records. Like you, I stood in awe of the different bins where the records were housed. I'd memorize where a certain album was in the store, and I'd flip to it to see if it was still there, almost like it was a friend of mine, even though I didn't own it.

There were intimations before the Doors that drifted to me via my brother, who was five years older and had already gone off to college. He was very particular about his records and magazines. He would accumulate a batch of them, and then he'd come home and leave them off to be stored where they'd be safe. Of course, he would say, "I will KILL you if you touch my records." Then he'd go off to college, and the first thing I'd do would be run in and grab his records and play them. He was into stuff like Left Banke and Lovin' Spoonful, which had a feel that was kind of different. Both of them had the beginnings of that sound. It wasn't blatant psychedelia, but it was an intelligent sort of stirring in that direction.

PP: The Turtles, Buffalo Springfield.

AB: God, yeah. "Itchycoo Park," by the Small Faces, was a real touchstone for me.

PP: To me the peak psychedelic musical work is *Anthem of the Sun*, by the Grateful Dead. Each side occupied 20 minutes. It was free-flowing. There were discernible songs, but they would fade in and out of this larger matrix. The way it was all strung together was really ingenious and inventive. If anything came out of the Acid Tests that was good, it was setting aside all this forethought and planning, and just surrendering to chance, trusting that some kind of coherent structure would emerge just by falling into synch with the cosmos. To this day, I think *Anthem of the Sun* is a masterpiece, an acid symphony. You can play it, sit back and go someplace else entirely. Especially the first side.

AB: I should've been more receptive to that than I was, and I don't know what it was about them. Maybe it was the sheer ugliness of the members of the band. You know how you'd stare at album covers? I couldn't stare at the Grateful Dead for very long. Nor did I like their voices very much.

PP: For me, staring at an album cover sure beat staring at a TV set. There was a period of about five years when I was so heavily into music that I hardly watched any TV at all.

AB: I felt the same way. It was a situation where I specifically would go to the TV at a set time if I knew someone was going to be on Ed Sullivan. I remember watching Jonathan Winters once, because the Doors were on it.

PP: That was the exception, when a musical performer was on a "variety show." I was pretty much a TV addict growing up as a kid. I gravitated to sitcoms. And then when I got heavily into music I gave it up, abruptly. It had nothing to say to me. I don't think it adapted to all the cultural upheavals of the '60s. If it did, those results weren't even seen until the '70s.

AB: Television in a suburban household is a group activity. But music was such that you only wanted to listen to it by yourself. It was like I would crawl under my rock into my room and listen to my records after dinner.

PP: I seriously read books then, too. I'd make lists of books I thought I ought to read, and then go down the list and read them.

AB: My brother, again, would bring his books home from college and store them at the house. He'd give me a mandate not to touch them, which of course would only encourage me to read them. When I was 13, I was reading *Catch-22* and Vonnegut, just wolfing the stuff down.

PP: If you had to name five albums from that time that could be branded psychedelic, what would they be and why?

AB: My definition of psychedelic is probably wider than most. To me, a really great psychedelic album was the first Procol Harum album. How much more exotic could those lyrics be? They were almost inscrutable, but they had enough intelligence in them that even if you weren't high you could sit back and ponder what they could possibly mean. It stretched your mind. It was a very mind-expanding kind of thing.

So the first Procol Harum album and the first Doors. *Happy Trails* by Quicksilver was a big one with me, side one especially. *I Feel Like I'm Fixin' to Die* by Country Joe and the Fish would be my fourth choice. There was something so ethereal and otherworldly about the sound they got on that particular album. That is truly a psychedelic album. Finally, I'd pick *Their Satanic Majesties Request* by the Rolling Stones. I listened to that and stared at the 3D cover endlessly. I loved that stuff.

PP: My five favorite acid-rock records would be the first Doors album; *Electric Music for the Mind and Body* by Country Joe and the Fish; *Piper at the Gates of Dawn* by Pink Floyd; *Anthem of the Sun* by the Grateful Dead; and *After Bathing at Baxter's* by Jefferson Airplane. I tripped without taking drugs to that music. I played those albums so much they look like somebody rubbed a sheet of sandpaper on them. That is the mark of an album that mattered.

AB: You know who we are leaving out: Jimi Hendrix. Personally, if I were looking at it objectively, I would have to put him up there in the top five somehow. But at the time, he scared me. There was something terrifying about him and his music.

PP: Whenever I would weigh the consequences of taking acid, you could hear in Hendrix's music that he'd been there, and it wasn't necessarily a place I wanted to visit because I didn't know if I'd ever come back.

AB: Well, when he asks, "Are You Experienced?" and you've got zits all over your face and you're overweight and nerdy and haven't kissed a girl, and this guy's performing cunnilingus on 20 of them every night, what are you supposed to think, you know? Burning his guitar, wearing outrageously exotic outfits. On the other hand, when I listen to him now I realize what a genius he was. I can listen to him safely now. But back then there was something terrifying. His music would come on at a high-school party, and it would change the entire tone. You could almost feel the tension in the air. It was like when Hendrix came on it was time to leave the party.

PP: I definitely had to catch up to him. I had to get older to understand that music. My choice of musical handholds probably had something to do with the culture

I came up in, so it was easier for me to get into Jefferson Airplane than Jimi Hendrix. There was another valid side that he embodied whereby psychedelia wasn't necessarily all comforting. It could be terrifying, too. It wasn't just benign pot-smoking and incense-sniffing. It was hard drugs and scuffling in the street and running away from home and finding out that Haight-Ashbury wasn't necessarily this velvet-lined love nest or learning firsthand that the Vietnam experience was a hell beyond words. Through Hendrix you could get vicarious glimpses of that other, darker side. Which at age 12 was a little hard for me to take. I just wasn't ready.

Which brings me to a final question I think we ought to ask ourselves. Being involved in the music of that era and willing to stretch our minds with the various expressions of psychedelic culture, why didn't we take acid? Why didn't you trip? I'm sure it wasn't for lack of opportunities.

AB: You know that thing Woody Allen said about marijuana—that he was afraid if he smoked pot he'd do something weird like try to take his pants off over his head—well, it was that way for me with LSD. I was afraid—and I had personal, family-related reasons for this—that I'd enter some mental nightmare from which I would never escape, or I'd start weeping and not be able to stop until I dehydrated and died, like in that Loudon Wainwright song. Plus, I was just enough of a contrarian even back then that when acid was readily available, it seemed to me that all the wrong people were taking it for all the wrong reasons. I wanted no part of that in-group's scene.

It's funny now, in retrospect, to think this. Here my parents must have thought I was some sort of Manson-in-the-making, with my secret, uncommunicative life in the basement. And, as it turns out, all along I was more "clean living" and a damn sight more hardworking than any member of the high-school football team or one of those pitiful boobs in Bible study class.

PP: I was afraid that I'd make like the Linkletter kid and try to fly out a fourth-story window if I took acid. I bought into some of the warnings circulated by "straight society" about the drug, which is to say I didn't want to wind up a mental misfit while my whole life still lay in front of me. Those warnings didn't seem entirely unfounded, because I did see my share of burned-out cases from high school on up. There was one guy in particular who I remember a bunch of us visiting on a college campus. He seemed a little unstable and disassociated to me, and people who knew him whispered about his having had a "bad trip." He suggested that we all go out for ice cream and when no one seemed inclined to do so he began insisting on it, visibly trembling and becoming unglued. I thought to myself, "This is not for me."

All the same, ·I enjoyed vicariously receiving the fruits of other people's visions through the music, artwork, literature, and conversations, which then triggered my own imagination. I don't think everyone necessarily had to be tripping for the whole culture to benefit from it. The other thing is that my father was a chemistry professor, so I understood a little bit about the molecular structure of LSD and the way it acted on the brain. In fact, I did a pretty scholarly term paper on the subject in the seventh grade! Having done my homework, so to speak, I resisted the idea of tripping, and no one really tried to force it on me. I was never "dosed," for instance, thank God, even though I was surrounded by people who were tripping their brains out.

In the end, I think you knew intuitively if this was something you could handle. It worked for some people, and for others it was risky business.

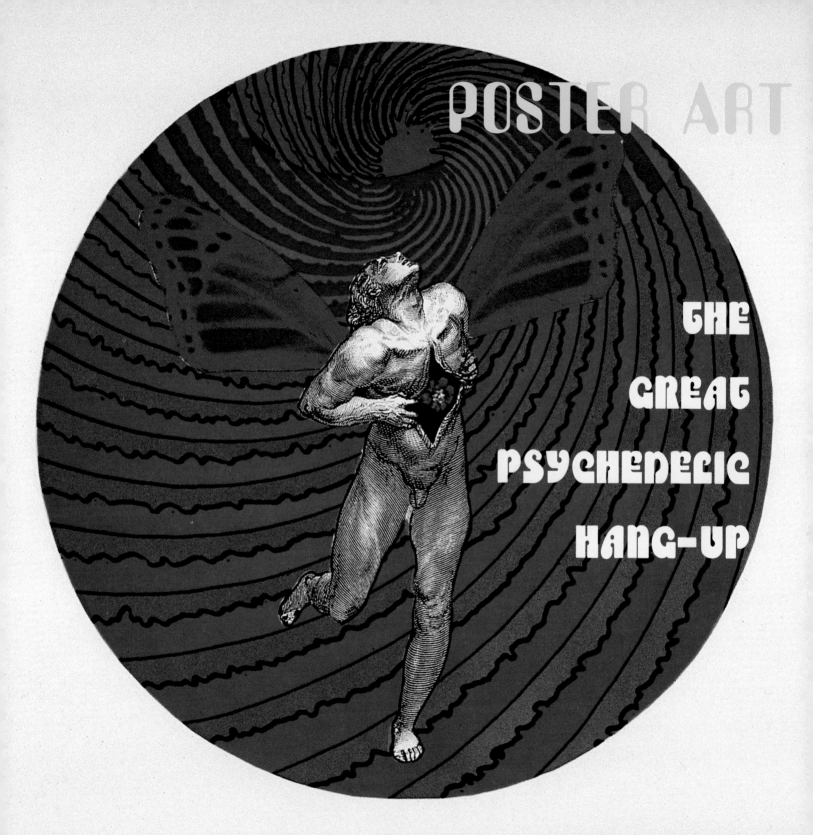

POSTER ART

THE
GREAT
PSYCHEDELIC
HANG-UP

M ost hippies in the know consider the peak of their collective experience to have been the first Human Be-In (full name: "A Gathering of Tribes for a Human Be-In"), held January 14, 1967, on the Polo Grounds of Golden Gate Park. The Be-In had been heralded for weeks in advance with assertive, polemical press releases that read: "A new nation has grown inside the robot flesh of the old....Berkeley political activists and the love generation of the Haight-Ashbury will join together." While such provocative rhetoric had a certain appeal, it was limited to those willing to make room in their Technicolor fantasies for the black-and-white lockstep of politics. From the perspective of many in the Love Generation, the pen was mightier than the sword but no match for a well-designed poster.

For the previous two years and on through the end of the decade, posters were the single most effective tool for rallying the cognoscenti. Brightly colored psychedelic poster art appeared in seemingly every shop window in the Haight, on every square foot of wall space inside each shop, and on every telephone pole and bulletin board. While the Haight's heads may have simply assumed this brilliant artistry and graphic design had sprouted like magic mushrooms after an acid rain, the truth is more intriguing.

For the visual artist, a new challenge had been presented by the musical goings-on in San Francisco, with ample opportunities for the most imaginative among their number. Naturally, they gravitated to the poster genre, a hybrid art form (commerce wedded to fine art) that had—with the exception of recruitment purposes and other propaganda—been out of favor for some time. To meet the needs of head shops, progressive causes, record companies, and concert promoters like Chet Helms and Bill Graham, new graphics studios popped up all over the Bay Area. In addition to Chet Helms' in-house Family Dog imprint, there were Bill Graham Presents, Berkeley Bonaparte, Neon Rose, The Food, Sparta Graphics, Mouse Studios, Western Front, and East Totem West.

One of the most fascinating and disturbing of all the psychedelic artists in the Bay Area was Wilfried Sätty (1939–1982). He started as a draftsman for the Bay Area Rapid Transit (BART), and then began publishing his work on posters and notecards for East Totem West. "Eternity" is one of his postcards. Sätty went on to great renown for his work in *Rolling Stone* and his illustrated editions of Poe's tales and Bram Stoker's *Dracula*. He and fellow artist David Singer shared a North Beach apartment that became a legendary psychedelic salon. They dug out the basement and turned it into a sort of underground headquarters that attracted avant-garde artists, musicians, and Hollywood stars. Sadly, Sätty fell to his death from the ladder leading into his basement salon in 1982.

A Pre-Raphaelite Collection.

Pictures by
D.G. ROSSETTI
F. MADOX BROWN
BURNE-JONES
HOLMAN HUNT

The Goupil Gallery
5 Regent Street
Waterloo Place S.W.
10 To 6. 1ˢ Illustrated Catalogue 1ˢ

J.S. VIRTUE & Cᵒ LTᴰ LITH

The Pre-Raphaelite Brotherhood, an impassioned circle of artists, writers, and bohemians in England during the mid-1800s, was one of the many forerunners of, and influences on, the psychedelic artists of the 1960s. Dante Gabriel Rossetti (1828–1882) was their Tim Leary, and his art inspired this retrospective poster and exhibition in 1898, at the peak of the Art Nouveau craze.

Though five separate posters for the aforementioned Be-In were circulated, Rick Griffin designed the most famous, depicting a Native American on horseback strumming an electric guitar. By then, such familiar and striking imagery seemed more trustworthy than TV or newsprint. Call it a secret language that only the truly enlightened could comprehend. In fact, a compelling history of psychedelia, at its most intense flowering (1966–1969), could be told without words. One could simply present an illustrated chronology of the posters created by artists like Griffin, Stanley Mouse (née Miller), Victor Moscoso, Alton Kelley, John Van Hamersveld, David Singer, Sätty, Bonnie MacLean, Wes Wilson, Joe and Irene McHugh, and Gary Grimshaw. What a feast!

As stated above, the poster medium was not new. It wasn't even American, having been born in Europe in the 1890s as a means of advertising dances, theater productions, books, and products. The *fin de siècle*'s version of psychedelia was Art Nouveau, an equally utopian flowering that took its inspiration from the Arts and Crafts movement of William Morris, Japanese flower arrangements, and an improbably wistful nostalgia for the art of the Middle Ages. The best known of the early poster artists were Jules Cheret, Alphonse Mucha, Maxfield Parrish, and Henri de Toulouse-Lautrec, all of whom would have fit in on Haight Street.

While the psychedelic artists were fully aware and appreciative of their precedents, they approached the old form with new ideas and from novel directions. Rick Griffin, for example, was a surfer boy, and his surfing decals, T-shirts, and cartoons were internationally known before he ever touched a psychedelic substance. Likewise, Stanley Mouse came to the rock poster genre from the world of hot rods and Ed "Big Daddy" Roth.

118

Victor Moscoso and Joe McHugh had extensive art-school training. And so on.

Regardless of how they arrived on the scene, the artists' goal was nothing less than visually interpreting an era that was unfolding on all fronts—an enormous explosion of light, sound, and motion—right beneath their noses. Obviously, they had a reverence for the work, a sense of being part of the fast-moving train of history and a kindred spirit with communal impulses. But they also had to eat and pay rent, so some element of commercialism in their work was inescapable.

One of the most intriguing aspects of their art is the tug-of-war within each poster artist's soul between pure self-expression and commercialism. This probably explains why psychedelic script was so hard to read. That it was the ostensible *raison d'être* of rock posters (after all, a viewer had to know the date, time, and place of the event advertised) seemed secondary to the artists, as if by obscuring the words they could further

blur the line between commercial and fine art and draw more attention to the amazing images they were creating. Equally amazing was the prolific output of the artists—as many as 10 different posters were created every weekend in San Francisco alone—and the benign and friendly aspect of their competition.

Nationwide, a so-called poster boom had been ignited in New York in 1966 when someone got the bright idea to blow Humphrey Bogart up to wall-size. A still from Casablanca (Rick with shot glass and wounded visage) became a huge seller and was followed by similar shots of Brando (on motorcycle with leather cap), Bardot, Harlow, Belmondo, W.C. Fields, Stokely Carmichael—all the product of Personality Posters. The same East Coast wave brought reproductions of Andy Warhol's pop-art iconography and Roy Lichtenstein's oversized cartoons, as well as nausea-inducing optical illusions (a.k.a. op art). Soon enough, *Life* would journalistically

The poster artists who developed the widely emulated Art Nouveau style in the 1890s didn't have rock concerts to advertise, so they found other products to suit their times. Some, like absinthe, in an 1896 ad by the Belgian Privat Livemont, seemed to forecast the trippy feed-your-head spirit of San Francisco, circa 1966.

119

Although he grew up in Philadelphia, studied in Europe, and never lived on the West Coast, Maxfield Parrish (1870–1966) helped mold a California impressionistic style that found its way onto psychedelic posters. All the elements of this style were firmly in place as early as 1897, in this ad for *Scribner's* magazine: exotic setting, erotic subject, otherworldly colors.

reduce it all to "The Big Poster Hang-Up."

By 1967 shops devoted entirely to the sale of posters were springing up all over the country. Some moved as many as 25,000 a month. Posters were sold at public events, too, with enterprising vendors filling the trunks of their cars and setting up makeshift stalls at music and arts festivals. They became staples of promotion for the burgeoning rock industry, papering the walls of virtually every record store, head shop, and suburban bedroom in America.

The poster boom was part of an even wider explosion of interest in the past, and yet that interest was ironic and coolly detached, part of some secret masquerade. That is, every phase of history, from antiquity to Victoriana to film noir,

was treated with the same mock reverence. The operative word is "camp," which Susan Sontag described—in her famous 1966 essay "Notes on Camp"—as "love of the unnatural, artifice, and exaggeration....Camp is esoteric, something of a private code, a badge of identity even, among small urban cliques."

The stylistic badge most honored in San Francisco was Victoriana, partly due to fashion statements made by the Charlatans and partly due to the architectural style of the Haight itself, a lavishly pure Victorian neighborhood. In fact, the best-known revival movie house in America (which thrived in the '60s and is, incidentally, still in business) was the Red Victorian, on Haight Street. Naturally, this *fin de siècle* flavor trickled down to the poster artists, who unabashedly borrowed from the 1890s originators of the poster genre. In short, "camp" to the hippies was epitomized by this revival of Art Nouveau, which Sontag called "the most typical and fully developed Camp style."

The "camp" aesthetic was not confined to the United States.

It may, in fact, have flourished to an even greater extent in the U.K. Art Nouveau was a rich part of the artistic tradition, and the Brits' vaunted love of goofiness for its own sake made them proto-Campers. Add to that rich back-drop the sudden availability of LSD and the explosion of fashion, music, and hip culture in Swinging London—hippiedom's immediate predecessor—and you didn't need to be Nostradamus to predict something weird, wild, and won-derful would happen in the visual realm. Even now, the visually rich alternative papers of the day— *International Times* and (especially) *Oz*—still look innovative. Founded by transplanted Aussies Richard Neville and Martin Sharp, *Oz* truly shook up the London scene, espe-cially with its dazzling psychedelic visuals. Years later, Philip Hodgson—one of Europe's earliest light-show operators—assessed the legacy of the London-based '60s psychedelic artists to chronicler Jonathon Green:

"The things they did with one-, two-, and three-color screen-ing have still not been bettered.

They pushed litho-printing and screen-printing a long, long way....It was one of the great positive things to come out of the era, some great graphics...and the nice breaky things of overprinting colors. Certainly in *Oz* they were prepared to run it, and if you couldn't read it, tough. Which is a very nice way of doing it. People don't have that freedom anymore."

In addition to the artistic precedents, there was the undeniable influence of psychedelic drugs. It would be a misrepresentation to ignore the role that LSD and other hallucinogens played in '60s poster art. In the words of Joe McHugh, founder of East Totem West and a pro-lific poster artist: "I always thought what I was doing with posters had something to do with LSD. The idea of a poster before then was to pro-mote something—a product or an event. I was promoting something, too, but it wasn't a product. It was that acid

Lewis Carroll's *Wonderland* was a touchstone for many psychedelic rangers, including Joe McHugh, founder and artist for East Totem West. McHugh created this wide-selling poster, *Cheshire Cat*, in early 1967, just before the Summer of Love brought an army of inno-cent Alices to San Francisco. As Carroll's treed cat told Alice, "We're all mad here. I'm mad. You're mad."

The psychedelic artwork found on rock and roll posters gradually trickled down, like Agent Orange, to the posters and broadsides created in protest of the Vietnam War. The legend on this one seemed particularly honest to those "young ones" facing a military draft belligerently overseen by dinosaur-like Gen. Lewis B. Hershey.

Stanley "Mouse" Miller worked closely with Alton Kelley, collaborating on a number of strikingly original posters for concerts at Bill Graham's Fillmore Auditorium. He echoed McHugh's sentiments in Jack McDonough's book *San Francisco Rock*, saying, "Graphics were coming apart at the seams, and Kelley and Mouse were there playing in the rubble. What we came up with out of the rubble was twentieth-century teenage hip Americana. It's electrical-age folk art."

Like the music that caressed the scene, psychedelic art eventually began to wane as exploiters, wannabes, and novelty artists elbowed their way onto the stage. "Unless the energy came from the images," McHugh notes, "I didn't want to continue supporting the cause. What with all the novelty stuff coming out on the market—you know, like pigs and rhinos fornicating—the fine-art stuff didn't stand a chance."

The main popularizer of psychedelic art was Peter Max, a self-promoting New York graphic designer (his name was clearly embossed on every work). He codified the style by using bold colors and clear lines, and he quite consciously sought out corporate clients, including infamous polluters like General Electric, for his version of psychedelia. Soon enough,

change of mind. And I felt proud of it, blessed to be part of that whole movement, privileged to have the opportunity. I took it seriously. As a publisher I felt responsible for putting out a spectrum of what was happening. We weren't representing rock music, per se. We were representing a time and a spirit."

his familiar style began to infiltrate Madison Avenue ad campaigns, too. It also showed up on every conceivable commodity, from scarves and towels to clocks and inflatable plastic pillows.

By late 1968, it was hard to find a mainstream magazine that did not feature elements of the Max style in their pages. Across the Atlantic, a German poster artist named Heinz Edelmann used a similar style to produce an animated film version of the Beatles' *Yellow Submarine*, a huge box-office smash in the United States the same year.

One final ironic note: While Madison Avenue and Wall Street both began banking on psychedelia, the artwork that was created—the real art of the times—was completely ignored by art galleries,

Bill Graham's production company enlisted the services of the Bay Area's finest artists to promote concerts at Fillmore Auditorium. These are two of the many created: (right) Rick Griffin's poster for a three-night stand by Big Brother and the Holding Company (whose singer, Janis Joplin, lived in Haight-Ashbury) and Santana, September 12–14, 1968; and (left) a three-night stand by the Grateful Dead, Big Mama Thornton, and Tim Rose, December 9–11, 1968.

art critics, and art journals. The lone exception was Thomas Albright, who wrote for the *San Francisco Chronicle* and *Rolling Stone*. Albright astutely performed the same role for Bay Area art scene that Ralph J. Gleason had for its music. Thanks partly to his efforts, this beautiful flowering that took place in San Francisco and then spread throughout the land is now highly valued by collectors. And the same old cry goes up from the artists: Where were you when we needed you?

WEARING YOUR VIEWS: BUTTONS, SYMBOLS, AND SLOGANS

Sixties people not only wore their art on their sleeve, they broadcast their feelings via buttons. Political views, lifestyle statements, favorite bands, and symbols and slogans of the '60s zeitgeist were all fair game for the button wearer. In a world where millions circulated anonymously through what a sociologist once termed "the lonely crowd," a button served as a little window into one's soul.

Here is a sampling of some of the more popular ones you might have seen on an under-30 person in the mid-to-late '60s:

Stop the Draft

Grass Is a Gas

God Is on a Trip

F*ck Censorship

I Am a Human Being; Do Not Fold, Spindle, or Mutilate

Legalize Spiritual Discovery

Love One Another

50/50 (a reference to half the country's population being under 30)

LOVE

Keep Your Laws off My Body

We Shall Overcome

War Is Not Healthy for Children and Other Living Things

Peace and Love

Watch Out I Vote

Work for Peace

Make Love Not War

Suppose They Gave a War and Nobody Came

Ban the Bomb

Ban the Bra

Flower Power

Student Power

Of course, the most popular button of all might have been the wordless one that simply showed the peace symbol.

ALL WE ARE SAYING IS GIVE PEACE A SIGN

The peace sign—that "broken cross" housed within an unbroken circle—was the semiotic (and semiautomatic) rebuttal to the endlessly escalating militarism of the Cold War era. While it was as ubiquitous in the '60s as the roach clip and the VW Bug, the peace sign was first used in the 1950s as the rallying flag of the Campaign for Nuclear Disarmament, a European pacifist organization headed by philosopher Bertrand Russell. Gerald Holtom is generally given credit for designing the peace symbol, unveiling it at a meeting of the Campaign for Nuclear Disarmament on February 21, 1958, but it had appeared even earlier—without Holtom's intended meaning—in *The Book of Signs* (1955), by German calligrapher Rudolph Koch.

Holtom decided on his "crow's foot" design because it incorporated the semaphore elements for the letters "N" and "D" (as in Nuclear Disarmament). Plus, it was a potent symbol that, much like atomic power, could be interpreted in two diametrically opposed ways: either as death (the broken cross) or infinity (the unbroken circle). Yet the peace sign was accused of possessing evil properties that predated Holtom's appropriation of it. The John Birch Society, those God-fearing Commie-bashers, claimed the peace symbol was the sign of the Antichrist. Of course, they also disseminated one of the most popular anti-hippie bumper stickers of the 1960s, consisting of the peace sign and the legend "Footprint of the American Chicken."

Hippies, on the other hand, like to claim full credit for the peace sign, perpetuating the myth that it was really a graphic rendering of the B-52 bombers that were wreaking havoc in Southeast Asia. The circle, so they claimed, symbolized their efforts to stop those gargantuan killing machines. Whichever account of its origins one believes, the peace sign was also a way to convey a very important message in symbolic shorthand. Just as hobos scrawled their own symbols on the sides of houses where free food was available, the presence of a peace sign affixed to a car, business, or home sent a semaphore signal to hippies and heads: "You are welcome here."

"ZAP! BAM! POW!"

UNDERGROUND COMICS STRIKE A BLOW

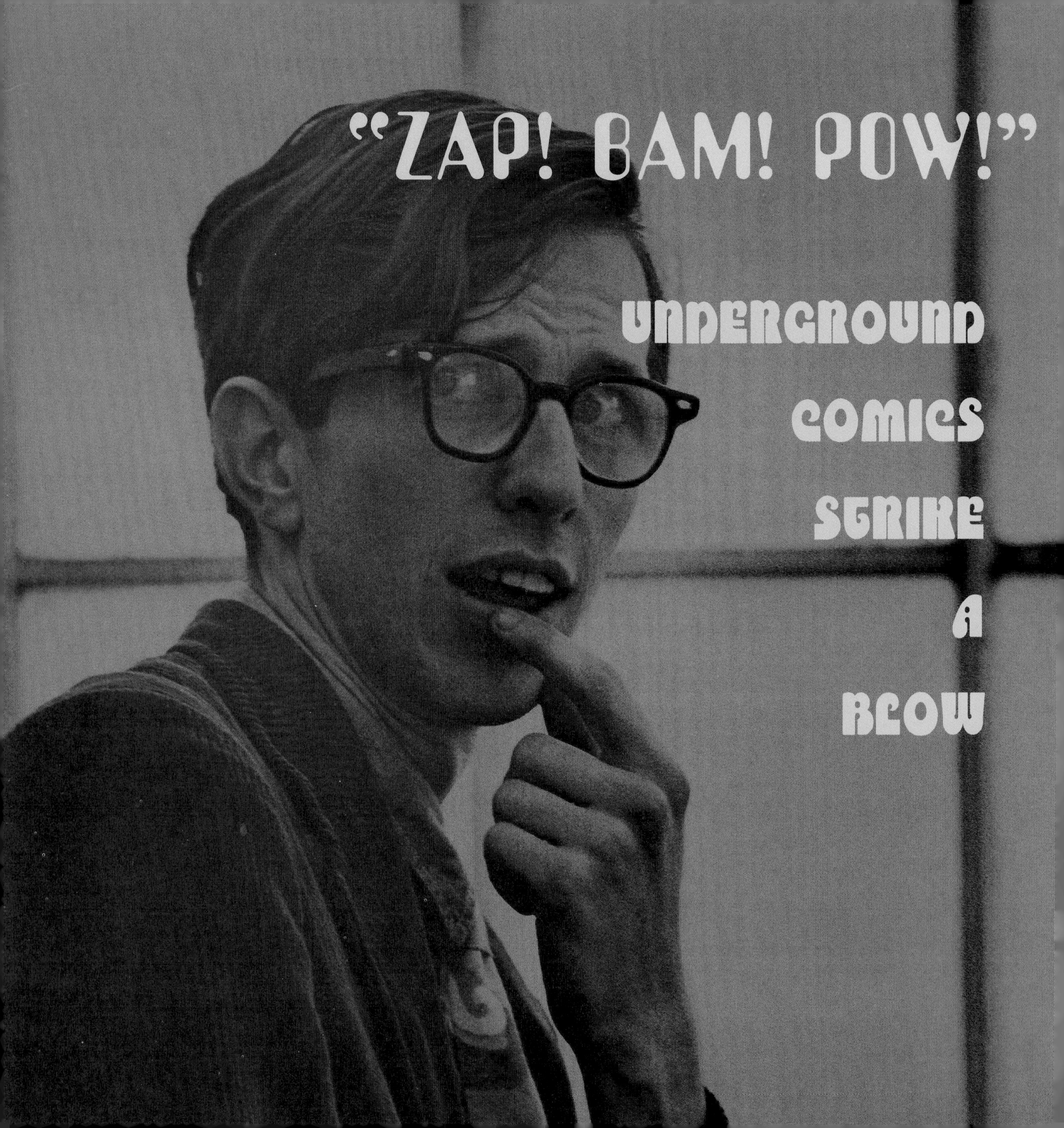

Bible verse frequently hurled at young people in the 1960s was First Corinthians 13:11. It was about putting away childish things, and it went like this: "When I was a child, I spake as a child, I understood as a child, I thought as a child, but when I became a man, I put away childish things." Right-thinking commentators and college presidents used it to castigate war protesters and "hairy

Portrait of the artist Robert Crumb as a young man living in Haight-Ashbury. Does this look like the face of a man about to give birth to an underground revolution?

hippies," and moms used it to prod wayward progeny into throwing away comic books.

The verse was delivered with such maddening condescension that it's little wonder now that kids—faced with a "manly" world of war, greed, and institutional lying—were turned into budding revolutionaries. As usual, parents didn't know or suspect that comic books were one of the "childish" things that were growing up right alongside their kids. If they'd only continued quoting from First Corinthians, they might have gotten a clue. The next verse begins, "For now we see through a glass, darkly."

Indeed, that verse could have been the unstated credo of a new breed of print animation. Comic books grew out of the daily comic strips that began appearing in newspapers in the 1890s. They became a well-established publishing venture with the first issue of *Action Comics* in June 1938, which introduced Superman to the world. Along with the caped crusader, heroic icons such as Batman and Captain Marvel scrambled the hormones of many a boy in America, as well as serving a benign and valuable propagandistic function as Nazi-killers, Commie-bashers, and crime-stoppers.

But in the 1960s mainstream comic books lost their appeal to the new generation simply because publishers wouldn't change with the times. True, they were hemmed in by a Comics Code—a legislated ratings authority resulting from Congressional hysteria in the 1950s over *EC Comics*, the gory precursor to *Mad* magazine. But even so, they approached their permissible subject matter with the black-or-white mind-set of the Cold War era and its patronizing *Father Knows Best* attitude. Even the dullest lad or lass could see that father didn't know shit anymore.

The only mainstream comic-book publisher that did change with the changing times was Marvel. Founded in 1939, Marvel changed dramatically in 1961 when a young, street-smart publisher named Stan Lee launched two new titles (with artwork by Jack Kirby) that found a ready audience: *The Fantastic Four* and *Amazing Adventures*. While continuing to adhere to the Comics Code rule that good must triumph over evil, Lee allowed artists and writers to mine their imaginations for new

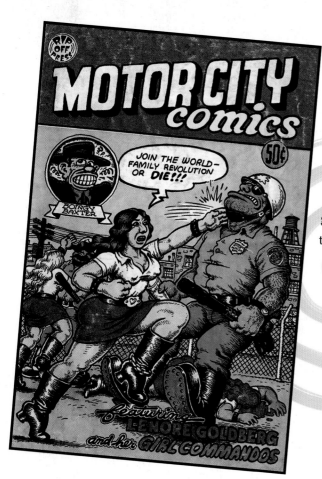

twists on old formulas. New "superhero" characters appeared, as complex and troubled as their times, including Spider-Man, Hulk, Silver Surfer, and Thor. They clicked, almost instantly, with college kids. A 1965 *Esquire* article proclaimed Spider-Man to be more popular among radicals than Che Guevara.

Besides the characters, a dramatic change was evident in Marvel artwork. Panels were expanded, graphics and ink overlapped into kaleidoscopic patterns, landscapes were more otherworldly than they'd

Two typical Crumb products are his seminal (and semen-filled) *Zap Comix* (right) and *Motor City Comics* (above). The original artwork for his *Zap* debut in 1967 was stolen and then relocated, but only in photocopied form. Using the copies, he redrew the whole thing and published it as *Zap* No. 0, following *Zap* No. 3, in 1969. *Motor City* had nothing to do with Detroit or cars but everything to do with Crumb's unrepentent disregard for feminism, embodying what he saw as its fascistic hypocrisy in the righteous form of Lenore Goldberg.

been since the glory days of George Herriman's *Krazy Kat* comic strip (a masterfully surrealistic cat-and-mouse saga that ran from 1914 to 1944). The greatest of the envelope-pushing comic-book artistry could be found in *Strange Tales*, starring Dr. Strange, beginning with the 10th issue (July 1963). As depicted by artist Steve Ditko, *Strange Tales* was a visual feast, and the character of Dr. Strange was, well, unusual. "Unlike the other Marvel heroes," writes Les Daniels in *Comix: A History of Comic Books in America*, "he never punched anyone. Instead he cast spells and entered weird dimensions....There can be little doubt that much of the psychedelic art that was to emerge from the West Coast two years later owed something to the vistas explored in the *Dr. Strange* pages." It was appropriate homage that the first communal rock dance in

Marvel's *Strange Tales* featured two heroes—Nick Fury and Doctor Strange—whose visual style and sense of mystery appealed to those under the sway of psychedelia. Doctor Strange was unsurpassably hip, a "Master of the Mystic Arts" and a resident of Greenwich Village. Nick Fury, Agent of S.H.I.E.L.D. (begun June 1968), was drawn by Jim Steranko, who later wrote an excellent multivolume history of comic books.

San Francisco—held at Longshoreman's Hall on October 16, 1965—was dubbed "A Tribute to Dr. Strange."

Sensing the obvious appeal his new comics were having on college campuses, Lee formed the dada-spirited Merry Marvel Marching Society (MMMS) in 1965. For a modest fee, one could join this antiorganization, read the tongue-in-cheek bulletins, and sport the requisite buttons and T-shirts. What, in effect, was created by this admittedly commercial gesture was the prototype for a playful group mind-set, later seen on Haight Street, at Be-Ins, and in the radical antics of Yippies and Diggers. (Abbie Hoffman was a big comics fan.) Along with quasi-uniforms, a new language

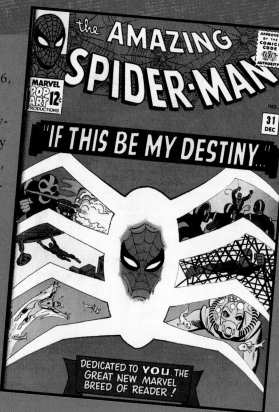

By issue No. 31 (January 1966), it was obvious the self-tormented but earnest Spider-Man had struck a timely chord, thus the dedication to "the great new Marvel breed of reader." By issue No. 68 (January 1969), Marvel was pushing hard to be "relevant." Though Stan Lee still personally wrote the scripts, the great artist of the former issue, Steve Ditko, left in a huff in late 1966—allegedly over the secret identity of Spidey's nemesis, Green Goblin—and was replaced by the competent John Romita.

was adopted, as was a feeling of being part of a fantasy universe much better than the real one.

On a personal level, the MMMS spirit can be found in an exchange of letters between one of our brothers, Jeb Bisbort, and his best friend in 1967–1968. Both were college students, both members in good standing of MMMS, and both heavily into psychedelia. Typical of their concerns about MMMS are the following excerpts:

"This explains why we can simultaneously hold dear Spidey [Spider-Man] and Hulk while viewing clods like Iron Man with interested disdain. That is, Hulk cannot react against World Bland Evil because he doesn't really know it. He's not of it. Likewise, Captain America is

Fantastic Four, begun in 1961, was the first of the "new Marvel" marquee titles, featuring a team of scientists turned superheroes when their rocket passed through "cosmic rays." Drawn by veteran Jack Kirby and written by Stan Lee, the long-running comic was a great vehicle to test out new characters. The "sentinel of the spaceways," Silver Surfer, created by Kirby in March 1966, turned up often, became hugely popular with college kids, and got his own comic in August 1968 (drawn by John Buscema). Kirby also drew the cover for the Merry Marvel Marching Society catalog (right).

The tabloid *Trashman*, created by Spain Rodriguez, appeared in 1969—a sort of Che Guevara on LSD. This was also proof that after the Summer of Love, things in America got progressively more heavy, as it were.

equally wonderful because he is hopelessly devoted to the unreal. He knows nothing of Bland America but only of the America of Good and Evil which, after all, only exists in our minds when we all sing together. The same goes for Spidey, except he's so unbelievably crapped-up. Likewise, the Sub-Mariner is an obverse of Iron Man. He reacts against Bland World (the 'surface' world) by trying to alter its blandness.

"Here I am on the verge of disbelief following (1) the disappearance of [Jim] Steranko [one of Marvel's greatest artists, creator of the psychedelic effects found in *Agent of S.H.I.E.L.D.*]; (2) my disillusionment with [Jack] Springer [a lesser Marvel artist]; (3) the cut-back of *Dr. Strange* to bimonthly; and (4) the lack of Dr. Doom getting his own mag, and you sit there all knowing and smug and tell me, 'Aw, I knew about it all the time.' You insinuate you have all this secret information....Why not in your next letter, as a generous, friendly, open thing to do, send me what you know about future Marvel developments?"

Future developments in comic books revolved around one man: Robert Crumb, who signed his work "R. Crumb." Though steeped in comic-book tradition, Crumb had no interest in adhering to any code of censorship. Lacking outlets for his work, he nonetheless pressed on, hanging out almost daily in the fledgling Haight-Ashbury community in the mid-1960s. Naturally, he came into contact with psychedelic drugs. The combination of hallucinatory visions and his own eccentric graphic style led to his remarkable artistry. Art critic Robert Hughes has called him "the Brueghel of the second half of the 20th century."

For various reasons, including a dysfunctional upbringing in one of those seemingly perfect (from the outside) *Father Knows Best* families, Crumb did, indeed, see "through a glass, darkly." He also created some archetypes for his age, including Mr. Natural, Eggs Ackley, Flakey Foont, the Vulture Women, and the "Keep on Truckin'" dude. He also started a trend in innovative album art with his cover design for *Cheap Thrills*, the huge-selling album by Big Brother and the Holding Company.

In Terry Zwigoff's riveting 1994 documentary *Crumb*, Robert Crumb explained the course of events that led from the coded wonders of Marvel Comics to the no-holds-barred curiosities of his own *Zap Comix*: "All these hippie underground papers started up in 1966 and 1967. Every town had one or two of them. They would print anything related to psychedelic experience or the hippie ethic. So, I started submitting some of the LSD-inspired drawings I'd been doing in my sketchbook, and they liked them. Then, this guy came along and suggested I do a whole book, *Yarrowstalks*, which went over big. Then, this other guy says,

'Hey, why don't you just do psychedelic comic books and I'll publish them.' So, I set to work and did two whole issues of *Zap Comix*."

Other comic artists followed his lead, and in a matter of weeks (according to Crumb) an underground comix revolution was born. Among the artists who entered this new uncharted, and unregulated, territory—the "x" in comix wasn't just a semantic affectation—were Gilbert Shelton (creator of *The Fabulous Furry Freak Brothers* and *Wonder Warthog*), Spain Rodriguez (*Trashman*), Victor Moscoso and Rick Griffin (both of whom also designed rock posters), Vaughan Bode, Kim Deitch, the Mad Peck (who also reviewed rock records in comic-strip form), Skip Williamson, S. Clay Wilson, Bill Griffith, and Art Spiegelman. These artists, in turn, inspired the renaissance of sophisticated comic-book art we see today, ushered in by the seminal *Raw* magazine in the 1980s.

Getting back to First Corinthians, maybe the Bible did prophesy this madness, after all. Not long after the verse about putting away childish things, Paul's epistle to the Corinthians asks, "If the trumpet give an uncertain sound, who shall prepare himself to the battle?" It then advises, "Let us eat and drink, for tomorrow we die." It certainly felt that way in the '60s.

Amen.

An "underground" press has existed on the edge of American society for most of its history. One might even say American journalism began as an underground press, with the first newspaper in the colonies, *Publick Occurrences*, suppressed by the government of Massachusetts Bay Colony in 1690 for "reflections of a very high nature." The same charges could be lev-

For the 1997 opening of an exhibit on the psychedelic era at the Rock and Roll Hall of Fame and Museum in Cleveland, the surviving Merry Pranksters arrived in a refurbished "magic bus" named FURTHER. The bus immortalized in "new journalist" Tom Wolfe's *The Electric Kool-Aid Acid Test* was misspelled FURTHUR.

eled against the underground press of the 1960s, with "high" being the buzzword of the newsroom in more ways than one.

Between those two historic wickets, of course, a lot of colorful balls got knocked, including Ben Franklin's *Poor Richard's Almanack* (humor, advice, sedition), John Peter Zenger's *New York Weekly Journal* (suppressed by the Colonial government in 1735), *Freedom's Journal* (the first black-controlled newspaper, 1827), *Cherokee Phoenix* (the first Indian newspaper, 1828), and the abolitionist papers of Frederick Douglass and William Lloyd Garrison. In this century alone, a number of important papers have operated on the fringes of the political spectrum, not just to push ideological agendas but to shed light on (or rake muck about) societal ills the mainstream press would otherwise ignore or dismiss. Among the best were *The Masses*, *Appeal to Reason*, *Daily Worker*, *The Progressive*, *Partisan Review*, and *The Guardian*. A bit later, snapping at the heels of the '60s, were *I.F. Stone's Weekly*, *Dissent*, and *Village Voice*.

While each of these broke ground that the underground press of the 1960s would claim as its own, they were too overtly and narrowly political to have any direct effect. More

influential, in fact, would be the proto-hepcat publications that flaunted the prevailing mores and, consequently, obscenity laws: *Evergreen Review*, *Nugget*, *Cavalier*, *Swank*, *Screw*, and (yes) *Playboy*, as well as those that pushed the envelope on graphic art: *EC Comics*, *Mad*, *Wild*, and the syndicated comic strips *Pogo* and *Krazy Kat*. Toss in more literary, artistic, and spirit-seeking journals like *Contact*, *Psychedelic Review*, *Yugen*, *Kulchur*, *Big Table*, *New Directions*, *Horizon*, and *View*, and you'd have to say the foundation was pretty well laid for a new type of underground journalism.

No publication created by adults spoke directly to the concerns held by the generation of kids born after World War II—you know, things like sex, drugs, rock and roll, the nature of reality, the meaning of life, and how to keep your van running. Each of these subjects had a sacramental aspect to it. Thus, such seemingly innocuous periodicals as comic books and teen music magazines were vital for surviving adolescence, while stroke mags provided the sexual insight that tight-lipped parents couldn't bring themselves to address. More seriously jolting to young minds were the rash of assassinations, civil-rights clashes, and an undeclared and escalating war that sent innocent Baby Boomers off to Southeast Asia to go boom as cannon fodder. So it was goodbye Peter Pan, hello sordid reality.

Arguably the first underground magazine that tried to make the leap into a new cultural epoch was *The Realist*, a monthly started by Paul Krassner in 1958. Krassner—a standup comic, writer for *Mad*, and intimate of Lenny Bruce (bona fides if ever there were any!)—was determined to create what he called "a *Mad* for grown-ups." The emphasis was on outrageous satire, taboo-trashing, and borderline libel. His most notorious sketch was a 1963 fantasy of LBJ having sex with JFK's corpse on the way back from Dallas. "Irreverence is the only sacred cow,"

preached Krassner, who soon found himself in hot water with the FBI but making fans (and contributors) of iconoclasts like Steve Allen, Henry Morgan, Kurt Vonnegut, Groucho Marx, and Joseph Heller.

He also found himself pulled into a new circle whose members were experimenting with hallucinogenic drugs: Tim Leary, Richard Alpert (later Baba Ram Dass), and Michael Hollingshead. As Krassner wrote in a 1993 memoir, "I became intrigued by the playful and subtle patterns of awareness that Leary and Alpert manifested. If their brains had been so damaged, how come their perceptions were so sharp? I began to research the LSD phenomenon, and in April 1965 I returned to Millbrook for my first acid experience. I was 33 years old, and I'd never been high." His guide was Hollingshead, "the baldheaded British rascal who had first turned Leary on," and his experience with pure Sandoz

Begun by Donald Allen and Barney Rossett in New York in 1957, *Evergreen Review* quickly established itself as the world's most influential avant-garde magazine. By No. 11 (1960), *Evergreen* was mingling old existentialists like Sartre, Artaud, and Beckett with new voices from the likes of Ginsberg, Burroughs, and Terry Southern. Kerouac's "The Railroad Earth" is among his finest work.

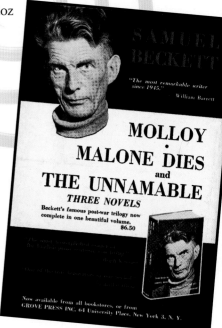

LSD was so life-altering that he shared every bit of it with his readers in *The Realist.* He also told his mom, who warned, "It could lead to marijuana."

Where it led was to the newsrooms of the underground press. Sexual boundaries had already been crossed in 1960, when the first oral contraceptive (Enovid) was introduced, and new horizons in rock and roll appeared imminent with the arrival of the Beatles in 1963. Thus, when the wonders of LSD began to be widely touted in 1965, it was only a matter of time before the spirit of psychedelia brought a new look to the old muckraking tradition.

Among the first and best of the underground papers that appeared regularly were the *L.A. Free Press* (begun in 1964), New York's *East Village Other* and *The Berkeley Barb.* The *Free Press* (or "Freep") was founded and edited by Art Kunkin, who ran it like a professional operation. That is, he paid his staff regularly and reasonably, which probably explains the paper's success. Moreover, Kunkin ran reliable and forthright news (local and national) and the take-no-prisoners views of Harlan Ellison, film critic Gene Youngblood, Lawrence Lipton (an old Beat), and cartoonist Ron Cobb, arguably the underground press' most talented graphic artist. The *Barb*, forged in the flames of the Free Speech Movement at the University of California at Berkeley, was as cantankerous as founder Max Scherr, a

Clayton Eshleman started *Caterpillar* in 1967 as a "dependable and generous outlet" for "difficult" poetry, using as his subtitle "a gathering of the tribes." Perhaps the most intriguing part of *Caterpillar* to these nebulous "tribes" was the cover art. The front and back covers of Number 8/9 featured collages by Jess, an L.A. artist too often overlooked in retrospectives of the times.

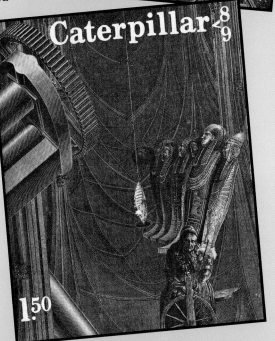

40-something labor activist and bar owner determined to produce a "people's paper." The *Barb* set precedents that were followed by other papers: shoestring budget, street-level reporting and vending. Soon enough, the Barb began to take notice of doings in a little neighborhood across the bay: Haight-Ashbury.

As Abe Peck, former editor of Chicago's *Seed*, wrote in *Uncovering the Sixties*, "The Haight was becoming the epicenter for an emerging Bay Area hip scene, for a new music network stretching from Santa Cruz to Marin County, and for acidheads seeking spirituality, community, and fun."

No truer picture of the psychedelic zeitgeist can be found than in the Haight's own homegrown paper, the *Oracle* (a.k.a. the *San Francisco Oracle*). Originally started in the summer of 1966 as *P.O. Frisco* (for "Psychedelic Oracle"), it ceased publication after one issue while the political radicals jumped ship. Then it resumed in the fall of 1966 as the *Oracle*, financially backed by Ron and Jay Thelin of the Psychedelic Shop and rock promoter Bill Graham. Though it lasted for only a dozen issues, the *Oracle*'s influence was huge, primarily because it so perfectly captured the utopian but utterly apolitical mind-set of psychedelia. Its content was driven by the explosion of art that had begun appearing on rock posters. The *Oracle*'s modus operandi said it all: "Designed to aid people on their trips."

High times in the Haight, like those of the *Oracle*, reached a peak with the Human Be-In in Golden Gate Park, on January 14, 1967. The *Oracle* was the driving force behind this monumental "gathering of the tribes," which counted acid gurus Timothy Leary and Richard Alpert among its organizers. The Be-In also connected the unnamed new movement with its spiritual antecedents. Present on the green that day were Zen master Alan Watts; Beat poets Allen Ginsberg, Gary Snyder, Michael McClure, and Lawrence Ferlinghetti (whose City Lights bookshop was a proto-hippie

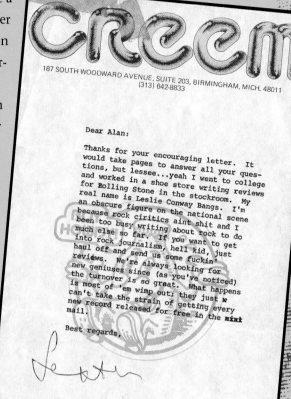

CREEM
187 SOUTH WOODWARD AVENUE, SUITE 203, BIRMINGHAM, MICH. 48011
(313) 642-8833

Dear Alan:

Thanks for your encouraging letter. It would take pages to answer all your questions, but lessee...yeah I went to college and worked in a shoe store writing reviews for Rolling Stone in the stockroom. My real name is Leslie Conway Bangs. I'm an obscure figure on the national scene because rock cirítics aint shit and I been too busy writing about rock to do much else so far. If you want to get into rock journalism, hell kid, just haul off and send us some fuckin' reviews. We're always looking for new geniuses since (as you've noticed) the turnover is so great. What happens is most of 'em wimp out; they just can't take the strain of getting every new record released for free in the maxi mail.

Best regards,

[signature]

LESTER BANGS

Like many Lester Bangs wanna-bes, one of us reviewed pop music for our college newspaper. A shameless fan letter and solicitation for advice prompted this candid, generous, and hilarious response from the great man himself.

The visually arresting *East Village Other* was started in 1965 by Walter Bowart, using his earnings as a bartender ($500). He thought of a newspaper "as a television set," about which Abe Peck wrote, "Its articles were less about Tammany Hall than Alpha Centauri, and energetic images sometimes resembled test patterns more than programs." By the time we got to Woodstock, the *EVO* was the paper of record for New York heads.

haven); radical leftists Jerry Rubin and Dick Gregory; and censored poet Lenore Kandel (whose explicitly erotic *The Love Book* was the subject of an obscenity trial). Of course, the most indispensable participants were the Grateful Dead, Quicksilver Messenger Service, and Big Brother and the Holding Company, who provided the music.

Of the scene, *Oracle* reporter Steve Levine wrote, "A generation considered by many to be the reincarnation of the American Indian has been born out of the ashes of World War Two, rising like a Phoenix in celebration of the slightly psychedelic zeitgeist of this brand-new Aquarian Age."

A phenomenon that revolutionary would not remain secret for long. The message was spread via an underground press network that included the following domestic publications:

Argus (Ann Arbor)
Avatar (Boston)
Big Fat (Ann Arbor)
Connections (Madison, Wisconsin)
Crocodile (Gainesville, Florida)
Distant Drummer (Philadelphia)
East Village Other (New York)
Fifth Estate (Detroit)
Free Press (Washington, Miami, Indianapolis, St. Louis, Columbus, Las Vegas, Baltimore)
Good Times (San Francisco)
Graffiti (Philadelphia)
Great Speckled Bird (Atlanta)
Guerrilla (Detroit)
Helix (Seattle)
Kaleidoscope (Milwaukee)
Kudzu (Jackson, Mississippi)
Open City (Los Angeles)

Sage (Santa Fe)
The Paper (East Lansing, Michigan)
The Rag (Austin)
The Rat (New York)
The Seed (Chicago)
View From the Bottom (New Haven)

Then there were a raft of international magazines, which likewise aimed themselves at a counterculture that had gone global:

Actuel (Paris)
Canadian Free Press (Ottawa)
Eco Contemporaneo (Buenos Aries)
International Times (London)
Om (Amsterdam)
Oz (London)
Puss (Stockholm)
Sanity (Montreal)
Satyrday (Toronto)

A correspondent from the *East Village Other* who reported on the Be-In declared San Francisco's seven hills to be "the Rome of a future world founded on love," as well as the "love-guerrilla training school for dropouts from mainstream America." With peaks like that, who needs valleys? But, inevitably, the valleys came. And they didn't necessarily wait for the Summer of Love to run its course. Early portents were forecast by Haight resident Chester Anderson, who printed and posted his own broadside and newsletter rants. In one particularly astute posting—headlined

"Uncle Tim's Children"—he dissed the head-in-the-sand mentality that pervaded the new street culture: "Minds & bodies are being maimed as we watch, a scale-model of Vietnam....And that goes for Uncle Tim, too, who turned you on & dropped you into this pit." Disturbed by what he saw as an inevitable crash, Anderson left town to help start his own rock and roll magazine, *Crawdaddy*.

The true bible of the rock revolution, *Rolling Stone*, was conceived and launched right across town from the Haight by 21-year-old Jann Wenner. Borrowing the seed money ($8,000), Wenner printed the first issue on November 6, 1967, with a press run of 40,000 (34,000 of which didn't sell). Wenner had previously written for *Ramparts*, a monthly magazine of radical politics and avant-garde arts that was politically born out of the Bay Area Catholic reform movement and was influenced, format-wise, by *Evergreen Review*. Though its reformist muckraking heart was in the right (that is, left) place, *Ramparts* was noticeably lacking in humor or a visceral connection with rock and roll culture. It was one thing to subscribe to *Ramparts*, quite another to have to read it.

Rolling Stone, on the other hand, instantly created rapport and established credibility with the new audience that arose out of the psychedelic scene. It was the first rock magazine to have a serious record-review section (overseen by the scholarly Jon Landau). Because the magazine professed to be about not just music, "but the things and attitudes that the music embraces," it also provided everything from incisive "new journalism" with a political slant to inside information on such subjects as drugs ("The Dope Pages," a regular column credited to "Smokestack El Ropo"), groupies, underground filmmakers, rock festivals, and any other serious rumblings in the counterculture. Instead of treating them as mindless, exchangeable commodities, *Rolling Stone* allowed rock musicians to talk candidly. Lengthy, thoughtful interviews were conducted with the likes of Pete Townshend, John Lennon, Eric Clapton, Mick Jagger, Bob Dylan, Jerry Garcia, and others in the pop pantheon. To a head, the magazine's masthead motto—"All the News That Fits"—rang true.

Wenner cultivated a stable of music writers that stands to this day as a who's who of rock jour-nalism: Landau (now Bruce Springsteen's manager), Greil Marcus, Lester Bangs, Ed Ward, Langdon Winner, Dave Marsh, Chet Flippo, Ben Fong-Torres, and more. Suffice it to say that rock journalism lagged way behind the furious pace of evolution in music until *Rolling Stone* came along.

Another in-the-know music magazine, *Creem* (out of Detroit), debuted on March 5, 1969. It served as an irreverent forum for Lester Bangs (who did his best writing there), Richard Meltzer, Nick Tosches, and many others who would not let rock and roll die at the hands of corporate strangulation. At its best, *Creem*'s journalistic approach captured the anarchic, liberating feeling of rock and roll in

The *Chicago Seed* began life in 1967 as an ardently radical rag and developed into one of the most visually interesting publications of the underground press. Most of the credit belongs to artist Karl Heinz Meschbach, who designed covers like this one and endlessly fascinating foldout collages.

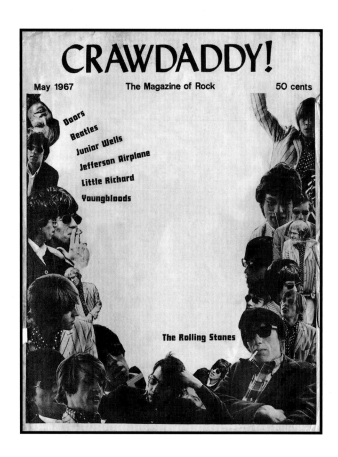

Rock and roll was taken seriously—as a celebration of life and a harbinger of a new youth culture—by *Crawdaddy!*, the first alternative music mag of its time. It was founded in January 1966 by Swarthmore student Paul Williams, who was soon joined by Chester Anderson. Together they shared a love of "rock"—no longer even calling it rock and roll—which Anderson dubbed "the glue of the new society, erasing false categories of art, class, race, privatism, and the gap between audience and performer."

After the Summer of Love, *Rolling Stone* ruled as the final word in music journalism, charting all the vital signs of the "new society" Chester Anderson longed for. Typical of its sweep is this early issue, which shows how the line between music and politics had blurred.

words. Consider this Kerouac-style passage by the late Bangs, excerpted from a long, undisciplined, largely fictional, and madly brilliant review-cum-essay that was ostensibly about the Count Five (one-hit psychedelic wonders who cut "Psychotic Reaction") but touched on larger themes:

"So perhaps the truest autobiography I could ever write, and I know this holds as well for many other people, would take place largely at record counters, jukeboxes, pushing forward in the driver's seat while AM walloped you on, alone under headphones with vast scenic bridges and angelic choirs in the brain through insomniac post-midnights, or just to sit at leisure stoned or not in the vast benign lap of America, slapping on sides and feeling good."

Obviously rock journalism crossed some kind of threshold with Bangs. You could call what he did record reviewing as an art form or as literature. Often he wrote hilarious epics that mocked musical pretense and celebrated rock at its most primitive. His 10,000-word masterpieces about Iggy Pop, Alice Cooper, and Lou Reed would run unedited in *Creem*. As Greil Marcus wrote in his intro to *Psychotic Reactions and Carburetor Dung*, a Bangs compendium that he edited: "Perhaps what this book demands from a reader is a willingness to accept that the best writer in America could write almost nothing but record reviews."

As two teens who got hooked on the underground press in general and Bangs in particular, we had no trouble accepting that last statement at all.

NOTES FROM THE MILITARY UNDERGROUND

Ultimately, how deeply did the underground press penetrate? You might find these examples hard to believe:

•*Fatigue Press*, out of Killeen, Texas, was an anti-military underground paper, written by members of the military (anonymously, of course). The editor was listed as Oleo Strut.

•*Om*, based in Washington, D.C., was a "liberation newsletter" first published out of the Pentagon (!) by Roger Lee Priest, a 25-year-old pacifist who also happened to be an apprentice seaman in the navy. One issue featured a cover picture of Secretary of Defense Melvin Laird, which bore the legend, "People's Enemy Number One—A Pig By Any Other Name Is Still a Pig." *Rolling Stone* called *Om* "one of the gutsiest of the military undergrounders (there are dozens)." Indeed, Priest earned his radical pinstripes, having to face court-martial on 14 separate counts of "disloyalty."

•J. Edgar Hoover, in an effort to counter alternative journalism's power, created two underground papers run by the FBI—*Armageddon News* (Indianapolis, 1968) and *Longhorn Tales* (San Antonio, 1969). One can only imagine the record section: five stars for Sgt. Barry Sadler's *Ballads of the Green Berets* and Victor Lundberg's *An Open Letter*, one star for Jefferson Airplane's *Volunteers* and Steppenwolf's *Monster*.

"STEAL THIS BOOK"

MUST-READS OF THE '60S

Abbie Hoffman

steal this book

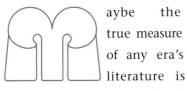aybe the true measure of any era's literature is how much more seriously it's taken by readers than by critics. By that yardstick (and certainly relative to today), the 1960s measure up as a literary renaissance. Books were like bombs whose ideas detonated in the minds of a new generation, filling them with the zeal and motivation to change the world—by seduction if possible,

Not the least of Abbie Hoffman's sins during the brutal Democratic Convention in Chicago, August 1968, was his daring fashion statement. He may as well have carried a sign inscribed: "Arrest Me! I've Crossed State Lines to Incite a Riot!"— precisely what he and seven others were later charged with. Read all about it in his book *Woodstock Nation*.

by force if necessary.

Every generation, of course, is eager to make its own mark, angry at the failures of its predecessors, and righteously optimistic about its own chances. As the French surrealist Alfred Jarry—author of *Ubu Roi* (1896), an enduring classic of the youth cult—put it: "And another lot of young people will appear, and consider us completely outdated, and they will write ballads to express their loathing of us, and there is no reason why this should ever end."

However, at the risk of sounding partial, the generation that came of age in the '60s broke the mold. They were unusually receptive to the brash ideas of a new literature. As their minds expanded (philosophically and chemically), the chain reaction was felt deep within the complacent folds of the academy. Genuine change seemed possible on all fronts—spiritual, political, racial, artistic—and books served as road maps into uncharted territory.

Allen Ginsberg, a driving force both among Beats and hippies, described the great schism in literature prior to the '60s in a 1996 interview: "When you opened one of the standard anthologies, you got Whitman as the representative of free verse, Pound and Eliot as the cut-up and montage guys, a little specimen of William Carlos Williams, and then you go back to John Crowe Ransom, Robert Penn Warren, and all the academic poets—Robert Lowell, Donald Hall, Louis Simpson, John Hollander, Richard Howard, blah-blah-blah. But the whole world of Frank O'Hara, Kenneth Koch, John Ashbery, Robert Creeley, Charles Olson, and their inheritors was eliminated, as well as Kerouac, Gregory Corso, and myself.

"In 1957, I came back to New York with manuscripts of Olson, Creeley, Kerouac, Corso, Denise Levertov, O'Hara, and myself, and I brought it all to Louis Simpson. He was putting together the Hall-Simpson-Pack anthology called *New Poets of England and America*. And between Pack, Simpson, and Hall, they rejected every single one of these poets, who are now big poetic figures and heroes. So Donald Allen at Grove Press, who was friends with O'Hara and Baraka and me, put together his anthology called *The New*

American Poetry. Both of those books came out the same year, 1960, and there was no crossover. That became known as the Battle of the Anthologies."

In such a climate, it is no surprise that most of the books deemed important by the academy were conspicuously absent from the list of what was considered essential reading in the minds of the restless young. A few titles crossed over—e.g., *Armies of the Night,* Norman Mailer's chronicle of an antiwar march on the Pentagon, as well as an exploration of gaps in America (between young and old, black and white, jaded academy and fearless activists).

Mostly, though, books read by true believers in Flower Power did not appear on college syllabi of the time, and relatively few have made it there in the years since.

The following is an admittedly subjective list of essential readings during the late '60s. These are the books that raised provocative questions, proposed intriguing answers, broke new ground, prodded and probed, or simply gave solace. Most were written in the 1960s, though some skirt other eras. *The Dharma Bums,* for example, was published in

1958 but pertained more to the hippie era with its gentle Eastern musings and call for a "rucksack revolution." Ralph Ellison's *Invisible Man* was published in 1953 but increased in relevance as the Civil Rights movement got snagged on issues raised by black militants. Books by the likes of Hesse, Blake, Baudelaire, and Rimbaud came from a previous century but still shot off sparks in the 1960s.

Given our constitutional First Amendment freedoms, it would be disingenuous to equate the role of these books to the *samizdat* literature in the Soviet Union. Still, like *samizdat* works, each was read and dog-eared, passages were underlined and memorized and recited to others, and the books themselves were passed along to friends or kindred spirits. Think of these books as the ones most likely to be found on the shelves of reasonably intelligent people who had tuned into the times in which they lived.

US was an innovative publishing venture, a paperback magazine with as many illustrations as stories. Unfortunately, it lasted all of three issues before Ballantine Books threw in the towel.

FICTION

Barth, John. *The Sot-Weed Factor, The Floating Opera*

Borges, Jorge Luis. *Labyrinths*

Brautigan, Richard. *A Confederate General from Big Sur, Trout Fishing in America*

Burroughs, William. *The Soft Machine, Nova Express*

Camus, Albert. *The Rebel*

Cohen, Leonard. *Beautiful Losers*

Didion, Joan. *Slouching Toward Bethlehem*

Donleavy, J.P. *The Ginger Man*

Dos Passos, John. *U.S.A.*

Dostoevsky, Fyodor. *Notes from Underground*

Ellison, Ralph. *Invisible Man*

Exley, Frederick. *A Fan's Notes*

Fariña, Richard. *Been Down So Long It Looks Like Up to Me*

Genet, Jean. *Our Lady of the Flowers*

Gogol, Nicolai V. *Dead Souls*

Gover, Robert. *100 Dollar Misunderstanding*

Heller, Joseph. *Catch-22*

Hesse, Herman. *Siddhartha, Steppenwolf*

Himes, Chester. *Pinktoes, Cotton Comes to Harlem*

Huxley, Aldous. *Island*

Joyce, James. *Portrait of the Artist as a Young Man, Ulysses*

Kafka, Franz. *The Penal Colony, The Trial*

Kerouac, Jack. *On the Road, The Dharma Bums*

Kesey, Ken. *One Flew Over the Cuckoo's Nest*

Larner, Jeremy. *Drive, He Said*

THE MADLY CAREENING NOVEL OF TODAY'S TURNED-ON, HUNG-UP YOUTH..."KNOWING... SAVAGE...ASSURED...AUDACIOUS...FILLED WITH VITALITY"
—LOS ANGELES TIMES

been down so long it looks like up to me

richard fariña

MacInnes, Colin. *Absolute Beginners*

Matthiessen, Peter. *At Play in the Fields of the Lord*

Miller, Henry. *Tropic of Cancer, Tropic of Capricorn*

Nabokov, Vladimir. *Lolita*

Paley, Grace. *The Little Disturbances of Man*

Patchen, Kenneth. *The Journal of Albion Moonlight*

Percy, Walker. *The Moviegoer*

Pynchon, Thomas. *The Crying of Lot 49, V, Gravity's Rainbow*

Reed, Ishmael. *The Free-Lance Pallbearers, Yellow Back Radio Broke-Down*

Robbins, Tom. *Another Roadside Attraction*

Roth, Philip. *Portnoy's Complaint; Goodbye, Columbus*

Salinger, J.D. *Catcher in the Rye*

Selby, Jr., Hubert. *Last Exit to Brooklyn*

Southern, Terry. *Candy, The Magic Christian, Red Dirt Marihuana*

Stone, Robert. *A Hall of Mirrors*

Styron, William. *The Confessions of Nat Turner*

John Updike. *Rabbit, Run; Couples*

Vonnegut, Jr., Kurt. *Cat's Cradle; Slaughterhouse-Five; God Bless You, Mr. Rosewater*

Warren, Robert Penn. *All the King's Men*

POETRY

Allen, Donald (ed.). *The New American Poetry*

Basho. *The Narrow Road to the Deep North*

Baudelaire, Charles. *Flowers of Evil*

Blake, William. *Songs of Innocence*

Bly, Robert. *The Light Around the Body*

Brautigan, Richard. *Rommel Drives Deep Into Egypt, The Pill Versus the Springhill Mine Disaster*

Corso, Gregory. *Long Live Man*

Creeley, Robert. *For Love, Words*

cummings, e.e. *Poems, The Enormous Room*

Ferlinghetti, Lawrence. *A Coney Island of the Mind*

Ginsberg, Allen. *Reality Sandwiches*

Giovanni, Nikki. *Black Feeling, Black Talk*

Hughes, Langston. *Selected Poems*

Jones, LeRoi (ed.). *The Moderns*

Kandel, Lenore. *The Love Book, Word Alchemy*

Lamantia, Philip. *Selected Poems*

Levertov, Denise. *O Taste and See, Sorrow Dance*

Patchen, Kenneth. *Hallelujah Anyway, Hurrah for Anything, Because It Is*

Plath, Sylvia. *Ariel*

Rich, Adrienne. *Necessities of Life*

Rimbaud, Arthur. *The Drunken Boat*

Sexton, Anne. *Live or Die, Love Poems*

Snyder, Gary. *The Back Country, Regarding Wave*

Wakoski, Diane. *Inside the Blood Factory*

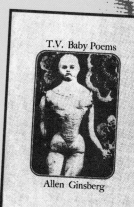

T.V. Baby Poems

Allen Ginsberg

Whalen, Philip. *On Bear's Head*

Whitman, Walt. *Leaves of Grass, Specimen Days*

Williams, William Carlos. *Paterson*

Yevtushenko, Yevgeny. *Bratsk Station*

SCIENCE FICTION AND FANTASY

Asimov, Isaac. *The Foundation Trilogy*

Baum, L. Frank. *Wizard of Oz* (series)

Beagle, Peter. *A Fine and Private Place, The Last Unicorn*

Bradbury, Ray. *The Martian Chronicles, Fahrenheit 451*

Burgess, Anthony. *A Clockwork Orange*

Capek, Karel. *War With the Newts*

Carroll, Lewis. *Alice in Wonderland, Through the Looking Glass*

Clarke, Arthur C. *Childhood's End*

Dick, Philip K. *The Man in the High Castle*

Eddison, E.R. *The Worm Ouroboros* (trilogy)

Ellison, Harlan (ed.) *Dangerous Visions*

Heinlein, Robert A. *Stranger in a Strange Land*

Herbert, Frank. *Dune*

Le Guin, Ursula K. *The Left Hand of Darkness*

Lovecraft, H.P. *The Dunwich Horror, The Call of Cthulhu*

Miller, Jr., Walter M. *A Canticle for Leibowitz*

Milne, A.A. *Winnie the Pooh*

Peake, Mervyn. *The Gormenghast Trilogy*

Sturgeon, Theodore. *More Than Human*

Tolkien, J.R.R. *The Hobbit, Fellowship of the Rings* (trilogy)

Wurlitzer, Rudolph. *Nog*

BLACK POWER

Brown, H. Rap. *Die Nigger Die!*

Carmichael, Stokely, and Charles V. Hamilton. *Black Power: The Politics of Liberation in America*

Cleaver, Eldridge. *Soul on Ice, Post-Prison Writings and Speeches*

DuBois, W.E.B. *The Souls of Black Folk*

Gregory, Dick. *Nigger*

Jackson, George. *Soledad Brother*

Malcolm X and Alex Haley. *The Autobiography of Malcolm X*

RADICAL POLITICS

Deloria, Jr., Vine. *Custer Died for Your Sins: A Manifesto*

Fanon, Franz. *Wretched of the Earth*

Guevara, Che. *Guerrilla Warfare*

Hoffman, Abbie. *Revolution for the Hell of It, Steal This Book, Woodstock Nation*

Kupferberg, Tuli, and

Robert Bashlow. *1001 Ways to Beat the Draft*

Marcuse, Herbert. *One-Dimensional Man*

Millett, Kate. *Sexual Politics*

Mungo, Raymond. *Total Loss Farm*

Thoreau, Henry D. *Walden, Civil Disobedience*

Tung, Mao Tse. *Quotations from Chairman Mao*

DRAMA

Albee, Edward. *Who's Afraid of Virginia Woolf?, The Zoo Story, The Sandbox*

Garson, Barbara. *MacBird*

Grotowski, Jerzy. *Towards a Poor Theatre*

Hansberry, Lorraine. *To Be Young, Gifted, and Black*

Ionesco, Eugene. *Rhinoceros*

Jones, LeRoi. *Dutchman and the Slave*

McClure, Michael. *The Beard*

Stoppard, Tom. *Rosencrantz and Guildenstern Are Dead*

Hair ("The Tribal Love-Rock Musical")

Oh Calcutta! (in which Broadway let its hair down and took its clothes off)

PSYCHEDELIC DRUGS

Burroughs, William, and Allen Ginsberg. *The Yage Letters*

Castaneda, Carlos. *The Teachings of Don Juan: A Yaqui Way of Knowledge*

Hoffer, A., and Humphrey Osmond. *The Hallucinogens*

Huxley, Aldous. *The Doors of Perception, Heaven and Hell*

Leary, Timothy. *The Psychedelic Reader, High Priest*

Ludlow, Fitz Hugh. *The Hasheesh Eater*

Margolis, Jack S., and Richard Clorfene. *A Child's Garden of Grass*

Metzner, Ralph. *The Psychedelic Experience, The Ecstatic Adventure*

Rose, Panama. *The Hashish Cookbook*

PHILOSOPHY AND RELIGION

Black Elk. *Black Elk Speaks*

Campbell, Joseph. *The Masks of God*

Chardin, Teilhard de. *The Phenomenon of Man*

Dass, Baba Ram. *Be Here Now*

Dubos, Rene. *So Human an Animal*

Eiseley, Loren. *The Immense Journey*

Fuller, Buckminster. *Operating Manual for Spaceship Earth, Utopia or Oblivion*

Gurdjieff, Georges I. *Meetings With Remarkable Men*

Jung, Carl G. *Man and His Symbols*

Koestler, Arthur. *The Ghost in the Machine*

Merton, Thomas. *Seeds of Contemplation*

Okakura, Kakuzo. *The Book of Tea*

Ouspensky, P.D. *Tertiam Organum, The Symbolism of the Tarot*

Tzu, Lao. *Tao Te Ching*

Watts, Alan. **The Book:** *On the Taboo of Knowing Who You Are*

Yogananda. *Autobiography of a Yogi*

Bhagavad-Gita

I Ching

Tibetan Book of the Dead

NONFICTION, ESSAYS, AND CULTURAL MISCELLANY

Boorstin, Daniel. *The Image*

Brand, Stewart. *The Whole Earth Catalog*

Brown, Dee. *Bury My Heart at Wounded Knee*

Bruce, Lenny. *How to Talk Dirty and Influence People*

Carson, Rachel. *The Silent Spring*

Commoner, Barry. *Science & Survival*

Cremer, Jan. *I, Jan Cremer*

Dylan, Bob. *Tarantula*

Ehrlich, Paul R. *The Population Bomb*

Gibbons, Euell. *Stalking the Wild Asparagus, Stalking the Healthful Herbs*

Goodman, Paul. *Growing Up Absurd*

Greer, Germaine. *The Female Eunuch*

Harrington, Michael. *The Other America*

Hughes, Langston. *The Sweet Flypaper of Life*

Laing, R.D. *Knots, The Politics of Experience*

Lennon, John. *In His Own Write*

Mailer, Norman. *Armies of the Night, Why Are We in Vietnam?*

May, Rollo. *Love and Will*

McLuhan, Marshall. *Understanding Media, Mechanical Bride, The Medium Is the Massage* (with Quentin Fiore)

Miller, Henry. *The Air-Conditioned Nightmare, Big Sur and the Oranges of Hieronymus Bosch*

Mills, C. Wright. *The Power Elite*

Muir, John. *How to Keep Your Volkswagen Alive*

Nader, Ralph. *Unsafe At Any Speed*

Nin, Anais. *Diaries*

Nuttall, Jeff. *Bomb Culture*

Perls, Frederick S. "Fritz." *In and Out of the Garbage Pail*

Reich, Wilhelm. *The Function of the Orgasm*

Roszak, Theodore. *The Making of a Counter Culture*

Schoenfeld, Eugene. *Dear Doctor Hippocrates*

Sontag, Susan. *Against Interpretation*

Steinbeck, John. *Travels With Charley*

Thompson, Hunter S. *Hell's Angels*

Wolfe, Tom. *The Kandy-Kolored Tangerine-Flake Streamline Baby, The Electric Kool-Aid Acid Test*

Marshall McLuhen was a Canadian thinker whose pioneering book on mass communication, *Understanding Media* (1964), was more talked about than read. One of its famous dictums, "the medium is the message," was altered for the title of this 1969 "inventory of pictures and words."

As a tireless and generous champion of progressive causes and other writers, Allen Ginsberg was never far from a camera or a telephone. In a 1996 interview with this book's authors, Ginsberg explained his motivations thusly: "William Carlos Williams answered me when I wrote him a note. He gave me good advice, turned me on to poetry, and gave me a direction in life. I've always felt it's up to me to pass that on."

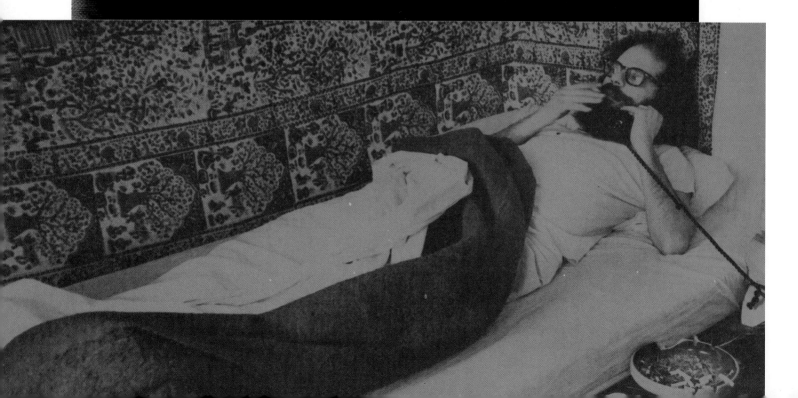

KESEY'S CRONIES

In 1971, upon the publication of *Kesey's Garage Sale*, Ken Kesey was asked to fill out an author's questionnaire by his publisher, Viking Press. This is standard publishing procedure. The information is used to generate interest in a book, prepare press releases, launch author tours, compile lists of those to whom review copies should be sent, formulate marketing strategy, and so forth. Never one for standard procedure on anything, Kesey took the opportunity to put Viking's publicity department through a different sort of acid test.

After filling in his name (Ken Kesey), the date (December 14, 1971), and his address (Pleasant Hill, Oregon), Kesey went into free fall, gluing portions of comic-book art onto each of the four pages of the document and answering questions about his education with enigmatic digressions like "Flutes all that I can see is if I'm to outdistance the picklocks I've either gotta keep changing doors or move into an unlisted cricket cage, while all the while swirling effluvium I admit in spite of advise [sic] to the contrary!" For his summary of his "other means of livelihood," he put, "I live in austere foolishness." His "brief summary of travels": "Over and back, sometimes tremulous, sometimes treacherous, sometimes tedious, like everybody's, I imagine...I been around, as they say." His "sports, skills, or other special pursuits": "I get high and pray a lot."

The portion of the questionnaire about which Kesey seemed most adamantly serious was the "brief list of people who will be interested in your book and whose influence is sufficient to warrant sending a complimentary copy in advance of publication." He filled two single-spaced pages with names. They are included here intact and verbatim—replete with misspellings and lack of punctuation—as a veritable who's who of the psychedelic years. The letters, too, are all capitalized, just as Kesey had it. The only part you'll have to imagine is his use of multicolored felt-tip pens.

"LEARY GINSERG FERLINGETTI BRAUTIGAN KRASSNER MCCLANAHAN MCMURTRY BERRY BOB STONE BOB KAUFMAN CAROLINE CASSIDY LENORE KANDEL BILLY FRITCH CARL LEHMAN HAUPT & SANDY MANSON WAVY GRAVY DONAVAN BESS GORDON LISH MAILER CRUMB GARCIA BRAND ROHAN COWLEY MCCLURE DYLAN KIRK DOUGLAS RINGO BABA RAM DAS TOM WOLFE TROCCHE TERMINAL ISLAND FEDERAL PRISON CALIFORNIA HERB CAEN CLEAVER GEORGE ODD BODKINS O'NEIL WAYNE MORSE PETE KNELL FRISCO HELL'S ANGELS ADELE DAVIS TOMMY SMOTHERS HENRY FONDA ROLAND KIRK CHIEF ROLLING THUNDER ZWERIN ANN HALPRIN JANN WERNER JACK KIRBY STEVE ALLEN DICK CAVETTE HELEN TAYLOR JOHN LENNON TINY TIM ED SANDERS GROUCHO MARX PAUL NEWMAN SALLY ELLIS WALT KELLY HUEY NEWTON FIEDLER ARLO GUTHRIE BECKETT DANNY KAYE GEORGIA O'KEEFE JERRY RUBIN MIKE MURPHY OZ IN LONDON A.R.E. ACLU CARLOS CASTANEDA JOHN SINCLAIR GILBERT SHELTON MOSCOSO S.CLAY WILSON ELVIS SPECTOR ANGELA "BUCKY" DR. HIP DAVID HARRIS ALI HAYAKAWA JACK CASSIDY JEFFERSON AIRPLANE MAMA CASS PAUL MCCARTNEY EMMET GROGAN JOAN BAEZ LORRE PAINE KAMLOOPS CANADA "HEAVY"—ANY BIKER HANGOUT IN EAST PALO ALTO LOU BRIEDENBACH JACKSON HOLE WHY JONI MITCHELL, all of whom are listed as bona fide switchboards for certain areas and reliable gossips anywhere."

THE MEDIUM MISSED THE MESSAGE

TV AND MOVIES IN THE '60S

RIGHTS, NOT FIGHTS

hen it came to psyche-delia, the conduits of mass communication with the deepest pockets and widest reach—film and television—were paradoxes as perplexing as an M.C. Escher drawing. On the one hand, a head was required to spend precious bread he or she generally didn't have to get into a movie theater. (There were no VCRs.) On the other hand, the televised emanations from three corporate networks—a simian out-pouring of what Frank Zappa called "the slime"—came free of

In this still from _Riot on Sunset Strip_ (1967), Hollywood takes aim at the generation gap and, as usual, misses the target.

charge and was accessible to every-one. Yet despite the fact that TV was the more democratized and afford-able medium, costing only precious time, big-screen flicks offered more accurate and insightful windows on the counterculture.

It was, in fact, no contest. TV fell mis-erably flat in this department, except as a medium for ironic entertainment—prefer-ably while drunk on cheap wine (Ripple, Boone's Farm, Richards Wild Irish Rose), stoned on weed, or high on both. Richard Meltzer, one of the wittiest and most wide-ly syndicated underground critics, used this aspect of TV wasteland as the hook for his columns. Writing about the medium under the pseudonym "Borneo Jimmy," he'd comb the channels of the Northeast, faithfully reporting on such staples of mainstream mass culture as televised bowling, roller derby, demoli-tion derby, boxing, game shows, pro wrestling (then a grunting blue-collar morality play, not today's slick specta-cle), suspense movies, cooking shows, and variety hours hosted by the likes of Lawrence Welk and Merv Griffin.

Meltzer reached the pinna-cle of antiestablishment fun in the May 1970 issue of _US: The Paperback Magazine_, which was devoted to "The Roots of Underground Culture." His "Lumpy Tomahawk Article" was ostensibly a review of _The Abbott & Costello Show_, a typically wrongheaded experiment whereby some of the duo's best

bits were chopped up and pack-aged as half-hour sitcoms (in hopes of snaring stoned hip-pies?). In it, Meltzer created a dead-on parody of _TV Guide_. Using the mag's familiar format, Meltzer interlaced capsule sum-maries of well-known shows—_Perry Mason, Jack Benny, Mr. Ed_—with those of his own invention: _Ruzz Whip_ (Western), _Marsh Fights_ (Science), _Dental Hints_ (Medicine), _Winky Dink & Me_ (Children).

In a "Close-up" of _The Web_ (Comedy), for instance, you find William Burroughs–style cut-up prose-nonsense that made an odd kind sense, if you were raised on TV: "Oliver buys 1,000 chicks as he tries to diversify the farm. The carpenters botch the building of a brooder. Only sightless passengers survive the crash of a plane carrying blind persons to a convention. Forced to depend on one another, they reveal Spot, the family's fire-breathing pet, in a household of mad-men seeking to obtain human heads for their ex-habit of murdering and robbing old men at seaside resorts."

In another of his columns, for Boston's _Fusion_ magazine,

The Rolling Stones perform on the oddly uncluttered stage of *The Ed Sullivan Show*, October 1964. "It took me 17 years to build this show," Ed fumed afterward. "I'm not going to have it destroyed in a matter of weeks....They'll never be back." But, of course, they were.

Meltzer nailed one of the telling moments of TV's inability to reach, or even to understand, its millions of young viewers. It occurred in late 1969 on *The Ed Sullivan Show*, a staple of live entertainment that was born with the medium (1948) and would soon die (1971). Ed had been burned in 1967 when Jim Morrison of the Doors ignored his order to amend a line with the word "higher" in it when the group performed "Light My Fire" on his show. But because his sagging ratings demanded that Ed give "the young people" another chance, he booked Steppenwolf. After they'd performed "Born to be Wild," Ed sidled over to the glowering, leather-clad band. In his famously wooden style, he chatted with bassist Nick St. Nicholas, the freakiest-looking of the bunch.

As Meltzer wrote: "When Nick St. Nicholas was asked by Ed Sullivan who his favorite rock group was, he answered, 'A group from Greenwich Village called the Fugs' just to make it real clear for Ed Sullivan, but Ed thought he said, 'the Frogs' so he hadta say it over again, 'the Fugs,' and then Ed knew it was 'Oh, the Fugs' and Nick affirmed it, 'Yeah, the Fugs.'"

It was live television at its most painful, although examples of musical myopia were legion. If you were young and into music in the '60s, you grew accustomed to cringing through an hour of gruesomely unhip entertainment and clueless hosts who often mocked their rock and roll guests. All that suffering just to get to those few moments when the squares ceased their blathering and actual music got played.

One classic example of rock and roll's mistreatment on the boob tube came during the Rolling Stones' appearance on the *Hollywood Palace*, hosted by crooner, boozer, and Rat Pack rodent Dean Martin. The July 3, 1964, appearance of the Stones took place on the third day of their first trip to America. What a rude welcome they received! As Stones bassist Bill Wyman recalled in his memoir *Stone Alone: The Story of a Rock 'n' Roll Band*: "It quickly transpired we'd been set up for ritual slaughter by Dean Martin, who seemed inebriated throughout the show. He persistently insulted us on the air to grab cheap laughs, and between songs and commercial breaks he made such jokes as: 'Their hair is not long, it's just smaller foreheads and higher eyebrows,' and 'Now don't go away, anybody, you wouldn't want to leave me with those Rolling Stones, would you?'"

Harlan Ellison was another hip overseer of TV. More renowned as a sci-fi writer and savvy editor (his *Dangerous Visions* anthologies were required reading), Ellison moonlighted for the *L.A. Free Press*, one of the most widely circulated underground papers. His regular column, "The Glass Teat," was an icepick to the heart of the TV industry next door in beautiful downtown Burbank. Ellison suffered no fools and cut against the hippie-dippy grain of most readers, who preferred their critics gentle, like Paul Williams, or prone to absurdity, like Meltzer and Lester Bangs.

Typical of Ellison's "Glass Teat" columns was one from 1969 entitled "Poisoned by the Fangs of Spiro," a three-part marathon response to Vice President Agnew's televised diatribes about liberals,

hippies, et al. Not only did Ellison rebut the VP with equal venom, he trained his sights on the kids who'd been "touched by the grave bone hands of their parents." He begins, "If you think the hope for tomorrow lies solely in the young—as did I—be advised the poison has seeped down through the veins of the society to them." He then pointedly addresses the underground audience, "What are you people training yourselves to be? Redemption-stamp center clerks?"

Call it an early dose of tough love, because Ellison was one of the last of the true believers in countercultural revolution. As he put it, in the same column: "Punching, punching, trying to get through, trying to tell them they are our last, best hope, and if THEY sat there with prognathous jaws and Little Orphan Annie eyeballs the whole COUNTRY was doomed." All this, in a feature subtitled, "A Column of Opinion About Television." With a beat like TV, it's no wonder Ellison was always pissed off.

TV OR NOT TV?

Its massive failings notwithstanding, TV did make a few attempts to reach a more with-it audience. Take *The Monkees*, a dizzying sitcom that picked up where *A Hard Day's Night* left off. Never mind that the Monkees were, by comparison, the Prefab Four: a quartet assembled from hundreds of aspirants who answered a casting call. Through serendipity or luck of the draw, they evolved into a viable rock and roll combo whose music, made with considerable input

Deadpan comic Pat Paulsen was a fixture on *The Smothers Brothers Comedy Hour*. Though his comedic shtick included a perennial tongue-in-cheek run for the presidency, he garnered more than a few votes from people who were sick of "serious" candidates like Nixon, Rockefeller, and Humphrey.

from some of the finest songwriters, producers, and studio musicians on the scene, was spirited, catchy, and fun.

The same could be said of their manic show, a kind of Marx Brothers for teenyboppers that began airing in the fall of 1966. The Monkees reflected the frenetic pace and surreal tenor of growing up in the '60s. Moreover, despite its silly and syrupy moments (e.g., Monkee Davy's cringeworthy ballads), it was hipper than anyone had reason to expect. A teen-oriented sitcom that could make room for a Tim Buckley performance in one of its segments was not just cool but visionary. When that same teen combo handpicked Jimi Hendrix as its opening act for a cross-country concert tour, those heads who paid attention realized that the Monkees were in their camp after all. Even a theosophical acid-steeped academic like Timothy Leary found cause to celebrate the Monkees. "Oh, you thought [the Monkees' TV show] was silly teenage entertainment?" wrote Leary in *Politics of Ecstasy*. "Don't be fooled. While it lasted, it was a classic Sufi put-on. An early-Christian electronic satire. A mystic-magic show. A jolly Buddha laugh at hypocrisy."

The youthful audience heard and saw rock and roll on the boob tube via such outlets as the soporific *American Bandstand*, which since 1957 had molded the mainstream's image of well-behaved young people. Yet *Bandstand* never really adapted to the changing face of rock and roll in the '60s, and as early as 1964 more credible musical offerings such as *Shindig* and *Hullabaloo* began turning up in prime time. Then there was *Where the Action Is*, a half hour of rock and roll in the afternoon full of high jinks from hosts Paul Revere and the Raiders and their groovy guests. The Raiders skits were as goofy as it got, but where else could you see sights like black-clad punk rockers the Music Machine lip-synching their gruff hit "Talk Talk"—even though they were "singing" into telephones and playing guitars that were obviously not plugged into anything.

It was all a little silly, but at least those shows took a step in the right direction. That is to say, Mark Lindsay made a hipper rock and roll host than Dick Clark, Lloyd Thaxton, Steve Allen, or Dean Martin. Still, timorous television never really kept pace or offered a forum for rock as it matured and manifested itself in more psychedelic ways. These things were incomprehensible and downright frightening to guardians of the boob tube's moral code. Of course, multiple murders on *Mannix* or Jackie Gleason's boozy allusions were A-OK. Can anyone say "double standard"?

More "relevant" (new buzzword) were shows like *Then Came Bronson* (starring Michael Parks as a peace-loving biker) and *The Mod Squad*. The latter debuted in the fall of 1968, a month after the police riot at the Democratic Convention in Chicago. This "Hair"-y drama featured a trio of hippie crime-stoppers, including right-on black dude Linc, groovy blonde chick Julie, and a frizzy-haired "head" named Pete. There were lots of pregnant pauses, nodding of heads, and hip platitudes uttered by these three sensitive young fuzz, who couldn't be further removed from the reality of the brutality-prone LAPD whose ranks they joined as undercover cops. The show was produced by Aaron Spelling and advertised with this hook: "One black, one white, and one blonde."

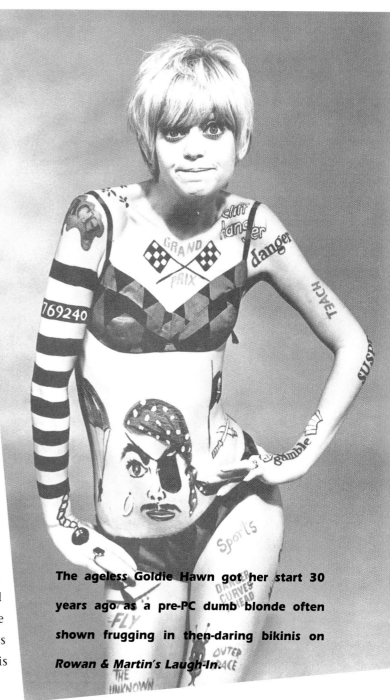

The ageless Goldie Hawn got her start 30 years ago as a pre-PC dumb blonde often shown frugging in then-daring bikinis on Rowan & Martin's Laugh-In.

157

A more authentic mirror of the counterculture could be found on two comedy shows: *The Smothers Brothers Comedy Hour* (1967–1975) and *Rowan & Martin's Laugh-In* (1968–1973). Tom and Dick Smothers rose from the ranks of the same politically aware folk-music crowd that spawned rebels like Bob Dylan, Phil Ochs, and Joan Baez. In fact, the latter's appearance on a March 1969 show got the Smothers' yanked off the air by their network, CBS, which objected to Baez's dedicating the song "Green Green Grass of Home" to "my husband David [Harris], who is going to prison soon." Harris was a draft resister, his imprisonment a *cause célèbre* within the antiwar movement.

Though soon reinstated, *The Smothers Brothers Comedy Hour* had a wobbly ride for the duration, eventually airing on—and being canceled by—all three networks. Nonetheless, regulars like Pat Paulsen, George Carlin, and Mason Williams piqued countercultural interest. Well in advance of Watergate, the late Paulsen's mock presidential campaigns reflected the degraded status of the highest office in the land in the eyes of an increasingly skeptical electorate. His campaign slogan: "We Can't Stand Pat." Song titles from his novelty record album, *Pat Paulsen for President*: "I Will Not Run," "I Will Not Serve," and "Freedom to Censor."

Laugh-In, as the name suggests, avoided serious politics, dealing with relevant topics through the comedic genius of regulars Lily Tomlin, Artie Johnson, and Henry Gibson (a proto-environmentalist), and the Smothers Brothers–style interplay of hosts Dan Rowan and Dick Martin. The latter duo were seasoned comics who'd lucked upon a new formula somewhere between pop art and psychedelia. The sets and costumes, particularly those worn by Goldie Hawn, were guaranteed to induce acid trails even if you were nowhere near a hit of windowpane.

Typical of *Laugh-In*'s big-umbrella approach was the September 16, 1968, appearance of Richard Nixon. Resorting to any stunt for a vote, he treated America to a rubbery nod of his head and a spirited "Sock it to me!" (a *Laugh-In* mantra, along with "You bet your sweet bippy!"). Maybe it helped put Nixon over the Hump(hrey) because, two months later, to our great collective misfortune, he was elected president. If so, that appearance would have reversed the media disaster of his 1960 campaign, which was sunk by his grim, oily appearance during televised debates with a suave, tanned, and telegenic JFK.

Oddly, some of the shows that never consciously tried to be hip became counterculture favorites. These include *The Twilight Zone*, hosted by Rod Serling. While the show originally ran from 1959 to 1965, it was just as popular in rerun syndication after that, as was *Outer Limits*—the precursor to *The X-Files*—which originally ran from 1963 to 1965. Some others that qualified as hip:

Mission: Impossible. Nifty theme song, incomprehensible plot lines (which made it all the more fun).

I Spy. Bill Cosby's first vehicle, which found him teamed with Robert

Culp in TV's first interracial "buddy" show.

Man From U.N.C.L.E. A sharp, sophisticated detective show featuring the well-coiffed David McCallum.

Get Smart. Smart, savvy satire of the spy game, complete with a bumbling intelligence agent (Maxwell Smart), his attractive counterpart (Agent 86), and the sort of inflated evil empire of an enemy (CHAOS) that could only have been dreamt up during the Cold War.

One can't, of course, forget *Star Trek.* Although it only lasted three years (1966–1969) and 78 episodes, it caught the imagination of heads and spawned a generation of Trekkies, as well as reincarnated spinoffs. In addition to playing captivating characters on the small screen, Leonard Nimoy (Spock) and William Shatner (Captain Kirk) made several of the most bizarre recordings of all time (see Rhino's *Golden Throats* anthologies).

Those with a well-cultivated sense of the absurd could enjoy the antiestablishment humor of *The Beverly Hillbillies*, especially its depiction of the shameless banker Milburn Drysdale. By making oil barons of the Clampetts, a decent but destitute family from the Ozarks, and relocating them to Beverly Hills, this sitcom classic was able to satirize the grasping, bankrupt materialism of affluent postwar urban dwellers. It was unfailingly hilarious on almost every subject, including the counterculture. Try meditating on this plot synopsis: "Jethro reads a book about yoga and decides to become a guru, much to Granny's disgust." There were also chuckles to be had watching those episodes in which Jethro, as the leader of a hippie cult, adopted the mantle of "Robin Hood of Griffith Park." When Granny informed them she was going home to fetch "a little pot," the hippies' eyes grew appreciatively large.

The most psychedelic shows of all might have been the sitcoms *Green Acres*, *Bewitched*, and *I Dream of Jeannie*. The first of these centered around the character of Oliver Douglas (played by Eddie Albert), a New York lawyer who opted out of the rat race to become a rural farmer. Instead of bucolic bliss, he found himself in an alternate universe where daily life meant stumbling through a parade of hilarious, Kafkaesque situations and misunderstandings. "Heads" were particularly amused by Arnold Ziffle, the talking pig.

Bewitched related the comic travails of the Stevens family. Husband Darrin was a straitlaced ad exec, wife Samantha a witch who could make things happen with a twitch of her nose. Those into theories of deconstruction might interpret *Bewitched* as an early treatise on the empowerment of women. Along the same lines, *I Dream of Jeannie*'s main character was a genie in a bottle who subverted reality with a brisk nod of her head. Her "master" was an air force major, and her antics often upended his world and the military. Countercultural wish fulfillment, perhaps?

TO BBC OR NOT TO BBC?

Despite the profound differences in broadcasting systems, popular

TV fare in the U.K. revealed much the same pattern as that in the States. The overwhelming amount of TV time in Britain was similarly boring and/or wrongheaded adult fare. Only a few shows spoke to the young either directly or in a more coded, clandestine manner. It should be noted that British TV, despite the government's direct control over content via the BBC, nonetheless had a rich tradition of broadcast satire. Predecessors to the no-holds-barred zaniness of *Monty Python's Flying Circus* (which began airing in 1969) included the radio comedy *The Goon Show* (1949–1960) starring Spike Milligan, and the comedy troupe *Beyond the Fringe*.

Originally a stage revue starring Peter Cook, Dudley Moore, Alan Bennett, and Jonathan Miller, *Beyond the Fringe* was so popular that it moved to TV, where it aired from 1962 to 1966. Simultaneously, a more strictly satiric political revue, *That Was the Week That Was* (or *TW3*), created a swirl of controversy from 1962 to 1964, before being yanked off the air. The parallels between the fate of *TW3* in the U.K. and *The Smothers Brothers Comedy Hour* in the States are inescapable.

For the real heads, there was the Carnaby Street cool of *The Avengers* and the inscrutable futurist drama of *The Prisoner*. For the kids there was *Do Not Adjust Your Set* (afternoon humor in an antic style that would later serve Pee-Wee Herman well) and musical variety shows like *Colour Me Pop* and *Top of the Pops*. Occasionally there'd be some odd special like the Beatles' *Magical Mystery Tour*, thoroughly trounced by the critics as the first outright Fab Four failure. *The Rolling Stones' Rock and Roll Circus*, an hourlong special filmed for the BBC in December 1968, would (alas) not be seen or heard until 1996. The Stones didn't like their own performance in it, which somehow seems a perfect commentary on the medium's inability to capture the dynamism of rock even in its liveliest moments. The tube just couldn't keep pace with the music.

That's about it for television and the counterculture. Even now, it seems amazing that television did not grasp the bankable concept of live rock and roll—despite record-breaking ratings for Elvis, the Beatles, the Stones, et al.—until the real rebellion was over. Even beyond TV's lame coverage of rock and roll, think of how the counterculture was ridiculed in almost every way on the boob tube, whose shows projected little more than ignorance on the part of its creators. In fact, television—with its uncanny knack for co-opting subversion—could be seen as the enemy. The dominant medium of our time did nothing but widen the Generation Gap while disillusioning the young to the point they found other places to go and things to do than lay around watching TV.

Perhaps the great CBS newsman Edward R. Murrow said it best at the start of the television age: "This instrument can teach, it can illuminate and, yes, it can inspire. But it can do so only to the extent that humans are determined to use it to those ends. Otherwise it is nothing but wires and lights in a box."

TEN REASONS WHY MOVIES WERE BETTER THAN TV IN THE '60S

1. Movie-making was an older, more mature medium of expression. Counter theory: The golden years of TV were its earliest days, when the possibilities of the new medium seemed boundless (see Murrow quote, above) and geniuses like Imogene Coca, Ernie Kovacs, and Milton Berle were able to indulge their proto-psychedelic imaginations. Modified theory: TV entered its troubled adolescence in the '60s, squandering its early promise by descending to formulaic pabulum.

2. TV advertisers would pull the plug on anything controversial or original. Movies, on the other hand, thrived on scandal and titillation.

3. Film-star personae were more culturally incisive, beginning with James Dean and Marlon Brando and then taking a giant rock-and-roll step forward with Elvis Presley. As early as 1959, Jack Kerouac was calling these three the avatars of a "revolution of love."

4. Despotic entertainment conglomerates like Disney-Capital Cities, Sony, and Time-Warner didn't exist. Most decisions were made by a monarchy of individuals, some of whom were enlightened. The shortsighted, cynical end of existing only to satisfy shareholders never entered into the, ahem, picture.

5. More talent was brought to bear on movies, which were seen as less ephemeral and thus more attractive to visionaries—i.e., directors who perceived themselves as auteurs, actors who considered themselves artists.

6. The lengthy process of making a film allowed more opportunity for a communal mind-set to emerge. The viewing of movies, too, had a ritualistic group-identity quality.

7. Hollywood had been quietly infiltrated by psychedelia as a recreational pastime (and spiritual quest). Pot, hashish, mescaline, peyote, and LSD were already in wide use among the film set by the late '50s.

8. The desire to see the latest foreign flick was deeply ingrained in the hip cognoscenti of the '60s. To supply that need, lovingly run repertory theaters emerged in urban centers and college towns, becoming hip havens.

9. The underground press allocated almost as much space to movies—particularly foreign, avant-garde, and radical ones—as they did to music, subtly reinforcing the priorities of "heads." Oddly, that pattern in the print media still survives at the expense of book review space, while the "product" of Hollywood grows ever more mindlessly crass—little more than fiery explosions, heinous plots, and cretinous characters (heroes and villains alike). As for film critics, those who aren't terminally jaded and disgruntled are essentially paid hirelings of studio publicity departments.

10. Finally, even if an avant-garde film made no sense, it was likely to have a good psychedelic soundtrack. Two cases in point:

Michelangelo Antonioni's *Zabriskie Point* and Jean-Luc Godard's *One Plus One*, apocalyptic films about revolution made in 1969. Though hip critics fell over themselves to praise them as "visionary" and "important," the films, in retrospect, are tedious and incoherent. Nonetheless, the former's soundtrack was composed by Jerry Garcia and Pink Floyd (among others), while the latter employed the music of the Stones. Both soundtracks still sounds fresh.

THE GOOD, THE BAD, AND THE UGLY

The role that films played in pushing the cultural revolution during the '60s is undeniable. But the decade itself was divided. Movies (like music) dropped hints of what was to come but really exploded after about 1967. As Richard Staehling, a freelance artist living in Hollywood in 1969, wrote in the December 27, 1969, issue of *Rolling Stone*: "The years 1955–1964 seem to be light years away from the world we live in today. Catch a few teen flicks on *The Late Show* and see just how long ago those years really are." In hindsight, the period 1960–1964 indeed had more in common with the late '50s' than with the '60s' furious finale, insofar as the way its realities were reflected in film.

Consider that dated juvenile-delinquent fare like *The Young Savages* ("As Timely As Today's Headlines!") was still being released in the early '60s. Parents were lulled by a different sort of genre film from 1963 to 1967: the simple-minded rebellion of "beach flicks" starring Fabian, Annette, and Frankie Avalon. These hugely popular films were often redeemed by the music that filled them (Beach Boys, Dick Dale, Elvis Presley) and for waxing the board for *Endless Summer* (1966). The latter was Bruce Brown's wave-breaking documentary on surfing that managed to capture the inexpressible longing of wayward youth—searching the world for the "perfect wave"—that would soon emerge on America's center stage.

Filmmakers and the film industry weren't necessarily better in the 1960s than in previous decades. Nor did they have any greater respect for defiant youth or alternative lifestyles (to borrow a latter-day phrase). We'd even go so far as to suggest that films in the '60s got it wrong as often as TV did. But with so much more youth-oriented cinema floating around, sooner or later some of it had to hit the target. Generally speaking, the films that did accurately mirror the cultural upheavals of the '60s were more sophisticated and experimental in technique and less blatantly exploitative of "teen culture."

As Richard Staehling rather hopefully put it, "The era when cheap and sleazy films sold well with kids is over. One may be able to make films for them, but the days of exploiting them have passed. Today you have to be good to make it; or at least you have to give the impression of being good. Assembly-line movie-making is over, the medium is the message, and so on and so forth."

Here is a list (offered with no pretense of being definitive) of some of the best films from the 1960s. Some are important, some may even be visionary, but all qualify as road maps through the psychedelic years:

Alice's Restaurant. Arlo's rambling draft-dodger parable struck a chord with "heads." Sometimes funny, sometimes poignant, sometimes boring.

Barbarella. Jane Fonda dolled up by hubby Roger Vadim as a futurist Barbie. As unpromising as that sounds, it's actually an arresting, quirky film, written by Terry Southern, with great light-show visuals.

Blow-Up. The ultimate flick about Swinging London that will leave you wondering, "What is reality?" Director Antonioni said, "I like everything today's young people do, even their mistakes, their doubts." Music by Herbie Hancock and the Yardbirds.

In *Blow-Up*, a hip photographer played by David Hemmings (standing) searches for the meaning of life and the nature of reality. He finds neither at this London pot party.

The latter were filmed live at a mod club, with Jeff Beck destroying a guitar.

Bonnie & Clyde. In retrospect, a cautionary tale for '60s radicals.

Butch Cassidy and the Sundance Kid. See *Bonnie and Clyde.*

Cool Hand Luke. Paul Newman never failed to communicate hipness.

Don't Look Back. Bob Dylan insulting everyone in sight on a London solo tour. Charisma + bile = genius.

Dr. Strangelove. Gallows humor for the nuclear age.

Easy Rider. An uneasy *On the Road* for the 1960s, in which biker brothers head off to find America and crash into its homicidal underside instead. Great soundtrack music by Steppenwolf, Roger McGuinn, and the Byrds.

The Good, the Bad and the Ugly. Spaghetti Western with soul. All of Clint Eastwood's sagebrush morality plays made super drive-in entertainment.

I Am Curious (yellow)
The complete scenario of the film by Vilgot Sjöman with over 250 illustration[s]

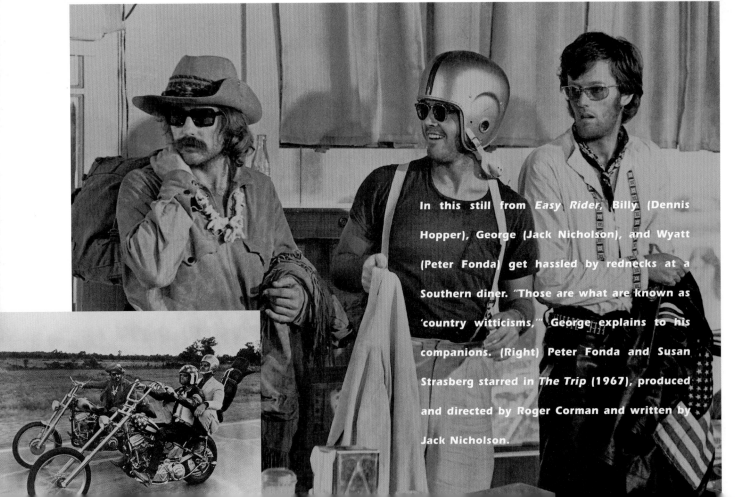

In this still from *Easy Rider*, Billy (Dennis Hopper), George (Jack Nicholson), and Wyatt (Peter Fonda) get hassled by rednecks at a Southern diner. "Those are what are known as 'country witticisms,'" George explains to his companions. (Right) Peter Fonda and Susan Strasberg starred in *The Trip* (1967), produced and directed by Roger Corman and written by Jack Nicholson.

The Graduate. In which the old generation tries to seduce the young. You could subliminally hear the Generation Gap widening in the songs of Simon and Garfunkel and the acting of Dustin Hoffman and Anne Bancroft.

Harold & Maude. Unfunny black comedy that became a cult-film staple of midnight shows.

Head. The Monkees experimental, film-length retort to those who didn't find them sufficiently hip.

How I Won the War. Antiwar satire by Richard Lester, with John Lennon as Private Gripweed (a still from which made the cover of *Rolling Stone*'s first issue).

I Am Curious (Yellow). A controversial and thus popular "art film" disguised as softcore porn then, and a total bore now.

If. A brainy slab of relevance from Britain's Lindsay Anderson, who later made *O Lucky Man.*

M*A*S*H. A slice of life during wartime, liberally dosed with the kind of wry humor it takes to get by under duress. Those who served or faced serving in Vietnam understood. *McCabe and Mrs. Miller* and *Brewster McCloud* completed a trilogy of great films written and directed by Robert Altman.

The Magic Christian. What a weird and wonderful crew hammered this together. Peter Sellers and Ringo Starr starred, Terry Southern wrote the script, Badfinger provided the soundtrack.

Medium Cool. Among the least dated films of the decade, this meditation on violence and TV looked back in horror at 1968 from the vantage point of '69. Written, directed, and filmed by Haskell Wexler, with an evocative soundtrack by Mike Bloomfield.

Midnight Cowboy. Outcasts Jon Voight and Dustin Hoffman slum around and barely survive the filthy, menacing streets of New York.

Monterey Pop. The counterculture's highwater mark and weekend-to-remember, with career-making exposure for Jimi Hendrix and Janis Joplin and explosive sets by the Who and Otis Redding.

Performance. An unnerving film in which a gangster on the lam hides out at the mansion of a decadent rock star (played by a typecast Mick Jagger). Phenomenal score involving a diverse cast: Jack Nitzsche, Randy Newman, Ry Cooder, Merry Clayton, the Last Poets, and Jagger.

Privilege. Rock star as Messiah; precursor to the Who's *Tommy.* The lead character was played by Paul Jones (singer for Manfred Mann), who wrested the part from Eric Burdon (of the Animals). The latter was deemed too short to play the role alongside costar Jean Shrimpton, the leggy model.

The Producers. Mad-like mayhem from Mel Brooks and Zero Mostel. The film-within-a-film *Springtime for Hitler* had "heads" rolling in the aisles.

Psych-Out. Jack Nicholson as "Stoney," ponytailed leader of a band called Ramblin' Jimi. Great period footage of the Haight, as a deaf girl searches crash pads for her lost brother. He kills himself, she winds up teetering about the Golden Gate Bridge on a bad trip. Groovy! Music by the Seeds and Strawberry Alarm Clock. Produced by Dick Clark. (Huh?)

Putney Swope. Demented "black humor" at the expense of the ad industry, by Robert Downey. Its chief virtue is a series of ad parodies.

Revolution. The movie isn't much, being the story of a beautiful blonde "who went to San Francisco and illegally changed her name from Louise to Today." (A good hippie chick, "Today believes that napalm is more harmful than LSD....Today learns more from talking with a little black kid on Haight Street than she did in school.") But the soundtrack featured vintage tracks by Quicksilver (an electrifying "Codine"), Mother Earth, and Steve Miller.

Trash. One of few watchable Andy Warhol films.

The Trip. Written by and starring Jack Nicholson, with Peter Fonda tripping his brains out to the music of the Electric Flag in hopes that an LSD experience might help him decide whether or not to divorce his wife. Directed by Roger Corman, king of the B movies.

Two-Lane Blacktop. James Taylor in a quixotic role, costarring Beach Boys drummer Dennis Wilson.

2001: A Space Odyssey. Stanley Kubrick's still mind-blowing masterpiece about mankind's past, present, and future. *2001* became one of the first "pothead" movies. It didn't do too spectacularly well on release, but word of mouth within the hip community made it a cult classic.

What's Up, Tiger Lily? Total comic subversion by Woody Allen, in which he obtained rights to a low-budget Japanese detective flick and overdubbed English-speaking voices uttering non sequiturs. (Sample dialogue: [pointing to blueprint] "This is Wingfat's house." "You mean he lives in that piece of paper?")

The Wild Angels. After directing countless horror films aimed at the drive-in crowd, Roger Corman turned to teen exploitation. This 1966 biker flick was a rumble-filled precursor to *Easy Rider*, without the social content, compassion, or message. In short, it was (and is) a great movie to watch with 10 of your drunkest friends.

Wild in the Streets. America's version of *Privilege*, in which a rock-star president named Max Frost marches all those over 30 into internment camps, where they are force-fed LSD. Inspired casting: Richard Pryor as a rock drummer.

Yellow Submarine. The Beatles' movie-length psychedelic cartoon.

On the foreign-film front, you can add to that list Fellini (*La Dolce Vita*, *8½*, and *Satyricon*), Bergman (*The Seventh Seal*), Godard (*Weekend* and *Breathless*), and Truffaut (*400 Blows*, *Jules and Jim*).

In addition, a number of films were made before the more tumultuous events of the '60s but got adopted (often ironically) by the counterculture as cult classics. While never intending to do so, they spoke—if only indirectly—to the psychedelic experience. These include *Fantasia*, *The Wizard of Oz*, *Reefer Madness*, *Freaks*, *Mondo Cane*, *Citizen Kane*, *Casablanca*, *Jason and the Golden Fleece*, *Night of the Living Dead*, *The Seven Samurai*, *Un Chien Andalou*, and any Japanese science-fiction movies featuring Godzilla or Mothra. And don't forget the bosom-flaunting oeuvre of trash-flick king Russ Meyer (*Vixen*, *Mudhoney*, *Faster Pussycat...Kill! Kill!*).

FILMED IN LIVING PATHECOLOR

A film that typically got it wrong in 1967 was a "shockumentary" called *Mary Jane*, starring the talentless Fabian. Dramatizing "the facts behind the marijuana controversy," the story line is simple: "Five kids smoked it—Two are in the hospital, One in jail...and the others have blown their minds!" Filmed in "Pathecolor" (as in pathetic), *Mary Jane* is so godawful it doesn't even qualify as *Reefer Madness*–style kitsch.

One film that does qualify for so-bad-it's-good honors is *Riot on Sunset Strip*. It employs quasi-documentary voiceovers ("Yes, today's youngsters are no different than they were in my day") while purporting to comment on the youth problem. So out of touch are the filmmakers that they have the wannabe hippie and main corrupting force drive a jalopy with "Rah-Rah" scribbled on its rumble seat. The action culminates in the ritual defrocking of a good but misguided girl (her parents are—gasp!—divorced) who has been slipped acid in her diet soda. Loosed from her middle-class moorings, she performs a sexy dance to some of the most comically skanky acid rock ever recorded. (You know, the kind of music that would be playing whenever Sgt. Joe Friday gravely invaded a crash-pad crime scene in *Dragnet*.) Then she was led upstairs in a rich boy's mansion to her moral decay. Neither the deflowering nor the riot are shown. On the bright side, the footage of the Standells' rave-up performance at Pandora's Box (the kids' fave club) is a garage-rock pinnacle.

Shortly after *Riot* the same crew (producer Sam Katzman, director Arthur Dreifuss) brought out *The Love-Ins*. It's an outraged take on an opportunistic Tim Leary figure named Jonathan Barnett. On a TV show hosted by Joe Pyne (the Rush Limbaugh of the '60s), Barnett urges everyone to take LSD. He then

Hauled down to the hoosegow in *Riot on Sunset Strip*.

The sci-fi flick *Barbarella* starred Jane Fonda, with screenplay by Terry Southern and production by Dino De Laurentis. The film's influence surfaced in an unlikely way in the '80s when one of the most popular groups of the New Wave era, Duran Duran, took its name from a robot in the film.

impregnates a college coed, who attempts suicide when he prods her into an abortion. Barnett is "destroyed" at one of his own happenings and becomes a hippie martyr. It's blatant propaganda but still a must-see for the ham-handed hippie happenings, with music by the Chocolate Watchband and the UFOs.

The bottom feeders who created this sort of fare are the same ones who thought nothing of using *Time-Life*–hyped hippie excess as an excuse for adult sexploitation flicks. Their films—which bore titles like *Sock It To Me Baby* (1968), *Love Commune* (1969), *Weird World of L.S.D.* (1969), and *Sweet Bird of Aquarius* (1970)—were really soft-core porn that revealed how jealous the older generation was of the "free love" of the young. But a retrospective immersion reveals them to be—underneath all the bobbing boobs, throbbing flesh, and headbands—as reactionary and anti-youth as the hard hats who routinely kicked the shit out of antiwar protesters.

Fairly typical is a 1968 film called *The Acid Eaters*, which billed itself as "Hollywood's first underground film." Directed by one B. Ron Elliott and starring Bucky Buck and Bob Wren, the plot involves a loose-knit gang of young couples who gather after work to blow off steam. They ride their Harleys in formation to a pond, disrobe (only their tops; bottoms demurely stay on). They frolic in the water. (Sample dialogue: "You got the pot?" "Yeah, four sticks....Ready to fly?") They see a pyramid. They wander over. They climb on. They eat chunks the size of ceiling tiles (made of Styrofoam, which crunch awkwardly). They enter the pyramid and find Satan, who tells them they're on LSD. Satan stokes their acid furies with his pitchfork. The chaos builds to a jam from Hell, culminating with the blonde bombshell jiggling toplessly to a bongo player.

Not to flog a dead jackass, but "stupid" doesn't begin to describe these films. Their only use is to show how everything—every single detail—about psychedelia was usually depicted inaccurately. For starters, the music by Billy Allen (who?)

is worse than anything you might hear at a roller rink—a shotgun wedding of Booker T. and Al Hirt. The actors look more like thugs or swingers, the very people who'd beat hippies up. They ride huge choppers in the manner of Hell's Angels—anti-hippies who symbolically ended the psychedelic era at Altamont when they went on a boot-stomping rampage. They speak in clichés that would have gotten them pegged as narcs in any crowd of real hippies.

Finally, Hollywood betrayed a lack of courage even when it tried to get it right. Always, it sided with the adult point of view, depicting the youth revolt as pointless or doomed. Two of the biggest blunders were *Getting Straight*, starring Elliott Gould as a liberal English professor (read: elbow patches and bushy mustache) caught in a student uprising, and *The Strawberry Statement*. How the latter wound up being so lame is a mystery, since it was based on a credible firsthand account by a participant in the uprising at Columbia University.

By and large, TV and movies missed what was going on in the '60s and have never really gotten it right in the decades since, even with benefit of hindsight. It is no mystery why the counterculture generally looked elsewhere—record albums, rock festivals, hallucinogenic drugs, underground writings, paintings and posters, the out-of-doors, and their own navels—for entertainment, enlightenment, and input.

CAN YOU DIG IT?

HIP LINGO OF THE PSYCHEDELIC ERA

For one blissful moment in time, psychedelia was a secret society with its own music, art, rituals, dress, attitude, and speech. The unenlightened "silent majority"—the latter a newspeak term coined by the wretched Richard Nixon—could only stand by the wayside and scratch their heads in confusion, wonder, or disgust. The waves of tourists who flocked to San Francisco during and after the Summer of Love did all of the above from the safety of their bus seats on Gray Line excursions through Haight-Ashbury. A

Suits-and-ties meet Sgt. Pepper's couture at the Electric Circus nightclub in New York City.

few people are probably still scratching their heads over some of the manifestations of Flower Power.

Nonetheless, in times of profound cultural upheaval—such as the psychedelic explosion of the late 1960s—mainstream society has a way of adapting to radical behavior. That is, they eventually co-opt and thereby tame it. The most visible aspects of cultural revolt are simply absorbed into fashion, design, and patterns of speech.

Sometimes it takes more than one revolt to introduce a term into common parlance. Take the word *groovy*. This hip coinage dates back to the late Thirties, when jazz musicians employed it as a shortened form of "in the groove," a phrase that meant somebody was playing with consummate ease, the way a phonograph needle glides in the groove of a record. Bing Crosby, of all people, offered this definition to San Francisco Chronicle columnist Herb Caen in 1938: "In the groove means just right, down the middle, riding lightly and politely, terrific, easy on the ears." The adjectival derivative groovey was adapted by the Beats (e.g., "A hip chick is a groovey chick") before falling from popular usage, only to be revived in the mid-Sixties as groovy, minus the "e." Dig? Groovy.

Lawrence Lipton's landmark study, *The Holy Barbarians* (1959) reveals that a number of terms alleged to be a part of every hippie's vocabulary were actually handed down from the Beats, who themselves borrowed heavily from the slang of inner-city blacks, as well as petty criminals and dope addicts like Herbert Huncke. The Beat terms most widely used by hippies include the following. The terms are taken from Lipton's 1959 glossary, while the definitions are ours:

Ax. A musical instrument, usually an electric guitar; as in "Hendrix set fire to his ax at Monterey!"

Ball. Sexual intercourse; as in "Did you ball that groovy chick you met in the park, man?"

Bread. Money, of which your average hippie had precious little, necessitating begging: "Brother, can you spare a little bread?" To which the typical response was, "Get a job."

Busted. Apprehended by the law, as in "I heard Panama Red got busted by the feds."

Chick. A female member of the species.

Dig. Not only to grasp fully the meaning of, but also to appreciate the beatific essence of, as in "Can you dig where I'm coming from?" Or, as the Friends of Distinction sang in "Grazing in the Grass": "I can dig it he can dig it she can dig it we can dig it they can dig it...."

Drag. A total bring-down. As

the Buckinghams sang, "Kind of a drag when your baby don't love you."

Far out. As Lipton so perfectly puts it, "If it sends you and you go, you may swing far out." The phrase almost went out of fashion after Arlo Guthrie and John Sebastian repeated it 800 times at Woodstock.

Flip out. Again Lipton nails it: "Anything from a fit of high enthusiasm to a stretch in the laughing academy." Hippies were known to flip out on acid, especially the suspect brown variety circulated at Woodstock.

Head. In Beat parlance, it meant someone who smoked pot. To hippies, it connoted someone who dropped acid or was generally hip to the scene. Synonyms: pothead, acidhead.

High. Euphoria, whether spontaneously induced (as in "natural high") or chemically stimulated (as in "I get high with a little help from my friends").

Holding. To be in possession of drugs, whether in your pocket, glove compartment, or posterior anatomical cavity.

Joint. To a beatnik, it could mean a place to hang out, but to a hippie it meant a marijuana cigarette, as in "Don't Bogart that joint, my friend." That last line comes from the chorus to "Don't Bogart Me," by the Fraternity of Man, which appeared in the soundtrack to *Easy Rider.*

Pad. The place where one crashed at the end of the day. A popular mock-sampler of the day read, "Bless This Pad."

Roach. The remaining end of a smoked joint, stuck in a clip and worth the risk of singeing your mustache because that's where all the THC got concentrated. "Be sure to hide the roaches," sang Crosby, Stills, and Nash in "Pre-Road Downs."

Split. As Robyn Hitchcock put it on his *Moss Elixir* album, "It's a quaint old-fashioned way to leave the room."

Stoned. To experience a chemically induced high, as in "I got stoned on some killer weed and forgot where I left my car keys." Synonym: wasted.

Turn on. One-third of Tim Leary's Holy Trinity ("Turn on, tune in, drop out"). It usually (but not necessarily) means to get high on drugs. It can also refer to scintillating new experience, as in "The new Tull album is a real turn-on!"

Of course, the psychedelic experience created a wealth of unique terms of its own that postdate the Beats. These include

Acid. Lysergic acid diethylamide, a.k.a. LSD. It is the drug that put a psychedelic gleam in the eyes of an entire generation. LSD also gave rise to its own musical subgenre: acid rock.

Bag. Any activity, thought process, or pursuit of a personal nature, as in "I'm into a back-to-nature bag now."

Blow my mind. To be so thoroughly overwhelmed that your mouth is left agape, as in "Santana's 20-minute guitar solo blew my mind!"

Bong. A bulky pot-smoking device that cools the smoke by bubbling it through a water chamber. One bong hit is worth several tokes off a rolled joint. Afterward the bong water can be drunk, if you're a truly desperate stoner.

Bring down. To sour the mood with inappropriate negativity; used as a verb or noun. If your parents were to return home early and discover a pot party in progress, the ensuing confrontation would be a major bring-down.

Bummer. Something that depresses the individual or group mood. The use of pool cues and knives by Hell's Angels at Altamont, for instance, was a bummer.

Burn. To cheat, often in a drug deal. Synonym: rip-off.

Burn out. To reach the edge of one's synaptic tether, usually from having overindulged in drugs.

Clean. The opposite of holding. Presumably, you wouldn't be hassled by the authorities if you were clean, unless they took exception to the length of your hair. Which was likely.

Colombian gold. The best-quality marijuana in general circulation at the time, since eclipsed by sinsemilla and numerous advancements in the science of pot cultivation. Often, *gold* was a generic dope peddler's term for what could be anything from the real thing to oregano.

Contact high. Secondhand euphoria, sans drugs, brought on by mere contact with a roomful of stoned comrades.

Cop. As ironic as it may seem, the noun form of the word means policeman; the verb, to score drugs.

Crash. To sleep, perchance to dream, often after coming down off drugs.

Crystal meth. A pure form of street-vended speed whose capacity to burn out those who used it gave rise to the cautionary phrase "Speed Kills."

Doobie. A joint; pals who share one are known as "doobie brothers."

Double bummer. Twice as bad, like the second Vanilla Fudge album.

Dynamite. Explosively good, as in "This homegrown weed is dynamite."

Flashback. The unscheduled rerun of an LSD experience, the contrived threat of which was cited by establishment types as further evidence of the drug's hidden dangers.

Flick. Movie. To many '60s college students, "free flicks" at the student union were the only affordable entertainment.

Fox. A woman who looks provocatively erotic; not surprisingly, the subject of many rock songs. Examples: "Foxy Lady," by the Jimi Hendrix Experience, and "Twentieth Century Fox," by the Doors.

Freak. A hippie, plain and simple. Think of Arlo Guthrie surveying the crowd at Woodstock and exclaiming, "Lotta freaks, man!"

Freak out. To lose one's mind or to behave in a disturbed or crazy way.

Free love. Though no such thing as "free love" existed on as broad a plane as popular myth would have you believe, an abiding fantasy persists to this day that hippies were amoral satyrs hell-bent on balling till the cows came home (which, in the case of the fields at Woodstock, may have been close to actual fact). However, to a lot of hippie-hating lowlifes, "free love" was taken as license to sexually harass any hippie chick whose path crossed theirs; hitchhiking was a particularly risky way to encounter such slime.

Getting off. To begin to feel the effects of a chemical stimulant.

Grok. A profound level of digging something, taken from Robert A. Heinlein's hugely popular science-fiction novel *Stranger in a Strange Land.* Like "soma" in Huxley's *Brave New World,* the word "grok" is such an integral part of Heinlein's book that it was incorporated onto the cover of the paperback edition.

Groupie. A young woman who balls rock and roll musicians, particularly those who play a mean ax.

Hang up, hung up. To be obsessed with something to one's detriment.

Happening. A real gone get-together, often one held in a public park.

Hash. Hashish. One step up the psycho-chemical scale from pot.

Hassle. To be given grief by either "the man" (the authorities) or "the old man" (one's father, often perceived as an adversary), as in "My old man hassled me about my hair again."

Heavy. Serious and deep, like a philosophical concept or a guitar solo. When the Beatles sang, "She's so heavy," they were not referring to the weight of their wives and girlfriends.

Hit. A toke, as in "Hey, man, can I have a hit off that joint?" It can also mean anything from a swig off a jug to a "hit of fresh air" (from a hit song by Quicksilver Messenger Service).

Lid. An ounce of pot.

Man. A hip, all-purpose word used as a running conjunction to link phrases and thoughts. When overused, as in Dennis Hopper's depiction of the character Billy in *Easy*

Rider (loosely based on the real-life David Crosby), it can lead to unintentional self-caricature. The following excerpt is taken from *The Fan Man*, by William Kotzwinkle, one of the great surreal reads: "And out I go, man, into the bright sunlight, man, which is too bright, man, I must put on my special shades, man...." You get the idea.

Munchies. Severe hunger pangs brought on by smoking pot, often inspiring new taste treats based on what paltry fixin's are lying around the kitchen, if the brownies and Bugles have all been eaten. Some improvised munchies that have been personally witnessed by the authors and editors of this book: raisin-bran sandwich, chicken-skin burger, bacon and syrup sandwich, chocolate chip omelette, peanut butter and spinach sandwich. Generally, such concoctions seem somewhat less appetizing in the cold light of day.

Narc. Similar to a pig, except it has a mustache and pretends to be hippie in order to make undercover drug busts. A narc (or nark) was the most vilified thing one could be from the point of view of the counter-culture. Suspicion that one was a narc, whether grounded or not, would lead to extreme social ostracizing—or, in the case of this recitation from a Bonzo Dog Band song, parody: "With a geranium behind each ear and his face painted with gay cabalistic symbols, six-foot-eight, seventeen-stone police sergeant Jeff Bull looked jolly convincing as he sweated and grunted through a vigorous twist routine....His hot serge trousers flapped wildly over his enormous plastic sandals as he jumped and

Enterprising hippies use their group house near Dupont Circle in Washington, D.C., as a jewelry workshop. This jewelry was sold at The Source, "a psychedelic art store" on K Street, N.W. Note the poster on the wall advertising the recent April 1, 1967, Human Be-In. This national event, which took place in verdant Rock Creek Park, was modeled on the successful first Human Be-In in San Francisco on January 14, 1967. (Below left) A window display for a Dupont Circle head shop, April 1967. Among the display items are rock posters, incense sticks, hookah pipes, inflatable pillows, and Tuli Kupferberg's indispensable tome, *1001 Ways to Beat the Draft.*

jumped and gyrated towards a long-haired man. 'Uh, excuse me, man, I have reason to believe that you can turn me on,' he leered suggestively."

Nickel bag. Five dollars' worth of pot. Nowadays, five dollars' worth of pot would fill a joint the width of a toothpick.

Number. A joint, as in, "Roll another number for the road."

Off. After the thrill of Flower Power waned, this term was adapted from militant blacks to mean "kill" (as in "Off the pigs!"), although it was militant protesters who more frequently wound up getting offed.

Old lady. Girlfriend, wife, or mother.

Old man. Boyfriend, husband, or father.

Organic. Wholesome and free of hormones, pesticides, and other chemicals. Watch out for specks of dirt or droppings, though.

Out of sight. Groovy to the max, as in "Everything is all right, uptight, out of sight," per Stevie Wonder. Often run together as a one-word exclamation: "Outtasight!" Synonym: "It's a gas" (as in "Jumping Jack Flash").

Paranoid. The title of an agonizing lude-rock song by Black Sabbath describing a mental state that was the flip side of Flower Power, usually induced by harder drugs and darker thoughts.

Peace. A term of good wishes, equivalent to "Take care," "Have a nice day," or (as they said in truly olden days) "Godspeed."

By September 1967, when this pamphlet was published, the hippie lifestyle had already been codified. The not unsympathetic author—though misspelling the designated subject as "hippy"—describes hippies as "two generations past the Rebel Without A Cause and one past the Cool Generation....They're passionate. They're Believers."

Peaking. That point at which a trip reaches its climax. While peaking, you'll no doubt see things that really aren't there: trails, colors, fantastic shapes and forms. If it's a bad trip, you might see dancing bats, an angry anaconda, or Spiro Agnew's face.

Pig. Derogatory term for peace officer, not generally used within earshot of one by anybody with brains.

Plastic. Anything or anyone that's phony and shallow (e.g., "*American Bandstand* is so totally plastic, man").

Right on. The verbal equivalent of a clenched fist, expressing solidarity.

Rip off. Used as a verb or noun, it refers to being cheated, robbed, taken advantage of, or otherwise, well, ripped off.

Roach clip. That funny metal thing dangling from a freak's neck that you thought was an Egyptian pendant.

Rush. What happens when a drug suddenly takes effect.

Score. To acquire something, usually drugs, as in "I scored some Colombian Gold. Now I think I'll go score some Pecan Twirls."

Solid. Hippie's version of "simpatico"; a favorite word of Linc's on *The Mod Squad.*

Spaced out. To become disoriented or to daydream, often after consecutive days of drug-taking while forgetting to eat, bathe, or sleep.

Spare change. The occupational alternative for hippies disinclined to work. Usually spoken by one or several members of a group while sitting on a sidewalk with a dog around whose neck a kerchief has been knotted.

Speed freak. An abuser of methamphetamine; i.e., Neil Cassady.

The Hippy's Handbook's myopic guide to sartorial splendor.

Presenting a hippy fashion guide, I realize, is antithetical to the basic tenets of hippydom. Nevertheless, there are certain styles

BOY

AUSTRALIAN DIGGER HAT
FLOWER
SHADES OR GRANNY GLASSES
HAIR: LONG
BEARD AND/OR MUSTACHE
BEADS
PEACE BUTTON "make love not war"
SKIN TATTOO
FLOWERED SHIRT
FLUTE
GARRISON BELT & HIP-HUGGER PANTS
PEACE EYE
BOOTS OR BAREFEET

**NINE
A HIP
FASHION
GUIDE**

OR: WEAR A TEE-SHIRT, WORK SHIRT & DUNGAREES

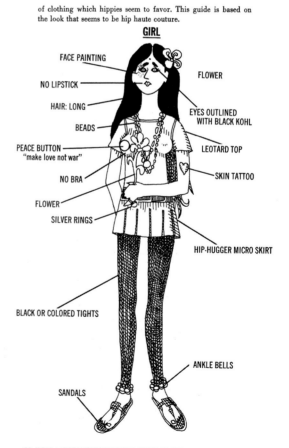

of clothing which hippies seem to favor. This guide is based on the look that seems to be hip haute couture.

GIRL

FACE PAINTING
NO LIPSTICK
HAIR: LONG
BEADS
PEACE BUTTON "make love not war"
NO BRA
FLOWER
SILVER RINGS
FLOWER
EYES OUTLINED WITH BLACK KOHL
LEOTARD TOP
SKIN TATTOO
HIP-HUGGER MICRO SKIRT
BLACK OR COLORED TIGHTS
ANKLE BELLS
SANDALS

OR: WEAR A LOOSE, FLOWER-PRINTED SMOCK OR ANKLE-LENGTH DRESS-PANTS

Stash. A hidden supply of drugs, often kept in one's stash box.

Strung out. A state of mental and physical fatigue brought on by excessive drug use, usually of harder drugs such as heroin and speed.

Toke. What Bill Clinton claims not to have done: that is, inhale a lungful of pot smoke.

Trails. Optical and spatial illusions brought on by acid.

Trip. A figurative journey under the influence of LSD. There are good trips and bad trips; one wished for the former and hoped to survive the latter.

Truckin'. The manner in which R. Crumb's cartoon characters walked, or the act of going about one's business as a matter of course. See the Grateful Dead anthem of the same name for further details.

Tube. Television; shortened from "Boob Tube."

Uptight. Having society's corncob up one's ass.

Vibe, vibes. The "vibrations," positive or negative, one senses in a given situation. The Beach Boys launched the term into general circulation with "Good Vibrations." Hippies, heads, and freaks often spoke of good vibes, meaning beatific radiance of the most positive sort. The antonym was bad vibes.

Wah-wah pedal. A psychedelic sound effect for the guitar operated by means of a foot pedal; cf. Cream's "Tales of Brave Ulysses."

Wasted. Too stoned to get off the couch and go to bed.

Weed. Marijuana.

Wiped out. Exhausted; borrowed from surfing lingo.

Wow. Delight or surprise beyond one's ability to express. Variation: "Oh, wow." Uttered a lot after Ten Years After played "Goin' Home" at Woodstock.

Zap. To paralyze someone with brilliance or chutzpah. Adapted by illustrator R. Crumb for his *Zap Comix* series.

Zonked, zonked out. Stoned or sleepy to the point of losing consciousness.

HIP CAPITALISM:
THIS IS NOT YOUR FATHER'S BUSINESS WORLD

After 1966, if you were the new longhair in town you did not need a road map or a set of intricate directions to locate the places you belonged. First, the smells would guide you: patchouli, musk, incense, cannabis, B.O. Then, the visuals would take over: Taoist yin-yang symbols, art nouveau swirls, peace signs, fluorescent paint, Hindu iconography, Tibetan mandalas, silhouettes of the Cheshire Cat and Mad Hatter, Asian calligraphy, inscrutable runes, cabalistic symbols, pyramids. Then, the sounds—often Jimi Hendrix Experience records—would serve as Sirens, calling you onto the rocks of psychedelia.

Some of these places called themselves "head shops." Head shops sold, according to Jeff Nuttall, "badges, beads, prayer wheels, joss sticks, and all the paraphernalia of pop Buddhism." (He left out rolling papers and posters.) At a head shop or other freak-friendly emporium, one could browse the merchandise for everything from hash pipes and roach clips to brown rice and megavitamins. You could outfit yourself for getting doped to the gills or take the organic, macrobiotic route. Or some strange combination thereof. There were no rules.

Barring any of the obvious sensory data above, one might simply recognize a head-friendly hangout by its very name. The following were handles employed by "hippie companies" in the '60s, all of them culled from underground papers.

Head Shops
The Zodiac, Head Imports, Fragile Sun, Four Heads, Do It, Ever-Lovin' Trading Post, the Psychedelic Shop, Mnasidika, Magic Theatre for Madmen Only, Middle Earth, Olfactory Incense Co., the Shrunken Head.

Clothing Shops
Fahrenheit, Dynamite & Co., Thee Sandal Cobbler, the Mod Shop, Sir Real, Awarehouse, Bottoms Up, the Great Pants Explosion, Wild Flower, Plaz, Chaldea, Merry Go Round, Skinnidippin, the Righteous Rag, Kicks & Lids, Shenanigans, the Mad Hatter, Rags and Riches, Biba, the Apple Boutique (Beatles-owned financial disaster), Granny Takes a Trip (run by artist-musician-designers Hapshash and the Coloured Coat), Zilch (Monkee Davy Jones' New York shop), Blimp (run by the Turtles' wives), Sat Purush (clothiers to the Strawberry Alarm Clock).

Record and Book Shops
Sights & Sounds, Gross National Product, Leaves of Grass, Circle of Sound, New Geology Rock Shop, Bookworm, Peace Eye, the Groove Company.

Music Clubs
Cats Cradle, Mr. Flood's Party, New Establishment, Childe Harold, the Matrix, Bottom of the Barrel, Psychedelly, Electric Circus, Kaleidoscope, the Trauma, Boston Tea Party, Cafe Wha?, the Travel Agency, the Trip, Cheetah.

Eats/Drinks
The Feedstore, Yellow Submarine, Eden Organic Foodstore, Noodle Nook, Drogstore Cafe, The I-Thou, the Blue Unicorn, Far-Fetched Foods, the Radiant Radish (Brian Wilson's short-lived health-food emporium!).

SILVER APPLES
CONTACT

A PLAGUE OF
CUTOUTS

THE
DREGS
OF
PSYCHEDELIA
UNEARTHED

STEREO

KAPP
KS-353

hings were very different for record buyers a few decades ago. For a long time we had cutout bins—clearinghouses for cheapie albums by staggeringly awful bands. These bins served as burial mounds for the wretched refuse of the late '60s, a time when an army of A&R men dragged every longhair with an electric guitar into a recording studio. Cutout bins served as the last stop before meltdown for unsold copies of these hapless releases.

The auteurs of Silver Apples, Simeon (left) and Dan Taylor, prepare for liftoff. Their final destination: K-mart cutout bins.

In their glory days, cutout bins offered a cornucopia of strange fruit to unwary adolescents such as ourselves. To comprehend all this, it is necessary to set the wayback machine to 1967 and take note of two pivotal events in the pop world: (1) the Beatles' turn to Nehru-jacketed psychedelia on *Sgt. Pepper's Lonely Hearts Club Band* and (2) the Top 10 success of Vanilla Fudge's debut album. A year later *In-A-Gadda-Da-Vida* by Iron Butterfly—an album whose title track was 17 minutes long!—shot to No. 4 and sold more than four million copies.

In the wake of these albums, record companies made haste to cop a slice of the lucrative magical mystery pie. Suburban garages and big-city crash pads were ransacked. Scores of barely rehearsed acts teamed up with staff producers accustomed to the likes of Al Martino and Bobbie Gentry. The results were pawned off as acid rock. It was not the shot heard round the world. It was the shot heard in the bedrooms of maladjusted adolescent males.

Though the bands and individuals responsible for these curios were soon forgotten, the records themselves refused to die. They returned as affordable cutouts, slashed to a mere fraction of their original list price. They would sit in discount department-store aisles, MIAs of a war now faded from memory. Their endless

baroque psychedelic covers—typified by mind-bending lettering and mind-boggling freaks cavorting against a background of jelly or Saran Wrap—lay limp in bins beside racks of madras beer visors and buckets of caramel corn.

And yet some of us actually purchased these artifacts. That is because in those days most any record that looked vaguely countercultural promised to be that philosopher's stone by which a frustrated adolescent living under the thumb of Mom and Dad might be transformed into the Wavy Gravy of his dreams. The cutout bins represented a veritable grail of treasures waiting to be unearthed for the price of a fountain Coke.

Given the sheer quantity of titles, there was one surefire criterion for getting straight to that 44-center that would free your mind (in hopes that your ass would follow): the album's jacket. Back then, any person who looked as if he would have been turned away from your parents' dinner table was presumed to be one step closer to bliss (or at least the West Coast) than you were. Moreover, that person was undoubtedly trying to tell you something important (e.g., "Hey mister please/I don't know your name/But I'll ask just the same/Have you seen my mind?"). The covers beckoned like decadent Sirens. A handful of bucolic longhairs strumming ukuleles beneath a rainbow of myriad hues was enough to entice an entire subculture to plunk down fistfuls of change.

On many a lonely adolescent K-mart Saturday, cutout addicts flipped through the bins with speed and agility, hoping some unfathomable gem lay buried between the endless piles of dreck: music of the Hawaiian islands, honky saxophone jive, singer/songwriters who made Bob Lind look manly, audio documentaries of the space program, and 10,000 copies of Sebastian Cabot reciting the poetry of Bob Dylan. (In hindsight, we should have snapped up the latter while we had the chance!) With the aid of a forklift, one carted his psychedelic bounty to the checkout counter, where a clueless matron with a hairy chin totaled the purchase: $4.32. Not bad for 18 albums.

What follows are capsule reviews of a small sampling of albums that got lost in the shuffle, only to turn up in cutout bins. It would be inaccurate to say you missed these LPs. But we suffered through this music. Now it's your turn.

The Fool by the Fool (Mercury). Filled with elfin, childlike imagery, *The Fool* sounds like what might have happened had Mister Rogers donned a Nehru jacket and tiptoed through Itchycoo Park. The Dutch hippies (two guys, two girls) who made up this wiggy band of designers worked for the Beatles' Apple firm—and should have stuck to artwork, based on this vapid release.

Resurrection by Aum (San Francisco). Those who frequent used record stores will recognize this mediocre title as a "repeater." The most noteworthy cut is the Gregorian chant–like "God Is Back in Town," a seven-minute epic capturing the religious views of swarthy guitarist Wayne Cevalos.

Phluph by Phluph (Verve). These cheerful lug nuts were hanging around the fringes of the ill-fated Bosstown Sound to wheel out some lame psychedelia. Despite a highly psychedelic cover splotched with blobs of greenish-yellow goo, the band members looked like bookish sorts who spent more time at MIT than on LSD.

Ambergris by Ambergris (Paramount). This nine-man, horn-oriented band surfaced and sank into a Sargasso Sea of oblivion on the hapless Paramount label. Blubber, Sweat & Tears, anyone?

Living the Blues by Canned Heat (Liberty). Clad in overalls large enough for a pod of whales, lead singer Bob "the Bear" Hite would grope and holler his way through huge festering mulch piles of boogie. A jam called "Endless Boogie" is split across two entire sides. Guest appearances on "Son of Refried Festival Boogie" by Furry Lewis, Fuzzy Thomas, and Foamy Edwards, with Orca on congas.

Mystic Number National Bank by Mystic Number National Bank (Probe). A habitual offender in the 2/$1.00 bins, the cover features circular punchouts and a wheel you could rotate; mindless fun when stoned. Inside, a Hefty bagful of stumblefoot, bovine blues-rock with psychedelic twinges.

High on Mount Rushmore by Mount Rushmore (Dot). This unhygienic pack of oafish longhairs weren't exactly presidential timber.

Contact by Silver Apples (Kapp). There were two Silver Apples. One handled percussion, while a chap named Simeon played "the simeon," a home-made synthesizer. In 1996, Simeon resurrected Silver Apples, which confirms our worst suspicions that nothing ever really goes away and that yesterday's cutout is tomorrow's collector's item.

Amon Duul by Amon Duul (Prophesy). In Germany, the '60s never ended. While acid passed from favor over here, our Teutonic brothers had skinny-dipping parties in the stuff. They brushed their teeth with it, dipped knackwurst in it, and made albums like this one, full of spacy jamming made with as much panache as German hippies can muster. At least they weren't as bad as Guru Guru. Ever hear of Guru Guru? Consider yourself fortunate.

Love Cycle by Crome Syrcus (Command). Though the jacket looks promisingly psychedelic, this album contains some of the most onerous music ever made. A monkish-looking band from Seattle—especially "Lee," the troglodytic hippie about whom the liner notes exclaim, "This cat is a freak for jewelry!"—Crome Syrcus uncorked a real bummer. Especially the bizarre and tedious title track, which took up an entire side.

Proud Flesh Soothseer by Linn County (Mercury). Linn County were a West Coast psyche-delic blues quintet whose specialty was long stretches of jamming as absorbing as TV bowling. Said jams would come in the midst of songs with titles like "Moon Food" and the nearly 15-minute "Protect and Serve/Bad Things" medley. Nice headbands, though.

AFTER THE BALL

UNRAVELING OF THE COUNTERCULTURE

For those with the eyes, ears, and stomach for it, the "real world" was never far beyond the outer limits of every college town or big city's psychedelic safe haven. Inside that zone—part neighborhood, part state of mind—things seemed peaceful enough, at least for the relatively brief period of time covered in this book. But even so, portents of doom were unavoidable and certainly could not be kept at bay forever.

This explains why, after the Death of Hippie parade in Haight-Ashbury, the most enlightened members of the tribe grabbed their copies of the Stewart Brand's *Whole Earth Catalog*, Buckminster Fuller's *Operating Manual for Spaceship Earth*, and any books by Scott Nearing or Euell Gibbons and headed for the hills, the desert, the backwoods, or another country.

On the national and international scene, battle lines were being drawn between generations, races, genders, spheres of influence, ideologies, and religions. When these same cracks— these same predatory power games—began to appear in hip communities themselves, the gig was up. The following are some of the black-letter dates, if you will, the portents, the low-water marks on the bong of hippie history, beginning with the bummer year of 1968. Call it the Bummers Parade:

January 30, 1968. The Viet Cong begin the "Tet Offensive," a bloody and prolonged campaign that turns the tide of battle in Vietnam.

April 4, 1968. Martin Luther King, Jr., is assassinated in Memphis by James Earl Ray.

April 23, 1968. Students at Columbia University begin an eight-day takeover of campus offices, eventually broken up by a police assault.

June 3, 1968. Valerie Solanis shoots Andy Warhol as a revolutionary act, a near-fatal assault approved by some radical feminists.

June 6, 1968. Robert F. Kennedy, moments after a victory speech in California's Democratic presidential primary, is assassinated in Los Angeles by Sirhan Sirhan.

August 8, 1968. Nixon and Agnew are nominated in Miami as the standard-bearers of the Republican Party.

The interior of a so-called group "psychedelic house" in Washington, D.C., April 1967, taken by *U.S. News & World Report* staff photographer Marion Trikosko. Note the telltale wasted expressions and wine bottle–turned–candleholder.

185

August 20, 1968. Soviet troops invade Czechoslovakia.

August 26–28, 1968. The whole world's watching as police riot at the Democratic presidential convention in Chicago, known derisively thereafter as "Czechago."

November 5, 1968. Nixon is elected president with 43.5 percent of the popular vote (less than Clinton's share of the popular vote in 1996).

January 28, 1969. One of the largest oil spills in U.S. history occurs off of Santa Barbara, wiping out marine life along a 200-mile stretch of coastline.

February 12, 1969. The governor of Wisconsin calls out the National Guard to quell a protest at the University of Wisconsin in Madison.

April 3, 1969. The death toll in Vietnam surpasses the body count in the Korean War.

May 15, 1969. Governor Ronald Reagan sends the National Guard to quell what had been a peaceful month of protest at the University of California at Berkeley over People's Park.

September 1969. The Chicago Seven's conspiracy trial opens.

November 16, 1969. It's reported that Lt. William Calley presided over the massacre of 500 people—many of them women and children—at My Lai, a Vietnamese farm village.

November 20, 1969. Native American activists take over Alcatraz Island.

December 4, 1969. Chicago police conduct an armed assault of an apartment shared by Black Panther leaders Fred Hampton and Mark Clark. Both are killed while in bed.

April 30, 1970. President Nixon announces the invasion of Cambodia and the drafting of 150,000 more troops for the undeclared Vietnam War.

May 4, 1970. Members of the National Guard open fire on a crowd of students during an antiwar protest at Kent State University in Ohio. Four are killed and nine wounded.

May 14, 1970. During a student protest at Jackson State University, an all-black school in Mississippi, police open fire on a dorm. Two are killed, nine wounded.

November 27, 1970. George Harrison releases his three-record set *All Things Must Pass.*

December 31, 1970. Paul McCartney began proceedings to dissolve the Beatles.

June 27–July 4, 1971. Bill Graham closes the Fillmore East and Fillmore West with a final series of concerts.

AFTERWORD

The spirit of the Sixties more or less died as the Rolling Stones played "Sympathy for the Devil" at Altamont Speedway. At the same time, the decade's zeitgeist-the agitated tenor of the music, the ongoing conflict over Vietnam, and the urge to tune in, turn on and drop out-continued to flap its injured wings through 1972 and even into '73, which is when the rot really set in. "Almost cut my hair/Happened just the other day," sang David Crosby in 1970, admitting that the jig looked to be up early in the new decade, but many a freak flag (including ours) flew well into the Seventies.

Still and all, the party was over. Whipped and weary from its clashes with the establishment, burned out on drugs, and lacking Great Causes like Vietnam, the counterculture atrophied and the shallow, antithetical mainstream culture of the Seventies reared its ugly head. You know how it all went down: greed, yuppies, bad TV, worse music, Watergate, Saturday Night Fever, shag carpeting, singles bars and smiley faces. The Seventies can be summed up in five words: "Billy, Don't Be a Hero."

To some degree, however, the Sixties never completely went away. Pockets of dropout culture remain scattered about the country. The first Earth Day observance took place on April 22, 1970. Environmentalism has since become an entrenched ethic and potent political issue. If nothing else survived the Sixties, environmental awareness would alone stand as a shining legacy. But the spirit of the decade infiltrated and continues to inform areas of literature, movies and music-especially music. Can you say "neopsychedelia"? And isn't a rave just a night at the Avalon Ballroom with new technology?

Many pined for the spirit of commitment and engagement that burned brightly in the Sixties. With tongue not entirely in cheek, Country Joe McDonald spoke for many when he cut a song called "Bring Back the Sixties, Man" in 1976, a year of endless jingoistic Bicentennial backslapping that seemed to celebrate all the wrong things. By and large, however, the Sixties' reputation has been subjected to hits from those who hated what the decade stood for or privately regretted they were too young to have lived in meaningful times.

Through revisionism and misrepresentation, heroes have become laughingstocks, loathsome politicians have been forgiven and reconsidered, and the brilliant works of artists operating in real time during the Sixties are now routinely abused for unworthy ends. Turn on the boob tube and you might hear a shrill voice massacring the Rascals' idealistic "People Got to Be Free" in a pitch for cellular phone service. Open a magazine and you might spy a rainbow-hued ad with wavy lettering that asks, "Don't you want some burger to love?" And so it goes, all the way to the muddy doorstep of the festival-turned- funeral pyre known as Woodstock '99.

But enough bad vibes. Our aim in this book has been to revisit and celebrate the Sixties without irony or lies, and to help set the record straight for those whose perspectives have been occluded by corporate ad campaigns, TV miniseries and other sources of cultural distortion. Our hope is that the worthiest parts of that long, strange trip will never be forgotten.

BIBLIOGRAPHY

In addition to interviews with many participants of the events related herein, we have relied heavily on an extensive archive collected during and since the '60s. These include the following newspapers and magazines: *Big Fat* (Ann Arbor), *Contact, Crawdaddy, Creem, Evergreen Review, Fusion, Good Times* (San Francisco), *Great Speckled Bird* (Atlanta), *L.A. Free Press* (Los Angeles), *New Times, Ramparts, Rolling Stone, The Seed* (Chicago), *The Whole Earth Catalog,* and *Zap Comix.* The following books were also invaluable:

Adams, Cecil. *More of the Straight Dope.* New York: Ballantine, 1988.

Albright, Thomas. *Art in the San Francisco Bay Area, 1945–1980: An Illustrated History.* Berkeley: Univ. of California. Press, 1987.

Bangs, Lester. (Greil Marcus, ed.) *Psychotic Reactions and Carburetor Dung.* New York: Alfred A. Knopf, 1987.

Bisbort, Alan. *The White Rabbit and Other Delights: East Totem West, A Hippie Company, 1967–1969.* San Francisco: Pomegranate Artbooks, 1996.

Castleman, Harry, and Walter J. Podrazik. *Watching TV: Four Decades of American Television.* New York: McGraw-Hill, 1982.

Cox, Stephen. *The Beverly Hillbillies.* New York: Harper Collins, 1993.

Daniels, Les. *Comix: A History of Comic Books in America.* New York: Bonanza, 1971.

Ehrenstein, David, and Bill Reed. *Rock on Film.* New York: Delilah, 1982.

Estren, Mark James. *A History of Underground Comics.* Berkeley: Ronin Publishing, 1993.

Ferlinghetti, Lawrence, and Nancy J. Peters. *Literary San Francisco.* San Francisco: City Lights and Harper & Row, 1980.

Ghiglione, Loren. *The American Journalist.* Washington, DC: Library of Congress, 1990.

Ginsberg, Allen. *Kaddish and Other Poems, 1958–1960.* San Francisco: City Lights, 1961.

Gleason, Ralph J. *The Jefferson Airplane and the San Francisco Sound.* New York: Ballantine, 1969.

Goldstein, Richard, ed. *US: A Paperback Magazine.* New York: Bantam, 1969.

Graham, Bill, and Robert Greenfield. *Bill Graham Presents.* New York: Doubleday, 1992.

Green, Jonathon. *Days in the Life: Voices from the English Underground, 1961–1971.* London: Minerva, 1989.

Grogan, Emmett. *Ringolevio: A Life Played for Keeps.* Boston: Little, Brown, 1972.

Grushkin, Paul D. *The Art of Rock: Posters from Presley to Punk.* New York: Abbeville Press, 1987.

Hewison, Robert. *Too Much: Art and Society in the Sixties.* London: Metheun, 1986.

Hopkins, Jerry, and Danny Sugarman. *No One Here Gets Out Alive.* New York: Warner Books, 1980.

Huxley, Aldous. *The Doors of Perception. Heaven and Hell.* New York: Harper Perennial, 1990.

Huxley, Aldous. (Michael Horowitz and Cynthia Palmer, eds.) *Moksha: Writings on Psychedelics and the Visionary Experience (1931–1963).* New York: Stonehill, 1977.

Isherwood, Christopher. *Diaries, Volume One, 1939–1960.* New York: Harper Collins, 1996.

Katzman, Allen, ed. *Our Time: Interviews from The East Village Other.* New York: Dial, 1972.

Krassner, Paul. *Confessions of a Raving Unconfined Nut: Misadventures in the Counter-Culture.* New York: Simon & Schuster, 1993.

Leary, Timothy. *Politics of Ecstasy.* New York: Putnam, 1968.

Lee, Martin A., and Bruce Shlain. *Acid Dreams: The CIA, LSD and the Sixties Rebellion.* New York: Grove Press, 1985.

Lipton, Lawrence. *The Holy Barbarians.* New York: Messner, 1959.

Makower, Joel. *BOOM!: Talkin' About Our Generation.* Chicago: Contemporary Books, 1985.

McDonnell, Patrick, et. al. *Krazy Kat: The Comic Art of George Herriman.* New York: Harry N. Abrams, 1986.

Nuttall, Jeff. *Bomb Culture.* New York: Dell, 1968.

Peck, Abe. *Uncovering the Sixties: The Life & Times of the Underground Press.* New York: Pantheon, 1985.

Rees, Dafydd, and Luke Crampton. *Encyclopedia of Rock Stars.* New York: DK Publishing, 1996.

Roxon, Lillian. *Rock Encyclopedia.* New York: Grosset and Dunlap, 1971.

Santelli, Robert. *Aquarius Rising: The Rock Festival Years.* New York: Dell, 1980.

Sätty. *The Cosmic Bicycle.* San Francisco: Straight Arrow Books, 1971.

Sätty. *Time Zone.* San Francisco: Straight Arrow Books, 1973.

Schoenfeld, Eugene. *Dear Doctor Hippocrates.* New York: Grove Press, 1968.

Schumacher, Michael. *Dharma Lion: A Critical Biography of Allen Ginsberg.* New

York: St. Martin's Press, 1992.

Scully, Rock, with David Dalton. *Living With the Dead.* New York: Little, Brown, 1996.

Snyder, Solomon H., ed. *Encyclopedia of Psychoactive Drugs. "LSD: Visions or Nightmares."* New York: Chelsea House, 1985.

Sontag, Susan. *Against Interpretation.* New York: Dell, 1969.

Stevens, Jay. *Storming Heaven: LSD and the American Dream.* New York: Harper & Row, 1987.

Taylor, Derek. *It Was Twenty Years Ago*

Today: An Anniversary Celebration of 1967. New York: Fireside, 1987.

Von Hoffman, Nicholas. *We Are the People Our Parents Warned Us Against.* Chicago: Quadrangle, 1968.

Walker, Cummings G., ed. *The Great Poster Trip: Art Eureka.* San Francisco: Coyne & Blanchard, 1968.

Watson, Steven. *The Birth of the Beat Generation: Visionaries, Rebels, and Hipsters, 1944–1960.* New York: Pantheon, 1995.

Whitburn, Joel. *Top Pop Albums, 1955–1996.* Menomonee Falls, Wisc.: Record Research, Inc., 1996.

Whitburn, Joel. *Top Pop Singles, 1955–1993.* Menomonee Falls, Wisc.: Record Research, Inc., 1994.

White, Timothy. *The Nearest Faraway Place: Brian Wilson, the Beach Boys, and the Southern California Experience.* New York: Henry Holt, 1994.

Williams, Paul. *Outlaw Blues.* New York: E.P. Dutton, 1969.

Wolfe, Burton H. *The Hippies.* New York: Signet, 1968.

Wyman, Bill. *Stone Alone: The Story of a Rock 'n' Roll Band.* New York: Viking, 1990.

PHOTO CREDITS

pages 8, 174, 175, and 184
Reproduced from the Collections of the Library of Congress

page 11
Library of Congress Publishing Office / Rosenwald Collection, Rare Book and Special Collections Division

pages 12, 13, 22, 76, 144, 150, 154, 157, 170, 173, and 178
UPI/Corbis-Bettman

page 164 (both Easy Rider images)
Springer/Corbis-Bettman

pages 26 (both images), 94, and 126
© Photo: Baron Wolfman

pages 34, 37, 43, and 45
Archive Photos

page 38
Archive Photos/Jim Wells

page 39
Archive Photos/The Platt Collection

pages 42 and 48 (bottom)
Blank Archives/Archive Photos

page 46
Express Newspapers/Archive Photos

page 49
Archive Photos/Popperfoto

pages 36, 54, 57, 60, 61, 66, 68 (top and bottom), 69, 70, 71, 72 (photo), 87, and 88
from the personal collection of Harold Bronson, Rhino Records

page 48 (top)
From *Alice's Adventures in Wonderland* by Lewis Carroll, illustrated by Arthur Rackham, William Heinemann (London), 1908, General Collections

pages 25 (bottom), 30, 32–33, 62, 82, 84, 86, 90, 95 (bottom inset), 97, 98–99 (plus inset on 99), 100 (three images), 101 (bottom), 102, and 103
Henry Diltz

pages 95 (top inset and background image), 96 (both images), 97 (inset), 98 (inset), 101 (top and center)
Henry Diltz/Onyx

page 64
MCA Records

pages 116 and 121
East Totem West, © Joe McHugh

page 123
(left) BG41 © Bill Graham Presents 1966
(right) BG136 © Bill Graham Presents 1968

page 128
ZAP No. 1, © Robert Crumb, 1968
MOTOR CITY No. 1, © Robert Crumb, 1969

pages 129, 130, and 131
reprinted with the kind permission of Stan Lee, Marvel Comics

page 134
Parke Puterbaugh

pages 152 and 167
Riot on Sunset Strip
An American International Release

page 165
The Trip, American International Pictures

page 168
Alan White Collection

All other images are from the authors' personal collections.

INDEX